# Test Scores and What They Mean

## Sixth Edition

**Howard B. Lyman**
*University of Cincinnati*

**Allyn and Bacon**

Boston  London  Toronto  Sydney  Tokyo  Singapore

Series Editor: Carla F. Daves
Series Editorial Assistant: Susan Hutchinson
Marketing Manager: Joyce Nilsen
Production Administrator: Deborah Brown
Editorial-Production Service: Saxon House Productions
Text Designer and Compositor: Glenna Collett
Composition and Prepress Buyer: Linda Cox
Manufacturing Buyer: Suzanne Lareau
Cover Administrator: Jenny Hart

Copyright © 1998, 1991, 1986, 1979, 1971, 1963 by Allyn & Bacon
A Viacom Company
160 Gould Street
Needham Heights, MA 02194

Internet: www.abacon.com
America Online: keyword: College Online

**Library of Congress Cataloging-in-Publication Data**

Lyman, Howard Burbeck.
    Test scores and what they mean / Howard B. Lyman. — 6th ed.
        p.    cm.
    Includes bibliographical references and index.
    ISBN 0-205-17539-2 (paper)
        1. Educational tests and measurements—United States—
Interpretation.    2. Educational tests and measurements—Validity—
United States.    3. Psychological tests—United States—Interpretation.
4. Psychological tests—Validity—United States.    5. Psychological
tests—United States—Data Processing.    I. Title.
LB3060.8.L85    1998
371.26—dc21                                                97-30509
                                                              CIP

Printed in the United States of America
15  14  13  12  11                        09  08

# Test Scores and What They Mean

2

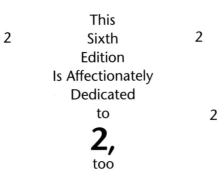

2                     2

2                                 2

This
Sixth
Edition
Is Affectionately
Dedicated
to
**2,**
too

2                     2

# Contents

Preface  *xiii*

### ONE
## *Learning About Test Scores*  *1*

Testing Today  *3*
No More Stalling!  *4*
    Now Is the Time for Learning  *5*
A Pretest  *5*
Answers to Pretest Questions  *5*

### TWO
## *Basic Attributes of the Test*  *9*

Validity  *9*
    Face Validity  *10*
    Content Validity (Logical Validity)  *10*
    Criterion-Related Validity (Empirical Validity)  *11*
    Factors Influencing Criterion-Related Validity  *11*
    Construct Validity  *13*
Reliability  *13*
    Lyman's Five Dimensions of Reliability  *14*
    Interrelationship of Sources of Error Variance  *17*
    Standard Error of Measurement  *17*
    Factors Affecting Reliability  *17*
    Comparing Validity and Reliability  *18*
Usability  *19*

**THREE**

### *The Language of Testing*   20

Maximum-Performance Tests   21
   Intelligence Tests   21
   Aptitude Tests   22
   Achievement Tests   22
Typical-Performance Tests   23
   Criterion Keying   24
   Forced-Choice Items   24
   Ambiguity of Items   25
Objective–Subjective–Projective Response   26
Select-Response—Supply-Response   26
Written–Oral–Performance Tests   27
Standardized–Informal Tests   27
Speed–Power Tests   27
Group–Individual Tests   28
Verbal–Nonverbal Tests   28
Culture Fair   29
How to Tell   29
This Book   30

**FOUR**

### *What's New in Testing Today?*   31

Computers and Testing   31
Criterion-Referenced Measurement   33
   Evaluation of Criterion-Referenced Testing   34
Test-Item Banks   34
Adaptive Testing   34
Latent Trait Scaling   35
Competency and Accountability   35
What Is Wrong?   36
Outcome-Based Education   37
Exceptional People: Those with Language and Physical Disabilities   37
Portfolios   38
New All Over Again?   38
Not Only in the United States   38

**FIVE**

### *Social Responsibility and Testing*   39

Tests Do Not Measure Innate Ability (Only)   40
Intelligence Tests Do Not Measure Creativity   41
People Use Tests to Label Children as Morons, etc.   42
Standardized Tests Favor the Glib and Penalize the Thoughtful   43
Tests Invade Privacy   43
Tests Give Changing Results   45

Tests Are Unfair    *45*
    Lake Wobegon Effect    *46*
Tests Are Misused and Misinterpreted    *47*


**SIX**

*A Few Statistics*    *49*

Introduction    *49*
    Frequency Distribution    *50*
    The Histogram    *52*
    Frequency Polygon    *53*
Descriptive Statistics    *53*
    Measures of Position (Other than Central Tendency)    *54*
    Measures of Central Tendency (Averages)    *55*
    Comparison of the Central Tendency Measures    *57*
    Measures of Variability    *57*
    Measures of Covariability    *59*
The Normal Probability Curve    *63*
    Points to Know    *63*
Inferential Statistics    *64*
    Standard Errors    *65*
Expectancy Tables    *68*
An Omission and an Explanation    *70*


**SEVEN**

*Information About Tests*    *71*

Test Catalogs    *71*
Test Publishers    *72*
Test Manuals    *73*
    Rationale    *74*
    Descriptions of the Test    *74*
    Purposes of the Test    *74*
    Development of the Test    *74*
    Directions for Administration    *75*
    Directions for Scoring    *75*
    Reliability Data    *76*
    Validity Data    *76*
    Norms and Norms Tables    *77*
    Interpretation of the Test    *86*
    Profiles    *86*
    References    *87*
Don't Overlook Your Personal Computer    *87*


**EIGHT**

*Derived Scores*    *88*

A Classification Scheme    *88*

Discussion of the Classification Scheme     *89*
**The Scores**     *95*
**Type I: Comparison with an "Absolute Standard," or Content Difficulty**     *95*
Type I A: Percentage Correct     *95*
Type I B: Letter Grades (Sometimes)     *96*
**Type II: Inter-Individual Comparisons**     *97*
Type II A: Inter-Individual Comparison Considering Mean and Standard Deviation     *97*
Type II B: Inter-Individual Comparison Considering Rank     *101*
Type II C: Inter-Individual Comparison Considering Range     *112*
Type II D: Inter-Individual Comparison Considering Status of Those Making Same Score     *112*
**Type III: Intra-Individual Comparisons**     *116*
Type III A: Ratio IQ (Intelligence Quotient)     *116*
Type III B: Intellectual Status Index     *117*
Type III C: Educational Quotients     *117*
Type III D: Accomplishment Quotients     *117*
**Type IV: Assorted Arbitrary Bases**     *118*
Type IV A: Nonmeaningful Scaled Scores     *118*
Type IV B: Long-Range Equi-Unit Scales     *118*
Type IV C: Deviation IQ (Otis-Style)     *119*
**A Final Word**     *119*

**NINE**

## *Test Profiles*     *121*

**General Profiles**     *124*
**The Good Profile**     *124*
**Significant Differences in Profile Points**     *126*
**Profile Analysis**     *126*

**TEN**

## *Don't Forget Common Sense*     *128*

**Institutional and Individual Decisions**     *130*
**Some Common Mistakes**     *131*
**Other Sources, Too!**     *131*

**ELEVEN**

## *What Can We Say?*     *133*

**Who Is Entitled to Test Information?**     *134*
The Examinee     *134*
Parents of Minors     *134*
Agency Policy     *134*
Schools and Colleges     *135*
Professional Colleagues     *135*
Personnel     *135*

In Conversation    *136*
**Communicating the Results**    *136*
To a Trained Professional Worker    *136*
To a Professional Person Untrained in Testing    *137*
To a Mature Examinee    *138*
To a Child    *140*
To Parents    *142*
**High and Low**    *142*
**In Summary**    *143*

## TWELVE

## *Closing Remarks*    144

**Things to Keep in Mind**    *144*
Know the Test    *144*
Know the Norms    *144*
Know the Score    *145*
Know the Background    *145*
Communicate Effectively    *145*
Use the Test    *145*
Use Caution    *145*
**Experts Still Needed**    *146*
**Go Ahead and Try!**    *148*

## *Appendix*    149

**Glossary of Terms**    *150*
**Selected Test Publishers**    *162*
**Bibliography**    *164*
**Code of Professional Responsibilities in Educational Measurement**    *167*
**Conversion Table**    *176*

**Index**    *183*

# *Preface*

There is as much need for *Test Scores and What They Mean* today as there was in 1963 when the first edition appeared. Increasingly, I am hearing of lay people being attracted to the book because of its ease of reading. I know personally of two attorneys who have used *Test Scores* for a "fast study" background for cases in which they were involved.

The first edition of *Test Scores and What They Mean* (1963) was written to give information about testing to people whose work gave them access to test results—for example, schoolteachers and principals, physicians, admission counselors, guidance counselors, social workers, and personnel workers—but whose training included little or nothing about the use and interpretation of tests.

It soon became apparent that the book was being used most often, not by in-service personnel, but by students in courses in psychological and educational measurement, industrial personnel, counseling, and the like. Therefore, I wrote the second edition (1971) with such students especially in mind.

My goal in the third (1979) and fourth editions (1986) was to update the content and make the book even easier to read. Reviewers have commented favorably that the book has been genuinely informative and full of illustrative examples. The fifth edition (1991) aimed at showing the ever-broadening applications of testing.

*Test Scores and What They Mean* has been so well accepted that several test publishers and industrial consulting firms have made it available to their own customers through their catalogs. One Briton, now retired, commented on when he had been named to head a test publisher's European office:

"Frankly, without your book, I wouldn't have known anything about tests." And one American publisher of tests has required all new employees to read the book.

Test publishers have been most helpful in keeping me up-to-date by answering my questions and by making sample copies of tests and test materials available to me. I want to thank personnel from The Psychological Corporation, Educational Testing Service, Consulting Psychologists Press, CTB/McGraw-Hill, Institute for Personality and Ability Testing, American Guidance Services, London House/Science Research Associates, National Computer Services, EDITS, Western Psychological Services, and Psychological Assessment Resources, among others, for their help over the years.

Even today my philosophy of testing is still evolving, for this is a dynamic and challenging field of study. As a student, I was influenced by J. McVicker Hunt, Donald B. Lindsley, Walter Hunter, Donald G. Paterson, C. Gilbert Wrenn, John G. Darley, Walter Cook, Ralph F. Berdie, Howard P. Longstaff, Robert North, Herbert Sorenson, Lysle Croft, et al. My views have been modified through years of using tests, teaching about testing, and consulting on testing problems with many individuals and agencies.

I want to thank the many colleagues and friends with whom I have discussed testing issues at one time or another: Peter Merenda, Goldine Gleser, John D. Black, John Holland, William Rusk, Frank Womer, Vytautus J. Bieliauskas, Richard Melton, Gerald Doppelt, William Mollenkopf, and Kenneth McLaughlin, among others. At times I have received helpful information from the psychometrists and counselors of the University of Cincinnati's Counseling Service.

I further thank the many users of the first five editions of *Test Scores and What They Mean,* especially those who have been kind enough to share their comments with me.

In the fifth edition (1991) I tried to emphasize some of the newer trends in measurement and to express my displeasure with certain current pedagogical movements. Once again, references were updated.

I have profited especially from the feedback given me by my own students over the past quarter century or longer, some of whom became psychologists and/or college professors in their own right—among them, Venus Bluestein and R. J. Senter (University of Cincinnati), Elizabeth Miller (Xavier University), Richard A. King (University of North Carolina), and Ronald Flaugher (Educational Testing Service). And I want to acknowledge especially a man who has functioned as my teaching assistant for more than ten years, William Bowles, Jr.

In this sixth edition, I have again updated content and references. The glossary of testing terms has been somewhat expanded, and a few outdated terms have been dropped. Additional attention has been paid to ethical issues in test usage. I am especially pleased to be able to include the *Code of Professional Responsibilities* (in the Appendix), developed by the National Council on Measurement in Education.

Many charges are still being made against testing. Some of these criticisms may be true. Some are not. Readers of *Test Scores and What They Mean* should be better able to judge which of the allegations have merit and which should be ignored.

I would like to acknowlege the following reviewers: John K. Conboy, University of Massachusetts, Dartmouth; Steven R. Kubacki, University of Wyoming, and Sandra L. Stein, Rider University.

Also, I would like to thank the Allyn and Bacon staff: Carla Daves, acquisitions editor, and Susan Hutchinson, editorial assistant; and Sydney Baily-Gould at Saxon House Productions, who handled the editorial production process. And finally, I give thanks to my wife, Pat, my inspiration for many years.

# Learning About Test Scores

According to a familiar adage, everyone complains about the weather, but no one does anything about it. In much the same way, it seems, everyone complains about American education, but not much is done to bring about *meaningful* change. Tests have improved over the years, but there hasn't been much improvement in the understanding of test scores or the interpretation of test results.

But recognition of the deteriorated state of American education is beginning to increase. In April of 1996, for example, a national conference of state leaders was convened to study educational needs—one conclusion being that our schools should be giving more challenge to students. Two other incidents that occurred early in the 1996–1997 academic year make me wonder at the lack of good judgment on the part of some of our nation's teachers and administrators:

> A six-year-old first-grade boy was punished for "sexual harassment" when he kissed a girl classmate on the cheek *at her request!* According to Dayton newspapers, a thirteen-year-old honor student in a suburb was suspended from school for two weeks "and recommended for expulsion." Her offense? She had taken a Midol tablet to school! (Her penalty was subsequently moderated, but only after much adverse publicity.) Yes, there are rules—but where has common

sense gone? I think that schools should pay less attention to such trivial offenses. Certainly there are more important matters for school administrators to be concerned with!

As we approach the twenty-first century, there is great confusion as to the appropriate role for educational and psychological tests. It is easy to believe that any tests that are used will automatically be interpreted properly. After all, with all the computers the schools have, there is no need for people, is there?

Unfortunately, perhaps, there is. There are techniques and devices for teasing meaning out of the results of testing. But there is no technique or device that will implant that understanding into the head of the examiner—let alone into the heads of the test takers themselves.

> "When am I going to start failing?" a student once asked me. Upon being questioned, he told me this story: "My high school teacher told me that I had an IQ of only 88. She said that I might be able to get into college because I was an All-State football player, but that I'd be certain to flunk out—with an IQ like that!" I pointed out to Don that he had been doing well in my course. I discovered that he had earned a B+ average during his first two years at our university. I reminded Don that the proof of a pudding lies in its eating—and that the proof of scholastic achievement lies in earned grades, not in a single test designed to predict grades. Two years later, Don graduated with honors.

> One eminent African American psychologist is an ardent disbeliever in the value of standardized tests—especially when given to minority students. Years before, a high school counselor had told him that his test scores showed that he should not plan to go to college. In spite of this unwarranted advice, he did go to college. He now has his Ph.D. and is a licensed psychologist.

These two stories raise many questions; for example:

> Were the test scores correct?
> Were there errors in the administration or in the scoring of the tests?
> Could the scores have been percentile ranks and not IQs?
> Should teachers give such precise scores without a thorough explanation?

One shouldn't make such wild assertions about test results; no test score (or anything else) predicts perfectly. No test score determines future performance. Demonstrated performance is better evidence than any test score, as both of the above students proved by their subsequent achievements.

Mistakes in test interpretation occur every day. Here are three more examples that come quickly to mind:

> A college freshman, told that she had "average ability," withdrew from college. Her counselor had not added, "when compared with other students at her top-flight college." The freshman reasoned that if she had only average ability compared with people in general, she must be very unintelligent when compared with college students. Rather than face that situation, she dropped out of college. (There may have been other reasons, too, but this seemed to be the principal one.)

A high school student who had high measured clerical and literary *interests* was told that this proved that he should become either a clerk or a writer!

A personnel manager, learning that one of her best workers had scored very low on tests that eventually would be used in selecting future employees, nearly discharged the worker: "The tests really opened our eyes about her. Why, she's worked here for several years, does good work, gets along well with the others. Those tests show how she had us fooled!"

None of these cases is fictitious. All involve real people. And we will see many more examples of test interpretation (and misinterpretation) throughout this book. Each is based on a true situation, mostly drawn from my personal experiences during years of working with people who use tests and who take tests.

No amount of anecdotal material, however, can show the thousands of instances every year in which the wrong persons are selected for jobs, admitted to schools and colleges, granted scholarships, and the like—merely because someone in authority is unable to interpret available test scores or, equally bad, places undue confidence in the results.

Nor will anecdotal material reveal the full scope of the misinformation being given to students and parents by teachers and others who are trying to help. Willingness to help is only the first step. There is also a great deal to know about the meaning of test scores. Even experts who work daily with tests must keep their wits about them, for this is no game for dullards.

## TESTING TODAY

The quality of tests has improved greatly during this century. Definite advances have been noted even in the past quarter century: novel approaches to achievement testing, electronic scoring and interpreting, varied approaches to the measurement of interests, etc. Most test authors and test publishers are competent and service-motivated; they subscribe to ethical standards that are commendably high. Each year universities turn out numbers of well-trained measurements people. More teachers and personnel workers are being taught the fundamentals of testing. In spite of these and other positive influences, we still find a desperate need for wider understanding of what test scores mean.

More than one million standardized tests are used each school day in American schools alone. Add to this number the tests that are being given in industry, clinics, the military, personnel offices, employment bureaus, hospitals, civil service agencies, etc., and we can conclude that there is a great deal of testing being done.

Who will interpret the test scores? Often, nobody. In millions of instances, test scores never progress beyond a file card or folder; indeed, this has been the official policy of many personnel offices and school systems. In other instances, the scores are made available to supervisors or teachers, who may, at their discretion, interpret the results.

Unfortunately, many people whose positions give them legitimate access to test results have had little training in test interpretation. People who are going to have access to test scores have an obligation to learn what those scores mean; however, many do not even realize the extent of their ignorance. I should not have been surprised at the following incident:

> When my son David was in junior high school, he took a battery of tests as part of a research project. At a conference with his homeroom teacher, I asked how he had scored. Ms. Whitfield located a report of David's test results after much searching in a locked file cabinet. But she did not know what tests had been administered, nor did she know whether David's scores were being compared with those of students nationally (national norms), with those of students from his school only (local norms), or with those of other students in the research study.

Although Ms. Whitfield was considered a good teacher, she knew very little about tests and test interpretation. She had not had so much as a single course in measurement during her studies for a teaching certificate. Usually, she told me, Mr. Hal Halone did any test interpreting that was done.
Mr. Halone was a certified school counselor, but even he had taken only one course in measurement. And, with responsibility for nearly 1,000 students, he had little time for working with any individual student.

Most students are never given much information about their test results. Who has time? Those teachers who have studied anything about tests are likely to have learned more about writing items for classroom tests than about the meaning of scores on standardized tests.

Personnel workers in industry usually have had no training in measurement. Test interpretation in industry is even worse than in education, except for one thing: Industry seldom gives tests for purposes of individual guidance; rather, most tests are used as a basis for institutional decisions.

## NO MORE STALLING!

Federal law demands that all schools at all levels, as well as all educational agencies that receive federal funds, *must* provide freedom of access to student records. Adult students and parents of minor students **must** be allowed to examine and challenge the contents of all school files relevant to the students if they so request. Companies that use tests **must** (for their own protection) be familiar with federal and state employment laws and policies.

School personnel have an ethical obligation to provide suitable interpretation when they release test scores. That, in turn, means that all school personnel have an additional ethical and professional obligation: to learn about tests and what test scores mean.

### Now Is the Time for Learning

This warning applies at least as well to personnel workers who are concerned with the selection and/or advancement of employees. Federal guidelines set by the Equal Employment Opportunity Commission require that we all must be able to demonstrate the validity of our selection procedures—including any tests that may be used.

## A PRETEST

As a test of your own ability to understand test scores, try the following questions, typical of those asked by test-naive teachers and personnel workers. If you answer the questions satisfactorily (answers at the end of this chapter), you may learn less than some others from this book. If you cannot understand the questions, you certainly need this book! Let us see how you do.

1. Why don't we use raw scores in test interpretation?
2. What is the difference between a percentile rank and a percentage-correct score?
3. Do IQs ever change, or do they remain constant throughout life?
4. Why are norms important?
5. What is the difference between reliability and validity?
6. What effect does the range of scores have on test reliability and validity?
7. Are tests fair to minorities?
8. Do tests measure innate (i.e., inborn) ability?
9. How big must a difference be in order to be called a "significant difference"?
10. How can test difficulty influence the apparent performance or improvement of a school class?

Did you take the pretest? If not, go back and take it **now**, before reading the answers that follow.

## ANSWERS TO PRETEST QUESTIONS

### 1. Why don't we use raw scores in test interpretation?

We do use the raw scores. Nothing is more important, for all derived scores are dependent on the raw scores' accuracy; however, a raw score depends so much on the number and difficulty of the test items that it is nearly valueless by itself.

There are a few instances in which the raw score does assume greater meaning. For example, in a typing speed test, the score typically is based on the number of words typed per minute (corrected for errors); that score, itself, is meaningful. And in some respects the scores on other criterion-referenced tests (see Chapter 4) seem to take on more meaning. But these are the exceptions; in most instances we need to go beyond raw scores for any sort of interpretation.

## 2. What is the difference between a percentile rank and a percentage-correct score?

A person's percentile rank describes his or her relative standing within a particular group; for example, a percentile rank of 80 ($P_{80}$) means that a person's score is equal to or higher than the scores made by 80 percent of the people in some specified group. A percentage-correct score, on the other hand, tells us nothing about a person's relative performance. It tells us only the percentage of items answered correctly; for example, a percentage-correct score of 80 means that a person has answered 80 percent of the test items correctly.

## 3. Do IQs ever change, or do they remain constant throughout life?

Certainly they change. Volumes could be written (and have been) on this topic. Even under ideal conditions (for example, a short time between testings of a highly motivated young adult, using the same test), we would expect to find slight differences in IQ from testing to testing. In general, changes in IQ tend to be greatest in the following situations: among young children, when a long time separates the first and subsequent testings, when different tests are used, when there has been a major change in environmental factors, and when there is a marked difference in the motivational level of the examinee at the different test sessions. Changes of five IQ points are common even under good conditions. Rarely will individuals vary so much as to be classified as normal or average at one time and either mentally retarded or near-genius at some other time. The IQ is only a type of test score. Any fluctuation or inaccuracy in test performance will be reflected in the scores and will cause differences in the IQ score.

## 4. Why are norms important?

Norms give meaning to our scores. They provide a basis for comparing one individual's score with the scores of others who have taken that same test. Ideally, the test publisher describes the norm groups as precisely as possible so that the user may decide how appropriate they are for reporting the performance of individuals of interest. Local norms, developed by the user, may be more appropriate in some situations than any of the publisher's norms. Norms tables are used to translate raw scores into derived scores such as percentiles, standard scores, grade-equivalent scores, IQs, and the like.

## 5. What is the difference between reliability and validity?

*Reliability* refers to the **reproduceability** of a set of test results under different conditions (that is, the stability or consistency of scores). *Validity* refers to a test's ability to measure what we want it to. High reliability is necessary for reasonable validity because a test that does not measure consistently cannot measure anything well; however, a test may be highly reliable without being able to do a specified task well.

## 6. What effect does the range of scores have on test reliability and validity?

Variability has a great effect on both reliability and validity. Other things being equal, a greater range in scores makes for higher reliability and validity coefficients. The sophisticated test user bears this fact in mind when reading reliability and validity coefficients in test manuals.

## 7. Are tests fair to minorities?

No. All tests are culture-bound to some extent. Most intelligence tests emphasize the sorts of material studied in school, and school-related test items are more likely to be familiar to children from upper- and middle-class families. It is possible to construct a test that will result in higher scores for Blacks than for Whites, but such a test may not reflect the skills and knowledge that most people feel are included as part of intelligence. Any test that is worthwhile must discriminate; after all, this is just another way of saying that it will reveal individual differences. But the intended discrimination should be on the basis of the trait being measured, not on the basis of racial or ethnic background.

## 8. Do tests measure innate (i.e., inborn) ability?

Only partly and indirectly. Any intelligence test (or aptitude or achievement test) does measure native ability—but only as it has been modified by the influence of the environment (including all training, experience, and learning) and by the motivation of the examinee at the time the test was taken. It is clearly a mistake to think of anyone's IQ as being *purely* inborn or as being determined solely by heredity; however, it is equally wrong to regard intelligence as determined entirely by environmental factors.

## 9. How big must a difference be in order to be called a "significant difference"?

There are statistics that give us some idea of how far apart a person's scores must be before we can be reasonably sure that they are truly different; however, no single statistic answers the question simply and satisfactorily in all situations.

## 10. How can test difficulty influence the apparent performance or improvement of a school class?

If a test is far too easy for a class, some pupils will obtain scores that are lower than they should be, because we cannot tell how much better the pupils might have done if there had been more items of suitable difficulty. If the pupils are given a test of appropriate difficulty some time later, they will appear to have made greater gains than we would expect; now they are not prohibited (by the very content of the test) from attempting items of reasonable difficulty, and fewer students will obtain perfect or near-perfect scores. There are many other facets to the problem of item difficulty. Some of these will be considered later in this book.

# *Basic Attributes of the Test*

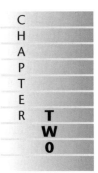

When evaluating a test, we need to consider three main attributes: validity, reliability, and usability. *Validity* refers to the ability of the test to do the job we want it to. *Reliability* means that a test gives dependable or consistent scores. *Usability* includes all such practical factors as cost, ease of scoring, time required, and the like. These attributes should never be considered as all-or-none characteristics, for they are relative to specific situations, uses, groups, etc.

## VALIDITY

Validity is the most important single attribute of a good test. Samuel Messick, the highly esteemed Educational Testing Service psychologist, defines validity as ". . . an overall evaluative judgment of the degree to which empirical evidence and theoretical rationales support the adequacy and appropriateness of interpretations and actions on the basis of test scores or other modes of assessment" (in Linn, *Educational Measurement,* 3rd ed.). Less

9

technically, validity refers to the evidence that a test gives us information that is useful for our purposes.

Nothing can be gained by testing unless the test has some validity for the use we wish to make of it. A test that has high validity for one purpose may have only moderate validity for another and negligible validity for a third.

> The hypothetical *Mechanical Applications and Practice Test (MAP)* has been found highly valid for predicting grades at the Manual Arts High School and for selection of people to be machinists' apprentices. It has reasonable, but low, validity for predicting performance in a plumbing training course and for the selection of people for industrial assembly jobs. The *MAP* is of no value, however, in predicting academic grade-point averages, in selecting industrial sales representatives, or in selecting students to enter engineering colleges. The *MAP*, for some reason that is not immediately apparent, even relates negatively to success in real estate selling; the better salespeople tend to score lower on the test.

There are no fixed rules for deciding what is meant by high validity, moderate validity, etc. Skill in making such judgments comes only through training and experience in dealing with tests. The study of a test's validity may be either primarily logical (*face* or *content*) or primarily empirical-statistical (*criterion-related* or *construct*).

## Face Validity

The term *face validity* means simply that the test items appear to be appropriate. Good face validity helps to keep motivation high, for examinees try harder when the test seems reasonable and fair. Additionally, good face validity may be important to public relations. Face validity is the least important indication of validity. Many psychologists do not regard this as validity at all, but only as a "practical factor."

## Content Validity (Logical Validity)

Somewhat similar, but more systematic and more sophisticated, is *content validity* (otherwise known as *logical validity*, *course validity*, *curricular validity*, or *textbook validity*). Like face validity, content validity is nonstatistical; here, however, the test content is examined in detail.

We may check a test to see whether each item covers an important bit of knowledge or involves an important skill related to a particular course or training program. Or we may start off with a detailed outline of our training program or course and see how thoroughly the test matches important points of that program. Either way, the evidence of content validity is the similarity of content between the training outline and the test. Content validity is most obviously important in achievement tests, but it can be important with other types of test as well. Content validity takes on added importance whenever it is impossible to establish criterion-related validity.

## Criterion-Related Validity (Empirical Validity)

*Criterion-related validity,* or *empirical validity,* is implied whenever validity is mentioned. This sort of validity is most important in any practical situation. How well does the test measure what we want it to? Empirical validity gives us an answer by indicating how closely the test relates to some criterion (that is, to some standard of performance that is external to the test). When empirical validity is high, we can use the test for predicting performance on the criterion variable.

Evidence for this type of validity typically is gained through a validity coefficient, a coefficient of correlation between the test scores and criterion values for a group of people.

A correlation coefficient is a statistic that expresses the tendency for values of two variables to change together systematically. It may take any value between 0.00 (no relationship) and +1.00 or –1.00 (each indicating a perfect relationship). Further information on this statistic will be found in Chapter 6.

## Factors Influencing Criterion-Related Validity

Skill is required to interpret validity coefficients. In general, the higher the correlation between the test and the criterion, the better; however, other factors do need to be considered:

### 1. Test variables differ

Some tests lend themselves more naturally to validation studies than do others. For example, school grades are a natural criterion to use in validating a scholastic aptitude test. On the other hand, what would we use as a good criterion for a sociability scale? Where good criteria are hard to find, we usually cannot expect high validity coefficients; sometimes, in fact, the test itself may be a better measure of the characteristic than any criterion is. For example, a standardized achievement test is usually superior to a teacher-made classroom achievement test or a teacher's grade in some course.

### 2. Criteria differ

The criterion used in one validation study may be more important or more relevant to our purposes than the criterion used in other validation studies.

> We want a test to help us in the selection of bookbinders. The hypothetical *Health Analysis Form* correlates 0.65 with record of attendance on the job; the *Hand Dexterity Test* correlates 0.30 with number of books bound during an observation period. Which test should we use? Should we use both? We would need more information, of course, but we would certainly want to consider which criterion (attendance record or production record) is more important to us.

### 3. Groups differ

For any number of reasons, a test that works well with one group may not do so with another group. A test that discriminates between bright and dull primary school pupils may be worthless when used with high school students because all high school students get near-perfect scores. Consider also the following:

> The *Aytown Advertiser* finds that the *Typographers Own Performance Scale (TOPS)* is very helpful in selecting good printers and in reducing turnover among printers, but that it is no good for selecting reporters or office workers. The *Beetown Bugle* finds that the *TOPS* is of little value in selecting its printers. (This is entirely possible, for the two newspapers may have different standards of quality, the labor markets in the two cities may differ, etc.)

### 4. Variability differs

Validity coefficients are likely to be higher when the group of examinees shows a wide range of scores. A casual glance may tell us that John (a basketball center) is taller than Bill (who is of average height), but it may take a close look to tell whether Bill is taller than Tom (who is also of about average height). In much the same way, a crude test can discriminate well if there are gross differences among those tested, but a much better test may not discriminate adequately if the group is highly homogeneous.

> Once, when consulting at a conservatory of music, I found that the best predictor of grades was a (not very good) intelligence test, not any measure of musical knowledge or judgment of musical ability. On these latter measures, the range (a variability statistic) was restricted, as all applicants were well above general population averages; however, there was a much wider range of scores on the intelligence test.

### 5. Practical factors

With today's emphasis on fairness in testing, the examiner may wish to determine empirical validity separately for different ethnic groups. A test that has high validity for one sex or for one race may not have comparable validity for the other sex or for another race; however, such differences may be less common than generally supposed.

### 6. Additional information

A validity coefficient must also be evaluated in terms of how much **additional** information it will give us. One test may have a very high correlation with a criterion variable, but still not help us much. This situation is likely to occur whenever the test also has a high correlation with information we already have (for example, scores from another test or previous school grades). In other words, the test will not be helpful unless it contributes something new to understanding the examinees; this increase is sometimes called *incremental* *validity.* (Note: If this were not so, we could give several different forms of a valid test to each examinee and, eventually, get perfect validity. In reality, we can get only a slight increase in validity in this manner.)

These six considerations only suggest why we cannot assert flatly, "The higher the validity coefficient, the better." Other things being equal, the statement will be true; however, we must be sure that other things *are* equal.

Criterion-related validity may be either concurrent or predictive. At times in the past, these were treated as separate types of validity, but they are better described as both being instances of empirical validity, for they differ only in time sequence. In *concurrent validity,* both test scores and criterion values are obtained at about the same time. In *predictive validity,* there is some lapse in time between testing and obtaining the criterion values.

## Construct Validity

With *construct validity,* there is no obvious criterion. There may be no natural criterion, for example, for an anxiety scale; however, we may be able to identify several groups of people who would seem to be more anxious (according to the test's definition of anxiety). Such groups might include students who ask questions of a teacher the day before a test, students who visit the campus counseling service, etc. A study showing that such people have higher scores than others in a control group would be some evidence of the test's construct validity. In short, construct validity is "the evidential basis for score interpretation" (Messick).

Construct validity involves an effort to understand the psychological meaningfulness of both the test and the rationale that lies behind the test. Increasingly, the term *construct validity* is coming to refer to the entire body of accumulated validity evidence about a test.

The topic of construct validity is a complex one. Further details may be obtained from a psychological or educational measurement textbook. See, especially, the text by Anne Anastasi or that by Lee Cronbach.

# RELIABILITY

Test reliability is very important to the test user, for it is necessary (but not sufficient) for good validity; that is, a test can be highly reliable without necessarily being valid for any stated purpose of interest to us.

A classroom teacher would have little confidence in a standardized achievement test in mathematics that placed Laura in the top 10 percent of her class last month but places her near the median today. An industrial personnel person would have little use for a selection test that ranked Travis Taylor in the bottom quarter of the applicants' norms group a few weeks ago but in the top quarter of the same group today.

Reliability refers to *the reproduceability of a set of test results under differing conditions or situations.*

Note that what is important is the order of the scores—not the exact score values. If everyone's score were to change by the same (or a proportional) amount under the two conditions, the reliability would be perfect between the original and revised sets of scores.

Any factor that tends to exert a different or varying influence on a set of test scores has an adverse effect on the reliability of the test. We say that such factors contribute to the *error variance* of the test. We can never tell exactly how much error variance is present in a set of scores. We can, however, estimate how much error variance there is. And that is essentially what we do when we compute reliability coefficients (i.e., correlation coefficients between two versions of the test scores for the same group of individuals). There are different types of reliability coefficients, each of which tells us something (but not everything) about the reliability of the test scores.

When we read test manuals, we need to look carefully at the reliability coefficients reported. We can sometimes get a good estimate of how stable and consistent we may expect the results from a test to be. There are some sources of error variance, however, that are not included in any of the common estimates of reliability. On the other hand, all sources of error operate to keep any validity coefficient from being unrealistically high.

## Lyman's Five Dimensions of Reliability

We can consider most sources of error reasonably well using a five-dimensional model that I think suggests most factors that influence reliability. But remember, **anything** that affects scores differentially increases the amount of error variance and lowers the reliability and (indirectly) the validity of the test.

### 1. Examinee-incurred

Some error variance is contributed more by the individual examinee than by anything else. Take, for example, the motivation of the examinee at the times tested—to the extent that motivation varies, the resulting test scores vary and will be unreliable. But individuals may also vary in other significant ways: in physical health, mental alertness, stamina, competitive spirit, willingness to ask questions when directions are incompletely understood, ability to follow directions, or efficiency of work habits. These are merely suggestive of the nearly infinite number of ways in which the examinees themselves may introduce variable influences that will tend to lower measured test reliability.

None of the common methods of estimating test reliability gets at these examinee-incurred influences; however, we try to minimize such influences whenever we have charge of a testing session by trying to ensure that all individuals are ready, willing, and desirous of doing their best on the test. We cannot eliminate this type of error variance, but we can try to keep it minimal.

## 2. Examiner-scorer influence

This source of error variance can be, and often is, negligible. Variable errors attributable to the examiner and scorer of most standardized paper-and-pencil tests are seldom of great magnitude; however, they can be. In their efforts to have their students do as well as they can on a standardized achievement test or an intelligence test, teachers sometimes invalidate the test by giving extra help, pointing out mistakes, or allowing additional time. An overly strict, rigid, or angry examiner may reduce the test's reliability, for this nonstandard behavior will be reacted to differentially by the various examinees. Examiner influences have the most adverse effects on the scores of young and inexperienced examinees. Relatively mature, test-wise examinees who are well motivated can tolerate a great deal without being adversely affected. Typically, persons who administer a standardized paper-and-pencil test contribute little to error variance if they follow test directions.

The examiner is likely to be a major source of error variance on individual tests (for example, the *Stanford-Binet,* the Wechsler tests, the *Rorschach,* etc.). The literature is full of research showing that there can be large differences in the test results obtained by different examiners, and this, of course, is just another way of saying that error variance may be relatively great in a set of results from such tests.

Notice that we have also included the scorer element here. If the test can be scored objectively, there can be perfect scorer reliability. Only when there is an element of subjectivity in the grading of tests does scorer reliability become a factor—as, for example, in the scoring of individual tests of intelligence and of personality. Where there is any subjectivity in scoring, the test manual should mention scorer reliability. Errors in recording or in copying results may be further sources of error.

## 3. Test content

Some of the most common reliability coefficients are those relating to test content. A test, being merely a sample of the items that might have been written over the same subject-matter domain, offers a major source of error variance. The scores obtained by a group of examinees might have been quite different if different questions had been asked. When there are alternate forms of a test, we can obtain an estimate of content reliability by administering both forms to the same group of people and determining the correlation between the two sets of scores.

Provided the test is not highly speeded, evidence of the content reliability may also be obtained from one administration of a single form of a test. One common way of doing this is through the use of an internal consistency measure such as one of the Kuder-Richardson formulas. These formulas involve assumptions about the test items and the total score, but these assumptions are reasonable to make about many tests.

Also common with nonspeeded tests is the *split-half* (sometimes called *odd-even*) reliability coefficient. We score each person's test twice: once for the odd-numbered items only and once for the even-numbered items only. We then compute the correlation between the odd-item and even-item scores; however, this correlation coefficient is an underestimate of the test's content reliability, for longer tests tend to be more reliable than shorter ones—and we have correlated two half-length tests. The full-length test's reliability can be estimated using a formula known as the *Spearman-Brown prophecy formula*.

### 4. Time influence

The fourth type of contribution to error variance is probably the best known of all: time influences. *Temporal reliability* is estimated by giving the same test to the same group at two different times, and correlating the scores made on the first and second administrations of the test. Coefficients of stability are almost always reported in test manuals and are reasonably well understood by most test users.

If the second administration takes place very soon after the first, some people may remember specific items, and this will influence the results. With some kinds of tests, the difficulty level of the items is changed considerably once a person has taken the test; for example, this is the case when much of the difficulty for the examinee involves determining how to solve some type of problem.

If the time interval between testings is very long, real changes may have taken place in the examinees and test scores *should* be different; in such situations, the ability of the test to reflect these real changes in the people will result in a spuriously low reliability *coefficient* because the changes in score are not the fault of the test. For example, fourth-grade pupils are tested at the beginning of the school year and retested at the end; all pupils will have learned something, but some will have learned much more than others. Inexperienced machinists, retested after six months on the job, will show the same sort of pattern—some people will have changed appreciably, and some will have changed little. People undergoing psychotherapy between the first and second testings may show markedly different scores.

### 5. Situation-induced

By the test situation, I am referring to those aspects of the total testing picture that are not clearly attributable elsewhere.

> At a testing conference years ago, one participant asked: "What is the effect on test reliability of a sudden, preseason, unexpected blizzard?" Would there be any effect on the test scores of a class of children being tested under such a condition? Certainly there would be, but it would be impossible to estimate just how much. Little Alicia Alvarez may be worried that her mother won't be able to get to the school to pick her up. Freckle-faced Timmy Tolpin may be stimulated to do his very best work as he looks forward to some after-school sledding. But Timmy's steady-minded sister, Tammy, probably will do just about the same as she would have done under normal weather conditions.

Testing conditions can make a great deal of difference in test results. Such conditions as ventilation, noise level, sound distractions, lighting, overcrowding, writing surface, and the like all can (but usually don't) have a major adverse effect on reliability.

> Take writing surface, for example. Suppose a highly speeded test is being taken by a group of high school students or by a group of job applicants. Suppose further that some examinees have those pencil-rutted, hand-carved desktops; some have to take the test while balancing lapboards; and some have good, roomy, smooth desktops on which to take their tests. Is there any question that some examinees will be unable to do their best work? The writing surface will contribute considerable error variance in this situation.

Cheating is another variable error. The examinee is helped by an indeterminate amount (perhaps even a negative amount) by cheating. For this reason (among others), cheating must not be allowed in the test room.

These testing-condition influences, although potentially important, are hard to estimate—-and do not enter into any of the common reliability estimates. Most of these influences are subject to control by the examiners if they plan carefully in advance of the testing session. In all fairness, too, most situational influences can be overcome by reasonably experienced and highly motivated examinees. They produce greater unreliability with younger, less experienced, and less confident examinees.

## Interrelationship of Sources of Error Variance

Some reliability coefficients take several sources of error variance into consideration. For example, some test manuals report test-retest reliability coefficients with alternate forms of the test being used—clearly taking cognizance of both content and temporal influences. In general, test publishers do a good job of reporting on content and temporal influences but do less well on the others.

## Standard Error of Measurement

The reliability of test scores may also be expressed in terms of the *standard error of measurement*. This standard error tells us how much one's obtained score is likely to differ from the examinee's hypothetical true score. This concept is explained further in Chapter 6, pages 65–68.

## Factors Affecting Reliability

Thousands of pages have been written on test reliability; we will do little more here than suggest a few of the factors that influence reliability.

### 1. Length increases reliability

The longer the test, the more reliable it will be—provided other factors are held constant (for example, the group tested is the same, the new items are of the same quality as those on the shorter test, and the test is not so long that fatigue becomes a consideration).

### 2. Heterogeneity increases reliability

The variability of the group tested is also important in evaluating any reliability coefficient. If everything else is the same, higher reliability coefficients will be found for groups that vary more in ability.

> We are going to demonstrate the temporal reliability of a *Reading Speed Test* (*RST*). From our school system we select at random one pupil from each grade, one through nine. We test each child in this sample; one week later, we test them all again. Inasmuch as speed of reading increases sharply through these grades, we should have a tremendous range in scores, and the differences among pupils should be so great that the order of score is not likely to change from one administration of the test to the next. The reliability coefficient then would prove to be very high—spuriously high, though. If, on the other hand, we were to select a small group of average ability second graders and test them twice (as above) on the *RST*, we should find a much lower reliability coefficient; these pupils probably would not differ much in their initial scores, and the order of score might very well change on the second testing, thereby reducing the size of the reliability coefficient. (This latter example is appropriate; the former is not.)

We need to note carefully the publisher's description of groups used and the conditions of testing in any reliability report.

### 3. The shorter the time, the higher the reliability

The length of time between the two testings in a temporal reliability coefficient is of obvious importance. Reliability is higher when the time between the two testings is short. That is one reason why IQs change most when there is a long period of time between testings.

### 4. Type of reliability estimate affects reliability

Reliability coefficients will differ according to the type of reliability estimate being used.

## Comparing Validity and Reliability

Validity is established through a statistical comparison of test scores with values on some *outside* variable. Any *constant* error in the test will have a direct adverse effect on the test's validity.

> We want to select power sewing machine operators. We use a test that includes many difficult words that are not necessary for good sewing machine operation.

Since this extraneous factor will influence each individual's score in a consistent fashion, the difficult words will reduce the test's validity for our purpose. (Note that the reliability is not necessarily reduced.)

No outside variable is involved in reliability, for reliability is not concerned with *what* a test measures—it is concerned only with the *reproduceability* of test results. Irregularities in testing procedures have a direct and adverse effect on reliability; indirectly, they may reduce validity as well. (These are *variable* errors. *Variable* here simply means nonconstant. In most other places throughout this book, *variable* is a general term referring to any characteristic, test, or the like that may assume different values.) The size of a validity coefficient is limited mathematically by the size of the reliability coefficient.

Note: A test must be reliable in order to be valid; however, the test can be reliable without being valid for our purposes.

## USABILITY

The third basic attribute of a test is *usability.* This includes all the many practical factors that go into our decision to use a particular test.

We are wondering whether to use the *Lyman Latin Verb Test* (*LLVT*) or the *Latin Original Verb Examination* (*LOVE*) in our high school Latin course. Since both tests are hypothetical, we may give them any characteristics we desire. My *LLVT*, therefore, has perfect reliability and validity. The *LOVE,* although not perfect, does have respectable validity and reliability for our purposes. We'll probably decide to use the *LOVE* in spite of the *LLVT*'s perfection, for the *LLVT* takes two weeks to administer and an additional week to score, can be administered to only one examinee at a time, and costs $10,000 per examinee, and only one person is considered qualified to administer and score it. The *LOVE,* on the other hand, can be given to a group of students simultaneously, has reusable test booklets that cost only eighty cents per copy (answer sheets cost ten cents apiece), and can be scored by a clerical worker in two or three minutes.

Under usability, we deal with all sorts of practical considerations. A longer test may be more reliable, and even more valid; however, if we have only a limited time available for testing, we may have to compromise with that ideal. If the preferred test is too expensive, we may have to buy a different one instead (or buy fewer copies of the first test), and so on.

I am **not** suggesting that validity and reliability are important only in theory, or in the abstract. They are vitally important. There is no point in testing unless we can have some confidence in the results. Practical factors must be considered, but only if the test has satisfactory reliability and validity.

# The Language of Testing

There are many different terms used in testing: aptitude, intelligence, achievement, attitude, personality, adjustment, etc. People sometimes find these terms confusing, but they do not all mean the same thing.

Some tests are known as maximum-performance; others are typical-performance. Tests of maximum performance ask examinees to do their best work; ability, either achieved or potential, is being tested. With tests of typical performance, we hope to obtain some ideas as to what the examinees are really like or what they actually do, rather than what they are capable of doing. These types of test should not be confused, for they are distinctly different.

> Mr. Beatty, school counselor, was reporting interest inventory results to a high school junior and his father: "John scored high on Computational and Mechanical. This means that he should go on to college and study mechanical engineering." Apparently Mr. Beatty had never read the computerized report of John's test! The report stated clearly in several places that the test measured only interests or preferences, and that other things (such as abilities) must be considered in career planning.

Maybe John will become a good mechanical engineer. Maybe not. No decision should be made solely on the basis of test scores—and most certainly not on the results of one preference inventory! What about John's intelligence? His aptitudes? His grades in school? His motivation? His willingness to study hard and consistently? Many factors besides interest-test scores must be considered in deciding on any educational or vocational objective.

Interest and aptitude are not synonymous, but some test users do confuse them. There are so many terms used in describing different kinds of test that it is easy to become confused.

> Years ago, one small test publisher listed an interest inventory under aptitude tests in his catalog. When I challenged him about it, he explained,"Well, it's the only interest test that I carry—and I didn't want to create another whole category in the catalog for just one test." P.S.: He doesn't need to worry any more—he is out of business.

## MAXIMUM-PERFORMANCE TESTS

Maximum-performance tests include tests of intelligence, aptitude, and achievement. In such tests, we assume that all examinees are equally and highly motivated. To the extent that this assumption is not justified, we must discount the results. Since we rarely know how well persons were motivated while taking a test, we usually must accept the assumption.

At least three determinants are involved in every score on tests of maximum performance: innate ability, environmental influences (including education), and motivation. There is no way to determine how much of a person's score is caused by any one of these three determinants—they are all necessarily involved in every maximum-performance score; that is, a person's test score necessarily depends in part on inborn potential as it has been modified by life experiences (education and training, the environment in general, etc.) and by motivation at the time of testing. In addition, of course, there is always some element of error in any measurement. (See Reliability in Chapter 2.)

### Intelligence Tests

Intelligence is an abstract concept. We all have ideas about its meaning, but there is little agreement on its precise meaning. Each of us, test authors included, has his or her own ideas as to what constitutes intelligence.

Intelligence tests reflect these differences in definition. Some contain only verbal items; others contain much nonverbal material. Some stress problem solving, while others emphasize memory. Some result in a single total score (probably an IQ), whereas others yield several scores.

These varying emphases may lead to diverse results. We should expect to find different IQs when the same person is tested with different tests. We may be obtaining several measures of intelligence, but in each case intelligence is being defined a little differently. Under the circumstances, perhaps we should be more surprised when different intelligence tests give us very similar results.

For most purposes, intelligence tests may be thought of as tests of general aptitude or scholastic aptitude. When so regarded, they are most typically used in predicting achievement in school, college, or training programs. Performance on intelligence tests is related to achievement. Even the ability to take an intelligence test depends on achievement (in reading and arithmetic, for example). And familiarity with different words, objects, places, and concepts differs from examinee to examinee. Lack of familiarity will put anyone at a disadvantage when taking an intelligence test—one factor that accounts for the lower scores we may find when testing minority youth.

## Aptitude Tests

All aptitude tests imply prediction. They give us a basis for predicting future level of performance. Aptitude tests often are used in selecting individuals for jobs, for admission to training programs, for scholarships, and for many other purposes. Sometimes aptitude tests are used for classifying individuals, as when students are assigned to different ability-grouped sections of the same course. Aptitude tests sometimes are substituted for intelligence tests.

The *Differential Aptitude Tests* (*DAT*) and the *Armed Services Vocational Aptitude Battery* (*ASVAB*) are two examples of aptitude test batteries designed to yield scholastic aptitude (or intelligence) scores in addition to the scores on the several aptitude measures. Aptitude measurement depends in part on achievement in such areas as reading and mathematics.

## Achievement Tests

Achievement tests are used in evaluating the examinee's present level of knowledge, skills, and competence. Unlike other types of test, many achievement tests are written locally; a teacher's classroom test is a good example. There are also many commercially developed achievement tests. Criterion-referenced tests are further examples of achievement tests. *Assessment* and *evaluation* are terms often used in connection with achievement testing.

The principal basis for differentiating aptitude and achievement tests lies in their use. The same sorts of item—indeed, even the identical test—may be used in different situations to measure either aptitude or achievement. The purpose of the testing, whether for assessing present attainment or for predicting future performance, is the best basis for the distinction.

With tests of maximum performance, we seldom have difficulty understanding what we are attempting to measure. With aptitude tests, we are trying to predict how well people will do. With achievement tests, we are trying to measure their present attainment. With intelligence tests, although we may disagree on specific definitions, we are trying to measure their current level of intellectual capacity or functioning.

## TYPICAL-PERFORMANCE TESTS

The situation is far less clear with typical-performance tests. There is less agreement about what is being measured or what should be measured. Again, we find a proliferation of terms: *adjustment, personality, temperament, interests, preferences, values;* there are *tests, scales, blanks, inventories, indexes,* as well as *Q-sorts, forced-choice methods,* etc.—to say nothing of *projective techniques, situational tests,* and the like.

What does a score mean? It is very hard to say, even after giving the matter careful thought. In the first place, the dimensions of a typical-performance test are likely to be vaguely defined: What is *sociable* to one author may not be to the next. The philosophy or rationale underlying typical-performance tests must necessarily be more involved and less obvious than the rationale for maximum-performance tests.

Whereas a person's ability is more or less stable, one's affective nature (especially, one's mood) may change over a short period of time. And it is this aspect of the individual that we are trying to get at through tests of typical performance. We are trying to find out *what Jay Leno or Oprah Winfrey is really like*—not how much Leno learned in his math classes or how much Oprah knows about music.

With maximum-performance tests, we are at least certain that people did not obtain higher scores than they are capable of. After all, one cannot fake knowing more algebra or fake being more intelligent. The examinees can, of course, perform far beneath their capabilities—by simply not trying, by paying little attention, or by many other means. With typical-performance tests, though, a person usually can fake in either direction (higher or lower, better adjustment or poorer adjustment, etc.). With such tests, we do not want examinees to do their best; instead, we want them to answer as honestly as they can. In fact, the purpose of these tests often is disguised. A *Sense of Humor Test* may in reality be an attempt to measure selected dimensions of personality and have relatively little to do with humor. And, as we shall note later, there are other means of disguising the true intent of typical-performance tests.

There would seem to be an assumption that an examinee is trying to answer honestly. Yet on some personality tests, the authors are concerned *only* with the response made, not with the examinee's reasons for having made it. Thus, the person who responds *yes* to an item may do so honestly, or to look better or to look worse than is true; it makes no difference, these test authors contend, for a person resembles specified other people at least to the extent of having made that same response.

## Criterion Keying

Some typical-performance tests are said to be *criterion keyed* because their scoring keys have been developed through the performance of two contrasting groups.

> Years ago a certain university football coach—I'll call him Sid Sylman—had a theory that paper-and-pencil tests measuring desire for hard physical contact could be used to differentiate good and less-good football players. We decided to test his theory. We had all freshman football players answer several hundred items from personality tests. At the end of the season, each coach was to rate each player on a five-point scale according to the intensity with which he had played. We would combine the ratings and divide the players into two extreme groups. I would then determine those items that discriminated between the two groups. The selected items would be used the following year to predict which freshmen would play hard-contact football. We would need to cross-validate (essentially, replicate the study) to be sure the new scale worked; if it did, we would have a very useful test. (The results? I don't know. The coach resigned at the end of the season and became a professional coach. The project had to be abandoned; the assistant coaches were not interested. Do you remember this, Sid?)

Typical-performance tests that are criterion keyed often seem superior to tests for which the scoring keys have been developed in other ways. The *Minnesota Multiphasic Personality Inventory* is an example of a test using this approach. Criterion-keyed tests sometimes are criticized because occasional items are scored in a way that seems to make little sense. They sometimes are criticized, too, for using a *shotgun approach,* rather than being developed in accordance with some theory. The irrefutable answer to the criticisms is, of course, that the scoring system "works."

## Forced-Choice Items

An item is forced choice if the alternatives have been matched for social acceptability, but only one alternative relates to a particular criterion. The simplest form of forced-choice item has two alternatives, each seeming to be equally desirable:

**Would you rather be: (a) honest; (b) loyal?**

I would like to be both—and so would you. Perhaps, though, some group (say, good bookkeepers) could be found statistically to answer (a) more often than another group (say, less-good bookkeepers). The *Edwards Personal Preference Schedule* uses this style of item.

Other forced-choice items may involve three or four alternatives, rather than only two. The several Kuder preference records are common examples.

Forced-choice items have the advantage of being somewhat disguised in intent, but they are not unanimously favored. They may be resented by examinees because of the fine discriminations demanded. When used in such a way that the items are scored for more than one variable, they result in an *ipsative* sort of score; that is, the strength of each variable depends not solely on that variable but on its strength relative to the strength of other variables. In other words, if one variable goes up, another must go down.

## Ambiguity of Items

With nearly all typical-performance test items, there is likely to be some ambiguity. Let us look at one item. Consider the following:

**I am a liberal.**

*Strongly Agree     Agree     Uncertain     Disagree     Strongly Disagree*

If I had to answer this item, my reasoning might go something like this: What do they mean by "liberal"? I might say "Strongly Agree," for I am strongly opposed to censorship. However, my political views are moderately conservative, so I could answer "Disagree." The truth is that sometimes I am liberal and sometimes I am not!  Does this describe you, too?

The indecisiveness of an examinee may be caused by the ambiguity of a term, or it may be a reflection of the individual's personality—or perhaps just of his or her mood at the time the test is taken.

In any case, the examinee may sometimes answer an item one way and sometimes another and be perfectly sincere each time. (As we saw in Chapter 2, such factors as these lower test reliability.)

Furthermore, the motivational pattern of each examinee becomes of great importance. Examinees who have much to gain by showing up well may try to answer the items so that they appear to be better than they really are; others may try to appear more disturbed than they really are if that would be to their advantage. Furthermore, such behaviors may be either deliberate or subconscious.

Still further, most typical-performance tests try to measure several different characteristics of the individual. A person who fakes responses with one scale in mind may inadvertently change the scores on other scales as well. For example, the person who tries to appear more *sociable* may inadvertently also score higher on the *aggressive* scale.

Often test norms are based on the performances of groups of people (perhaps students) in nonthreatening situations. To compare the performance of a person under stress (such as fear of not being selected or having severe personal problems) with the performance of such groups may be unrealistic.

Typical-performance tests, of course, can be useful to psychologists, experienced counselors, trained psychiatrists, etc.; however, these tests rarely should be used by people with limited backgrounds in testing and psychology. There are too many pitfalls to be aware of. These tests do have their place—but that place is not in the hands of the amateur. Many psychologists believe that less confidence should be placed in typical-performance tests than in the maximum-performance tests with which this book is principally concerned.

## OBJECTIVE–SUBJECTIVE–PROJECTIVE RESPONSE

Another way of looking at tests is to classify them according to the form of response called for. One familiar classification is *objective* versus *essay* or, better, *objective* versus *subjective,* and I would add *projective*. A little later I will mention a similar classification that I prefer, even though it is less common.

An item is *objective* if the complete scoring procedure is prescribed in advance of the testing. Thus multiple-choice and true-false tests are usually objective, for the test writer can draft a scoring key that contains the right (or best) answer for each item on the test before the test is ever used. Except for mistakes or for difficulties in reading responses, we can be completely objective. When answered on special answer sheets, such items can be scored by machine. *Subjective* indicates that some element of personal judgment will be involved in the scoring. Completion and essay items are examples of subjective items, for the tester rarely can anticipate every response that may be scored as correct.

I have stressed objectivity of scoring. Any time that we prepare a test, whether for local use or for national distribution, we must make such decisions as what items to write, what elements of information to include, and what wording to use. Inevitably there is always some degree of subjectivity in test construction.

*Projective* items are, in a sense, subjective items—but they are something more. They are items that are deliberately made ambiguous in order to demand individualistic responses. The *Rorschach* inkblots and Murray's *Thematic Apperception Test* are examples. Verbal material may be used projectively, too; Rotter, for example, presents the examinee with stems of sentences to be completed, thereby making a person project his or her personality into the response. Typical of Rotter's items are:

I like to . . .

One thing I dread is . . .

My mother . . .

## SELECT-RESPONSE—SUPPLY-RESPONSE

A classification that I prefer when looking at test items is select-response versus supply-response. This classification, it seems to me, is self-defining: If the examinees may select from among the alternatives given to them, the item is *select-response*; otherwise, it is a *supply-response* item. Thus the multiple-choice test is select-response; the essay is supply-response.

## WRITTEN–ORAL–PERFORMANCE TESTS

Another basis for test classification is the medium used for presenting the directions and the item material. Most typically, test items are printed or *written,* and the examinee responds by writing answers or by making marks that correspond to chosen answers. Directions sometimes are given orally, but most frequently they are given both orally and in writing.

Few tests are *oral;* teacher-prepared spelling tests are the most common example. A few tests are available on sound recordings. There are tests for blind people, some of which were especially developed for them and others that are simply adaptations of tests for the sighted. There are trade tests prepared for oral presentation and oral response, used almost exclusively in employment offices. Nonstandardized oral exams are given in graduate school and other settings. Recently we have seen the development of a few oral aptitude tests for adults who are functionally illiterate.

*Performance* tests usually involve special apparatus (as opposed to only paper and pencil) and may involve a work sample.

## STANDARDIZED–INFORMAL TESTS

*Standardized* tests have been developed, usually by specialists, to be used more extensively than by the test writer and his or her immediate colleagues. The test content is set, the directions are prescribed, and the scoring procedure is completely specified. And there are norms against which we may compare the scores of our examinees (except on criterion-referenced tests).

*Informal* tests, on the other hand, refer primarily to tests written by the examiner for local use only. Classroom achievement tests, teacher-prepared, are the most common examples. We are not concerned with such tests in this book; however, much that is said about standardized tests does have some application to informal tests.

## SPEED–POWER TESTS

*Speeded* tests are maximum-performance tests in which speed plays an important part in determining a person's score; however, a test may have a time limit and still not be speeded. If there is no time limit, or if the time limit is so generous that most examinees are able to finish the test, the test is said to be a *power* test.

Most achievement tests should be power tests, for we usually are more concerned with assessing our examinees' levels of attainment than with finding out how rapidly they respond. Even here, though, there are exceptions—for example, an achievement test in shorthand or typing. Power and speed are opposite ends of a continuum. Some tests are almost purely power (having no time limit), and other tests are almost purely speed (having items of such little difficulty that everyone could answer them perfectly if given enough time); but in between these extremes are many tests with time limits, some generous and some limited. Such in-between tests have some characteristics of both speed and power tests and are classified as one or the other depending upon whether the time allowed makes speed an *important* determinant of score.

## GROUP–INDIVIDUAL TESTS

This classification is perhaps the most obvious of all. An *individual* test is one that can be administered to only one individual at a time. Common examples are individual tests of intelligence, such as the *Stanford-Binet* and the Wechsler tests. Projective tests of personality are almost always individual tests. Some tests that involve special apparatus, such as manual dexterity tests, usually are administered individually; however, such tests sometimes can be administered simultaneously to small groups if proper conditions exist and if the examiner has multiple copies of the test. For example:

> Mary Marston, a former student of mine, was the psychometrist in an industrial personnel office. She had tables arranged in a U shape with herself in the middle of the open area. With this arrangement, she was able to administer paper-and-pencil or apparatus tests to as many as twelve applicants at a time.

*Group* tests can be administered simultaneously to more than one person; usually they can be administered simultaneously to a group of any size. Group tests are usually, but not necessarily, paper-and-pencil (the only materials involved). Individual tests, however, commonly involve materials other than paper and pencil.

## VERBAL–NONVERBAL TESTS

A *verbal* test has verbal items; that is, the items involve words (either oral or written). So-called *nonverbal* tests contain no verbal items; however, words almost always are used in the directions. Some writers prefer the term *non-language* to describe tests that have no verbal items but for which the directions are given either orally or in writing; these writers use *nonverbal* only for tests in which no words are used, even in the directions.

## CULTURE FAIR

Some tests are said to be *culture fair* or *culture free*. The latter term should be avoided, for no test can be developed that is completely free from cultural influences. Some tests are relatively independent of cultural or environmental influences and may be thought of as being *fair* to people of most societies; however, these tests may do less well than others in measuring behavior within our own society. Tests that use items that are relatively culture free may not be measuring any characteristic within any given culture very effectively.

> Robert Williams, a well-known Black psychologist, has introduced the concept of *cultural homogeneity*, by which he seems to mean simply items that work well within a single culture or subculture. For example, if a Black girl does poorly on a standard intelligence test (a test that probably best reflects an upper-middle-class White culture), we might well test her with a Black-oriented test [for example, Williams's *BITCH* (*Black Intelligence Test Culturally Homogeneous*, formerly the *Black Intelligence Test Counterbalanced for Honkies*)].

For many years, I have used with my own classes a test that contains blocks of items that discriminate against either Black or White examinees. Because there are alternating blocks of five Black and five White items, I used to call it my *Checkerboard Test*; however, a respected tutor of mine, thinking that title undignified, prefers to call it the *American Cross Cultural Ethnic Nomenclature Test* (*ACCENT*). By either title, the test does a beautiful job of discriminating between my African American and White students.

## HOW TO TELL

How can we tell what a test is like? We can learn something about available tests by reading the catalogs of the various test publishers; however, a test catalog is printed to show the tests a publisher has for sale and is not the most objective source of information.

Nor is the test title the best means for telling the purpose of a test. In the past there have been many examples of tests with misleading titles; however, test publishers today tend to do a much better job of giving their tests descriptive titles (except where they are deliberately disguised, as in some personality tests).

The test manual is usually the best source for detailed information about a test. (See Chapter 7.) This has been especially true since 1954, when the American Psychological Association (in cooperation with the American Educational Research Association and the American Personnel and Guidance Association) first published technical recommendations for publishers. Those recommendations have been revised several times, and are generally accepted as authoritative. Also of great value is *Principles for the Validation and Use of*

*Personnel Selection Procedures,* a booklet published in 1975 by APA's Society for Industrial and Organizational Psychology.

The major reference for critical and objective reviews of most psychological tests is provided by the *Mental Measurements Yearbooks,* edited by the late Oscar K. Buros. At this writing there are eleven bound editions in the series: the 1938,1940, Third, Fourth, Fifth, Sixth, Seventh, Eighth, Ninth, Tenth, and Eleventh; all are needed, for they are essentially nonduplicative. Tests ordinarily are reviewed in subsequent editions only when there is additional evidence to consider. Buros's *MMYs* are also an excellent source for references to articles about specific tests.

Another excellent reference source is published by the Test Corporation of America: *Test Critiques I, II, III, IV,* and *V.* Another valuable book from the same publisher is *Tests, Second Edition.*

## THIS BOOK

This book is concerned mainly with maximum-performance, objective, select-response, written, standardized group psychometric tests, which may be power or speeded and hand- or machine-scored. The book is concerned primarily with norms-referenced—as opposed to criterion-referenced—measurement.

# *What's New in Testing Today?*

CHAPTER **FOUR**

These are exciting times for people who work with tests. Computer usage has become commonplace. Criterion-referenced testing became more accepted during the late 1980s, but it is probably still used less today than many of us had anticipated back in the 1970s. Adaptive testing has started to show its promise; I believe that this approach will become much more widespread as we head into the twenty-first century. Other new trends in testing include competency, accountability, accessibility of test results, the educational use of portfolios, outcome-based education, and so forth.

## COMPUTERS AND TESTING

At one time machine scoring of tests required a special answer sheet that had pairs of parallel lines. When marked with a number two (soft) lead pencil, the answer sheet could be scored by the IBM 805 Test Scoring Machine. With electrically sensitive sensors, the machine could "pick up" and count marks corresponding to the correct responses (the mark-sensing process). The machine operator read the score off the dial and wrote the score on the test paper.

Next came the work of Hankes in Minnesota and Lindquist in Iowa, and the electronic scoring age had begun. Such machines, used by major test publishers and several scoring services, depend on optical scanning (instead of actual electric contacts as in the mark-sensing process) and can operate at very rapid speeds. Machines are capable of scoring and printing simultaneously the scores from several different tests (or parts of tests) on both sides of the answer sheets, reading off examinee names, preparing rosters, and performing related operations.

The 1970s and 1980s saw the continued development of electronic scoring, reporting, and interpreting of test results. When computers in line with the scoring machines are fed relevant information, very helpful statistical material can be generated.

Computer-based test interpretation (CBTI) progressed during the 1980s to the point where it accounted for a major share of test usage in this country. Today the catalogs of many test publishers actually contain more pages describing computer services and computer software than pages describing the tests available from that publisher.

The development and growth of CBTI in the 1980s paralleled the development of powerful personal computers. CBTI programs are now available for the tests that are most widely used, including the following: *Differential Aptitude Tests, Strong-Campbell Interest Inventory, Kuder Occupational Interest Schedule, Minnesota Multiphasic Personality Inventory, California Psychological Inventory, Iowa Tests of Basic Skills,* and even the *Rorschach (Inkblot) Test.* The Psychological Corporation, California Test Bureau (CTB/McGraw-Hill), Institute for Personality and Ability Testing, Riverside Press, Psychological Assessment Resources, London House/Science Research Associates, National Computer Services, and Educational and Industrial Testing Service (EDITS) are among the major companies that offer such services.

Test publishers and others have feared that the increased use of computers in test interpretation might result in programs written by unauthorized and unqualified individuals. For that reason some publishers developed a logo to identify those programs that have been authorized by the respective test publisher; however, this logo has had very limited acceptance and use.

In one case (at least), the rights of a publisher to control the interpretation programs for its tests have been upheld by federal courts. The value of any test interpretation, of course, depends upon the knowledge, skill, and sophistication of the person who does the interpreting. But that is only part of the situation. Even when the CBTI program has been prepared by a well-qualified and knowledgeable authority, well-trained people are still needed to fine-tune the interpretation to the individual examinee. This is especially true in clinical settings. Knowledgeable examiners are still needed.

# CRITERION-REFERENCED MEASUREMENT

Criterion-referenced testing is not new. Dubois, in his *History of Psychological Testing,* credits the Chinese of about four thousand years ago with the first known use of standardized tests. Some of these tests (for example, tests of calligraphy and horsemanship) were almost certainly criterion-referenced tests.

A *criterion-referenced* test (also called *edumetric, content-, domain-,* or *objective-referenced*) is one in which scores are expressed in terms of the skills or behaviors achieved, rather than in terms of a comparison with other people (i.e., tests that are *norm-referenced*). For example, most shorthand and typing tests are reported in terms of words per minute, rather than as a comparison of an examinee's speed with the speeds of other examinees. Some of the earliest tests in this country were criterion-referenced. The *Ayers Handwriting Scale* (in 1912), for example, provided the teacher with a set of penmanship specimens against which to compare each pupil's handwriting. The score was based directly on the quality of the child's performance relative to the quality of the standard specimens; there was no between-pupil comparison involved.

As adapted to general school use today, the criterion-referenced test is typically one of a series of coordinated achievement tests that is designed to measure a single behavioral objective within a course of study. Ideally, the pupils would have no knowledge of the unit's content before instruction and complete knowledge after instruction.

In practice, the teacher strives for pupil *mastery* of the material. Mastery, though, does not necessarily mean complete knowledge of the content; rather, mastery is defined (usually by the test publisher) as obtaining a score of at least 80 percent (or perhaps 75 percent) correct.

**Warning: Do not confuse criterion-referenced tests with criterion-related validity or criterion-keyed development of test items.**

A criterion-referenced approach involves identifying (usually very small) units of knowledge or skill (much as one would do in developing a program for a teaching machine). A test is used to evaluate pupil mastery of each unit. Only when the pupil has demonstrated mastery (as defined) may the pupil proceed to the next unit of study.

Such an approach is said to encourage greater teacher emphasis on individualized instruction and to enable each pupil to work at her or his own pace. The approach allegedly discourages stereotyping individual pupils as dull or slow, and it clearly does discourage comparison of the relative performance of the various pupils.

The criterion-referenced approach leads to a philosophy that people differ not so much in intelligence as in the speed with which they can acquire facts and skills. Presumably this view helps teachers to be more patient and understanding with pupils who learn more slowly. Enthusiasts believe that teachers who are more concerned with a norm-referenced point of view are likely to neglect slower learners in order to spend more time with average and above-average pupils.

### Evaluation of Criterion-Referenced Testing

This reasoning may sound intriguing, but it has limitations. Some edumetric theorists try to give different meanings to validity and reliability (important measurement concepts defined more fully in Chapter 2), but this seems to be wishful thinking; validity and reliability, as the terms are commonly used, are still important. Major test publishers do pay attention to these concepts, but some tests produced by new publishers are weak—particularly because they use so few items that satisfactory reliability and validity (however they are defined) are impossible to attain. This approach to educational measurement may be useful in evaluating educational progress in the early stages of learning, but it seems to me to be completely inappropriate beyond the elementary grades.

## TEST-ITEM BANKS

Item banks have been commonplace for years. The publisher of every introductory psychology text, for example, prints an instructor's manual; this manual usually contains a large number of test items covering each chapter of the text. These items comprise a test-item bank—that is, a collection of test items from which the individual instructor may withdraw specific items to make up examinations for the course being taught. Many teachers and professors have developed item banks of their own. Some include such information as date(s) an item was used, percentage of students answering the item correctly, and how well the item discriminiates between the better and the poorer students.

The development and use of computers have added dimensions to the item banks. For example:

> Let's suppose that we have five teachers, each teaching one section of a geography course. The teachers have stored many test items in the system's main computer—some written by the teachers themselves and some supplied by a textbook publisher. Using a master list of the items, each teacher can draft a quiz or test simply by indicating the items desired. This general approach is being used in many larger high schools, colleges, and universities.

## ADAPTIVE TESTING

Adaptive testing is not completely new. In some respects, even the familiar *Stanford-Binet Scales* are adaptive. With the widespread use of computers, adaptive testing is certain to become more commonplace.

In adaptive testing, examinees are presented with one or more items of average difficulty. Examinees who answer correctly are presented with more difficult items; those who answer incorrectly are given easier items. This procedure is repeated until each examinee is responding to items of appropriate difficulty.

Such testing has obvious advantages. Fewer items are administered to any one examinee, and testing takes less time. A less obvious advantage is the fact that different examinees answer different items, thereby ensuring greater security of the pool of available test items. Other terms synonymous with adaptive testing include *branched, programmed, staged, selective, tailored, dynamic, individualized,* and *response-contingent.*

The adaptive approach is easier to develop for individual tests than for tests to be given simultaneously to more than one person. Because of the technical/statistical effort involved, the approach lends itself more readily to standardized testing than to informal testing.

## LATENT TRAIT SCALING

Latent trait scaling refers to various procedures in the development of test items. These procedures purport to yield items that have common discriminating ability across groups that differ widely in ability. The statistical methodologies are very sophisticated and go well beyond the limits of this book. Latent trait scaling has many enthusiastic supporters; however, some psychometricians note that there is little research so far to establish the validity or the utility of the procedures in coping with the challenges of real (rather than theoretical) data.

If latent trait scaling realizes the promise that some people believe it has, we may expect to see marked improvement in tests in the future. Alternatively, it may prove to be just another promising, but unrealized, fad. Further information may be found under the following library listings: *item response theory, item characteristics curve theory,* and *Rasch model.*

The well-informed test user will want to know that latent trait scaling exists, but only the psychometrician with a sound background in statistics and mathematics will be able to develop tests in this fashion.

## COMPETENCY AND ACCOUNTABILITY

These two words still are heard frequently in educational circles. The Buckley Amendment (Family Educational Rights and Privacy Act of 1974) mandated that student records (including test results) **must** be open to students and their parents. The Equal Employment Opportunity Commission (EEOC) provides some guarantees against racial and sexual discrimination in the workplace. Some states have introduced competency requirements for pupils and teachers. Still more needs to be done, for in many ways American education is in a deplorable state.

Many schools are unruly. Attendance is poor. Dropout rates are high. Teachers complain of poor morale. School systems in many cities are administratively top-heavy, burdening teachers with an unconscionable load of reports to be written and forms to be filled out. Racial tensions show little abatement, and violence seems to be at an all-time high.

The main difficulty, though, is that our students are not learning as much as they should. Countless studies support this allegation, including cross-cultural studies that compare American students with students in other countries. Lower scores are reported for the American students in subjects ranging from geography to the sciences. Performance is especially poor in mathematics and the sciences. Many companies complain of the necessity for training even new entry-level employees who are high school graduates.

Fifty-five percent of the finalists in the prestigious Westinghouse High School Science Competition in 1988 were either foreign-born or children of parents who were born outside the United States. In one recent year, valedictorians at 13 of Boston's 17 public high schools were foreign-born.

A January 1990 report to the Association of American Universities indicated that the shortage of Ph.D.s in this country is widespread and is getting worse. Primarily concerned with the number of people with the Ph.D. degree who will be available for university teaching, the researchers predicted an annual shortage of 7,500 natural science and engineering doctorates by the year 2000. The report said that shortages in the humanities and social sciences will occur even sooner. Of those people currently earning doctorates, less than half are now selecting academic positions. An educational conference of state governors held in March of 1996 urged schools and individual teachers to demand more of their students.

## WHAT IS WRONG?

In some cases it may be the environment for learning. Contrast these two situations:

> A few years ago I visited a city high school near my home. Although class was in session, the corridors were so crowded with students that it was difficult to make my way to the principal's office. There were other clusters of students in the boys' room, where the smell of cigarette (only?) smoke struck me immediately upon opening the door.

We need, instead, to have more situations such as the following:

> Again a few years ago, I made an unannounced visit to the high school [Athol (Massachusetts) High School] from which I had graduated more than fifty years

earlier. The principal showed me the entire plant of his 900-student school. In every room we visited, there was a cordial exchange between principal and teacher and/or students. The only person we saw in any of the hallways was the head custodian.

It helps, too, when textbooks are not watered down to oversimplify topics and to avoid controversial ones. As parents and teachers, we must start expecting more and higher performance from our students. Students do best when they are properly motivated to do so, and when they are expected to do so.

## OUTCOME-BASED EDUCATION

Evidence abounds that in many school systems—indeed, in some states—the prevailing educational philosophy is something called *outcome-based education.* Unfortunately, the "outcome" these educationists seem to have in mind is concerned less with educational excellence than with positive self-image. Certainly positive self-images are desirable, but most of us believe that such images are best when supported by earned achievement.

This outcome-based philosophy even extends to the field of athletics, if a story related to me recently is true:

> Daisy, a ninth grader, is a sprinter on her junior high track team. In a recent interscholastic meet, Daisy had won two races. Her coach told her that she would not be running in the third race, as she had planned. "Dorcas," he explained, "should be given a chance to win one of these races—and you've already won two. We'll let her have this one." I wonder how much Dorcas will value her victory—if, indeed, she did win.

## EXCEPTIONAL PEOPLE: THOSE WITH LANGUAGE AND PHYSICAL DISABILITIES

Although standardized testing works reasonably well for the vast majority of Americans, people with language disabilities ("challenged") are at a disadvantage. Some of the more popular tests are published in a second language (usually Spanish), and a few nonverbal tests exist; however, these are probably of only minimal value to teachers and personnel workers. English is the preferred language in the United States and the language people need in order to compete successfully in school and at work. I understand that most Hispanic parents prefer to have their children taught in English-only classes in the belief and hope that this will permit their children to achieve more than they would otherwise.

My good friend John Holland has met the language challenge in admirable fashion. His *Self Directed Search* is available not only in English and

Spanish, but also in two other versions standardized on Canadians: Canadian English and Canadian French. There are some other tests available in additional language forms, but fewer than we might wish.

People with physical disabilities are also at a disadvantage when taking standardized tests. Some suitable tests are available, and others are being developed. Typically, special education teachers and rehabilitation counselors are most knowledgeable about the relatively few special tests that are available; many of them are also skilled at adapting standard tests to cope with the specific limitations of the handicapped individual. Special educators, in fact, have such a splendid reputation for excellent teaching that many parents are striving to have their children declared eligible for special education classes.

*Note: Whenever possible, testing of handicapped individuals should be done only by qualified examiners.*

## PORTFOLIOS

One current fad is the use of portfolios in evaluation. In one sense, they, too, are not new. For example, a July 1995 issue of the British *Antique Trade Gazette* described an elaborate framed 19th-century sampler (being offered at auction) as essentially a portfolio prepared by a young female orphan to demonstrate her deftness in needlework. And, of course, portfolios have been widely used in the arts for many years: Actors, artists, models, photographers, and some others have always maintained portfolios. In the same way most university personnel keep their academic résumés (vitas) current.

But using portfolios on a large scale for general use as measuring devices is new. There is a little literature available in the various measurement and testing journals about the systematic use of portfolios in the evaluation of students. The articles suggest that the use of portfolios is expensive, time-consuming, of low reliability, and otherwise not generally useful as an evaluation tool. Later, perhaps—but not now.

## NEW ALL OVER AGAIN?

In the 1990s we heard of some "new" discoveries, advances, theories, etc., that somehow sounded awfully familiar. I guess that is all part of progress.

## NOT ONLY IN THE UNITED STATES

Many of the difficulties with American education that we have noted can also be found in Canada and in Great Britain—and probably in many other countries, too. For example, great controversy is currently raging in England on how best to teach and—especially—test pupils on British history!

# *Social Responsibility and Testing*

If testing is going to be effective and appropriate, we need to select good tests and to administer and interpret them correctly. Professional-ethical considerations are involved in all of these processes.

Testing is in a schizophrenic age. Although attacks on testing are still being made frequently and are ever more virulent, people are using more tests today than ever before.

Among other allegations, tests have been accused of:

1. Not measuring innate (inborn) intelligence
2. Not measuring creativity
3. Labeling children as morons, dopes, slow learners, and so on
4. Favoring the glib individual and penalizing the thoughtful person
5. Invading privacy
6. Giving inconsistent results
7. Being unfair
8. Being grossly misinterpreted

et cetera, et cetera, et cetera

How can we explain the increased use of tests in view of all these criticisms?

Part of the explanation may be that there has been a slight change in the emphasis of tests. There may be less intelligence testing today, but there has been a decided increase in aptitude and (especially) achievement testing. Aptitude batteries (such as the *Iowa Tests of Basic Skills* and the *Differential Aptitude Tests*) are tending to replace intelligence tests. After all, we don't have to worry about a precise definition of intelligence if we are trying to measure aptitude or achievement.

The increase in achievement testing has been phenomenal. Not only is there a steady demand for the norms-referenced achievement batteries, but development of criterion-referenced testing (especially at the primary level) has continued throughout the past decade. Additionally, there have been numerous local scandals as high school graduates in various states have been found lacking in seemingly basic skills. This latter situation has resulted in increased demands for proficiency tests to demonstrate that schools are developing at least minimum skills in students before graduating them. Most states now have some sort of statewide assessment program.

Many of the negative comments are true—or partly so. Much of the legislative attention has been an effort to guarantee that tests are used responsibly, and I believe that this will have a long-term beneficial influence on both education and testing. There still is a great need to educate people in the responsible and intelligent use of tests. Tests can be helpful in many situations, but they are not the complete and ultimate answer to every problem.

One big difficulty that most critics tend to ignore is this: The elimination of testing would solve very little. One cannot legitimately evaluate tests against a criterion of perfection; sometimes the absence of tests has disadvantages of another sort.

## TESTS DO NOT MEASURE INNATE ABILITY (ONLY)

Of course they don't. At any rate, that isn't all that they measure. They measure a great deal more. Any maximum-performance test (aptitude, intelligence, or achievement) always measures some combination of innate ability, the influences of environment, and the examinee's motivation when tested (and perhaps other factors as well). Environmental influences include all kinds of experiences (education, travel, etc.).

I was giving a short series of lectures on testing to a class of first-year psychiatric residents. These are people who have an M.D. degree and are now starting their training to become psychiatrists. In this particular group were several foreign-born physicians who had been in this country for only a brief period of time. I was illustrating the administration of one of the most popular individual tests of intelligence. As I went around the table asking sample questions of each resident, I received failures on these (simulated) items: "In what direction would I be going if I traveled from Detroit to Dallas?", "What is a child labor law?", and

"What does the word 'collect' mean?" The questions were asked respectively of an Iraqi, a Greek, and a Brazilian. I had little difficulty in making this class appreciate that tests are necessarily at least partially culture bound!

Rather obviously, people who have survived the educational system (in the United States or elsewhere) for long enough to obtain a medical degree are clearly above average in intelligence, regardless of their performance on specific items of this (or any) intelligence test. The professional literature on the relative importance of genetic and cultural bases of intelligence fills many volumes. The controversy is sometimes very bitter, and I shall not perpetuate it here; I believe that both heredity and environment are important—both in the determination of intelligence *test scores* and in the determination of a person's *effective intelligence*. Neither factor is sufficient by itself.

## INTELLIGENCE TESTS DO NOT MEASURE CREATIVITY

No knowledgeable authority claims that they do, but some critics denounce intelligence tests for not measuring creativity. No intelligence test gets at all cognitive functions, but some do report more than a single overall IQ. David Wechsler provides for separate measures of "Verbal" and "Performance" IQs on his intelligence tests.

Howard Gardner has developed a Theory of Multiple Intelligences that is attracting some attention in the late 1990s. Currently he identifies linguistic, musical, logical-mathematical, bodily-kinesthetic, spatial, interpersonal, and intrapersonal intelligences.

I believe that the late J. P. Guilford is the only psychmetrician of note to include any sort of creativity measure in his intelligence research. Guilford contended that he had identified at least 120 recognizably different intellective factors. Several of these were described as "measures of divergent thinking" and certainly might be considered measures of creativity. The fact remains that there is no widely used intelligence test that contains any measures of creativity.

Intelligence tests, starting with Binet (about 1905), have tended to be school-related. Most present-day intelligence tests have a similar school orientation, although some tests are slanted more toward use in an industrial personnel setting or in a clinical situation. Even for these latter uses, intelligence tests rarely include much that could be considered a measure of creativity.

We may question whether intelligence tests should measure creativity. There is less agreement among various definitions of creativity than there is among definitions of intelligence. (And there are certainly different definitions for that concept!)

Creativity may be important; however, until we have more evidence of the validity of creativity tests, we should not be too dismayed that intelligence tests make no effort to measure it.

# PEOPLE USE TESTS TO LABEL CHILDREN AS MORONS, ETC.

Unfortunately, people do sometimes *misuse tests* in this way. Tests are best viewed as sources of information. As such, they are appropriately used to help with decisions about people by people (individual and institutional decisions defined further in Chapter 10, starting on page 130).

It is morally indefensible, except in extreme or emergency situations, to use any single test as the sole basis for making a decision. In the clinical application, it is conceivable that a licensed psychologist might make a recommendation on the basis of a single test if the clinical signs were extreme enough to warrant it. In the school, a teacher or administrator might make a tentative placement on the basis of an achievement test. But both the psychologist and the educationist should be ready to reverse the decisions if behavior warrants. If the child (or adult) proves able to do the work, that individual should not be kept from doing the work because of some test score. Tests may reflect or predict ability; they do not cause ability!

> Harriet Hughes, a teacher in nearby Hume High School, is dismayed with what is happening to one of her students, Holly. Despite the fact that Holly has earned As in almost every course she has taken, the school counselor has insisted that she must not take the academic courses that would permit her to qualify for admission to college because Holly's tests show that "she cannot do quality work in school."
>
> What can we do about such a situation? In the first place, we check its credibility. Is the story true? Are there circumstances that modify its accuracy? In Holly's case, after checking, I called the city's supervisor of counseling and discussed the matter with her. She arranged to go to the Hume High School and review proper test usage with all the counselors at the school. Holly's case will be discussed with her counselor to see whether the girl should be allowed to take higher-level courses.

Along somewhat similar lines, I have heard people criticize maximum-performance tests because they have caused a person to form a low self-concept. True, but concepts of self and of others will be formed even in the absence of any testing. The emphasis should be placed, I feel, on the correct interpretation of test results. There is no place for the assertions that tests prove that one has little ability, that one has too little ability to go to college, and the like. Tests do not *prove* any such thing. In the extreme, they may *reflect* the fact that a person has limited ability. Even in extreme cases, however, the skilled test interpreter allows a generous margin for possible error.

Test debunkers seem to forget two things: Mistakes in classification can be made (and have often been made in the past) without the aid of tests; and tests sometimes reveal abilities that had not been suspected beforehand. For example:

Newspapers and magazines report occasionally that an elderly man (or, less often, an elderly woman) has been released from years of confinement in an institution for the mentally retarded. Years before, these stories go, a child considered stupid by parents or teacher was admitted to the institution. Now, testing has revealed that the person is not markedly deficient and consequently has been released from confinement. In school settings, something similar happens from time to time. A test may reveal that the pupil has much more mental ability than either teacher or parents had thought.

## STANDARDIZED TESTS FAVOR THE GLIB AND PENALIZE THE THOUGHTFUL

This line of reasoning argues that standardized tests (usually multiple-choice tests) give extra advantage to the person who can come up with a quick, superficial response and they penalize the person who is capable of more thoughtful analysis of the questions.

Although some multiple-choice questions deserve this criticism, it is no more generally true than the charge that essay examinations favor fast writers because they can write longer responses in the time available for testing.

There is ample evidence that good multiple-choice items may demand reasoning, interpretation, and other high-level mental processes. As the late Professor D. G. Paterson, of the University of Minnesota, used to say: "Short-answer questions, such as the multiple-choice, demand that the instructor substitute a skill in writing good items for a skill in grading answers."

## TESTS INVADE PRIVACY

This criticism has usually been leveled against personality tests that are used in nonclinical settings. The individual in counseling should be at least as interested as the examiner in revealing whatever can be revealed by the test. When criminal matters are involved, the privacy of the individual may be of less importance than other considerations.

But there are real questions in the minds of many people about the required use of personality tests in school, in employment offices, in civil and military government service, and so on. Does the school have a right to invade the privacy of its students? If so, under what conditions? All students, or just some?

In my opinion, the routine personality testing of students is not advisable. I don't believe it is ordinarily worth the time and the expense. In school settings, I am less concerned with the issue of whether the school has the right to give such tests, for—as any schoolteacher knows—students reveal themselves in many ways, from the "show and tell" sessions of primary pupils to the compositions and themes of secondary students.

The information that is likely to be obtained from routine personality testing in schools is not, in my opinion, worthwhile. I might feel differently if more schools had sufficient personnel who were skilled in the interpretation of personality test results. But there are too many false positives and false negatives (that is, misleading results) that require sophisticated understanding. Unless one understands personality tests, the examiner may tend to find disturbances where there are none and to overlook youngsters who really do have severe problems. Untrained school personnel are likely to hurt more than to help when they attempt to use personality test data. In my opinion, most school systems have better uses for their money than to spend it on mandatory routine personality testing.

Add to these objections the fact that parents may resent the personality tests, and I believe that we have compelling arguments against their routine use. But school psychologists and others with adequate test training should be allowed to use such tests in the study of individual children. Such an application, of course, is consistent with clinical usage.

I have less definite feelings about the issue of personality tests in government or private employment. The examinee at least has some freedom of choice, although refusal to take the tests may mean that the individual cannot compete for the position(s) available.

Should a private employer have the right to require an applicant for work to take a personality test? And should all applicants be tested or just those about whom there are "doubts"? After all, the employer may invest considerable time and money in training a new worker. Beyond that, the employer has a business to operate. Is it unreasonable for the employer to want to get the best possible employees—employees who are likely to do good work? May not the employer also be concerned with his or her future employee's ability to get along with coworkers, customers or clients, and the like?

Or, viewed differently, does the employer have any right to pry into an applicant's feelings and values? Should an employer be allowed to reject applicants who give "different" responses to personality test items? Should all nonconformists be rejected? We now have laws to protect against certain discriminatory hiring practices (for example, on the basis of sex or race). Should employers be permitted to safeguard the company image by requiring applicants for work to take personality tests? Tests are not the only vehicles for getting at personal information, of course. There are other means, such as the application blank and the interview. I once completed an application blank that asked whether I "use tobacco in any form," "use alcohol in any form," and would "be willing to teach Sunday School."

I believe that employers should have some voice in the selection of their employees and that they may legitimately use personality tests; however, they may be called upon to demonstrate a test's validity.

In summary, I believe that personality tests, when used unwisely, do constitute an unfair invasion of privacy; however, I think that they can be helpful in a wide variety of applications when interpreted by someone who is appropriately trained.

## TESTS GIVE CHANGING RESULTS

Naturally—and for many reasons—tests give changing results. Tests are not perfect. Neither are other evaluative techniques: the personal interview, the rating scale, direct observation, and so on. One should not evaluate any test against a criterion of perfection—only against other possible techniques. If a test gives useful information that we would not otherwise have, and does so without prohibitive cost, the test would seem to be desirable.

Also, individuals change over time. We may reasonably expect that test results will change along lines similar to the ways in which people change. And remember, people change in knowledge, in skills, in personality characteristics. They also change in the motivation that they bring to the testing room at different times.

Under the best conditions, test results show some variation. It has always seemed strange to me that a person whose bowling score may vary by forty to fifty points from one game to the next expresses surprise at hearing that someone's IQ has changed by ten to fifteen points over several years when tested with different tests. (See the discussion of standard error of measurement in Chapter 6, pages 65–66.)

## TESTS ARE UNFAIR

Probably the most vehement antitest criticisms are those related to fairness. Tests are alleged to be unfair to minorities and to women. This latter charge usually refers to the fact that girls and women tend to score lower than boys and men on math tests; however, research studies show that the differences are slight when mathematical training is equated.

For some reason, girls have tended to score lower on the *Preliminary Scholastic Aptitude Test (PSAT)/National Merit Scholarship Qualifying Test,* an examination used frequently as a basis for awarding scholarship money. The Educational Testing Service (ETS), which administers the *PSAT* program, added a test of writing skills in 1997, hoping to correct that apparent unfairness.

The charge of unfairness to minorities (especially African Americans) is less easily dismissed. The fact is that most minority students score lower than most white students on most maximum-performance tests. These differences lessen, but do not entirely disappear, when socioeconomic factors are equated. Although it is possible to develop tests on which Blacks outscore Whites, the content of such tests is generally not relevant to either educational or occupational goals. The cause of lower scores for Blacks is open to different interpretations. Socially conscious individuals leap immediately to the conclusion that the tests are unfair. Racists have the ready interpretation that the differences prove that Whites are superior to Blacks (though they are less eager to conclude from similar data that Asians are intellectually superior to Whites).

All the major publishers try to eliminate those test items that are clearly biased, but some differences in score still remain. If there are no inherent racial differences in ability, the average score differences should disappear unless there are differences in environmental factors (including schooling) and motivational factors (aspiration and expectation levels, and so on).

But fairness in testing also involves fairness in interpretation and application. Even if true differences in average ability exist between racial groups, there still is no excuse for discrimination—for treating people as second-class citizens. The variation in intellectual ability within each racial group is far greater than the average difference between groups.

Fairness must work in both directions, too. No bonus should be granted merely because of ethnic background.

## Lake Wobegon Effect

A new charge arose in 1987, with the publication of a report by John J. Cannell that contended that there was a gigantic conspiracy between educators and test publishers to create a "Lake Wobegon effect." Lake Wobegon refers to an imaginary community in rural Minnesota where, according to folk humorist Garrison Keillor, "all children are above average."

Cannell contended that state departments of education in all fifty states were reporting that their students had achieved above the national median on standardized achievement tests. Several test publishers have responded publicly to that accusation. So, too, has the U. S. Department of Education in a study by Robert L. Linn, M. Elizabeth Graue, and Nancy M. Sanders (Center for Research on Evaluation, Standards, and Student Testing, University of Colorado).

They point out that, although there was some validity to Cannell's accusation, there are several factors that tend to explain the apparent phenomenon: (1) the use of old norms (some improved performance is expected each year); (2) the practice at some schools of eliminating some pupils (e.g., language handicapped and special education pupils) from test sessions; and (3) the practice of using the same test each year (with some loss of security of the test items).

There are some other practices that play at least a minor role in the seemingly impossible results reported by Cannell. For example, for years I have had students tell me of teachers who study the tests to be given and then teach the specific content of those tests to their pupils. CBS-TV's 60 *Minutes* program of March 25, 1990, in a segment on test cheating in the school, contained these assertions: "'Teacher is a cheater' is an open secret in school districts all over the country . . . and the principal encourages them to cheat."

There is evidence, too, that African Americans are achieving in school—regardless of whether tests are fair to them. A news release by the United States Census Bureau in mid-September 1996 stated that for the first time in history, the percentage of Blacks and Whites who have graduated from high school is the same. The data are based on young adults (ages 25–29) in a demographically representative sample of 55,000 homes (125,000 people) nationwide.

## TESTS ARE MISUSED AND MISINTERPRETED

This is absolutely true! The remedy lies, however, in better education about testing, not in the abolition of tests. We have substantial evidence that tests do sometimes help in some situations. Let's concentrate on how tests can be used more intelligently and more efficiently, so that we can get more true meaning (and less nonsense) out of the test results.

How? I have no magical formula, but I do think that a better understanding of tests can be sought at all levels:

1. Test publishers can be encouraged to continue their good work in making test manuals and materials readable and intelligible. They need constantly to remember, also, to remind test users of the practical shortcomings of tests.
2. School and business administrators need to insist that their respective personnel offices use tests wisely and employ suitable safeguards to keep tests, test equipment, and test results secure. Test results should be available only to the individual tested and to qualified personnel. When appropriate, administrators should encourage or support in-service training on the meaning of test scores.
3. Counselors, guidance workers, school psychologists, personnel workers, and the like should take time occasionally to review the manuals of the tests they use, to restudy test statistics, and to look at new tests. Such people should plan occasional in-service training efforts to instruct individuals who receive test results about the meaning of test scores.
4. Teachers, supervisors, and others who may have easy or natural access to test results should be encouraged to learn what they can about the nature of tests and test results. We should require training in test interpretation for all people whose positions involve the use of test results.
5. All interested adults should be encouraged to read about tests, their strengths, and their limitations. There is a shortage of good material for general reading, although plenty of irresponsible nonsense is

poured out by less than fully informed writers. An occasional PTA meeting might be devoted to explanations of tests and testing.

6.  Schoolchildren can be trained to be somewhat sophisticated about the meaning of test results. They have already learned to inquire about time limits and whether tests are "corrected for guessing" whenever they take standardized tests. Why not teach them some measurement theory in their mathematics? Or a bit about evaluation and assessment in their social studies? Or something about the fallibility of observation in their sciences? Such efforts could, within a very short time, bring schoolchildren to a point of being able to recognize the strengths and weaknesses of standardized tests.

7.  All personnel who deal with tests should be reminded that cheating is unprofessional and unethical.

**There is nothing wrong with most testing that educating the user won't cure.**

All readers who expect to do much testing (administering, interpreting, or whatever) should study carefully the *Code of Professional Responsibilities in Educational Measurement* in the Appendix. It was first published in October 1985 by the Board of Directors of the National Council on Measurement in Education.

# A Few Statistics

Statistics is a study with a lurid past, a fascinating present, and a limitless future. What is more important for us right here is the fact that it is easy for a person to understand basic statistics. If you've completed eighth-grade mathematics, you should have no difficulty with this chapter.

## INTRODUCTION

Fifty people who applied for jobs at the hypothetical Culinary Crafts Company took the *Cooking Arts Test* (*CAT*). They earned the following scores (where one point was given for each correct answer):

| Name | Score | Name | Score | Name | Score | Name | Score | Name | Score |
|------|-------|------|-------|------|-------|------|-------|------|-------|
| AA | 65 | AK | 33 | AU | 35 | BE | 43 | BO | 34 |
| AB | 40 | AL | 50 | AV | 54 | BF | 43 | BP | 49 |
| AC | 55 | AM | 26 | AW | 44 | BG | 35 | BQ | 30 |
| AD | 49 | AN | 54 | AX | 50 | BH | 54 | BR | 38 |
| AE | 24 | AO | 42 | AY | 45 | BI | 44 | BS | 62 |
| AF | 48 | AP | 26 | AZ | 44 | BJ | 52 | BT | 42 |
| AG | 56 | AQ | 47 | BA | 41 | BK | 47 | BU | 48 |
| AH | 37 | AR | 31 | BB | 48 | BL | 50 | BV | 61 |
| AI | 50 | AS | 47 | BC | 62 | BM | 31 | BW | 50 |
| AJ | 29 | AT | 51 | BD | 43 | BN | 38 | BX | 46 |

*TABLE 6.1*    **Scores Made by 50 Job Applicants at the Culinary Crafts Company on the** *Cooking Arts Test**

| Score | Tallies | f | Score | Tallies | f | Score | Tallies | f | Score | Tallies | f |
|-------|---------|---|-------|---------|---|-------|---------|---|-------|---------|---|
| 65 | I | 1 | 54 | III | 3 | 43 | III | 3 | 33 | I | 1 |
| 64 |  | 0 | 53 |  | 0 | 42 | II | 2 | 32 |  | 0 |
| 63 |  | 0 | 52 | I | 1 | 41 | I | 1 | 31 | II | 2 |
| 62 | II | 2 | 51 | I | 1 | 40 | I | 1 | 30 | I | 1 |
| 61 | I | 1 | 50 | IIIII | 5 | 39 |  | 0 | 29 | I | 1 |
| 60 |  | 0 | 49 | II | 2 | 38 | II | 2 | 28 |  | 0 |
| 59 |  | 0 | 48 | III | 3 | 37 | I | 1 | 27 |  | 0 |
| 58 |  | 0 | 47 | III | 3 | 36 |  | 0 | 26 | II | 2 |
| 57 |  | 0 | 46 | I | 1 | 35 | II | 2 | 25 |  | 0 |
| 56 | I | 1 | 45 | I | 1 | 34 | I | 1 | 24 | I | 1 |
| 55 | I | 1 | 44 | III | 3 |  |  |  |  |  |  |

*Hypothetical data.

## Frequency Distribution

To visualize those *CAT* scores better, we might put them into a *frequency distribution,* an orderly arrangement, usually from highest to lowest, showing the frequency with which each score occurs (as in Table 6.1).

Often we can get an even better idea of the scores if we arrange them in *class intervals*; that is, the units (usually greater than one) used in a frequency distribution. The use of class intervals gives us a method for grouping together several adjacent score values, to enable us to (1) graph the distribution meaningfully, and (2) compute certain statistics more easily.

We aim for approximately fifteen intervals (a good compromise between too few and too many) to span the range of scores. We try to have each interval an odd-numbered width, so that the *midpoint* of each interval will be an *integer* (whole number).

For these data, Range = 65 – 24 = 41, and 41 ÷ 15 is approximately 3 (an odd number). Thus, we select 64–66 as the interval 3 units in width that is to contain score values of 64, 65, and 66. Since we are treating these scores as *continuous* (see the following), the *real limits* of the interval are 63.5 and 66.5; checking, we find that those values are 3 units apart, 66.5 – 63.5 = 3. The frequency distribution using these class intervals is shown in Table 6.2.

*Continuous* values are the results of measuring, rather than counting. We can never have absolute accuracy in measurement, for we might always use still finer instruments to obtain greater precision. We can measure relatively tangible variables such as length and weight with considerable accuracy, but such intangibles as intelligence, attitude, and neuroticism are harder to measure accurately. The principle is the same: Absolute precision of measurement

TABLE 6.2    Use of Class Intervals (of 3 Units Each) for Data
in Table 6.1

| Class Interval | f | Class Interval | f | Class Interval | f |
|---|---|---|---|---|---|
| 64–66 | 1 | 49–51 | 8 | 34–36 | 3 |
| 61–63 | 3 | 46–48 | 7 | 31–33 | 3 |
| 58–60 | 0 | 43–45 | 7 | 28–30 | 2 |
| 55–57 | 2 | 40–42 | 4 | 25–27 | 2 |
| 52–54 | 4 | 37–39 | 3 | 22–24 | 1 |

is not possible with any continuous variable. The degree of accuracy depends on the nature of the variable itself, the precision of the instrument, and the nature of the situation.

See how this works with length. In discussing the size of my office, I may use dimensions that are accurate to the nearest foot. I may note my desk size to the nearest inch. I measure the height of my grandchildren to the nearest quarter-inch. My model-builder friends do work that is accurate to the nearest one one-hundredth inch. And scientists working on our space program at NASA need even greater precision.

Some variables can be expressed only as *discrete* values: Number of volumes in the public libraries of Montana, number of students in each room at Walnut Hills High School, number of seats in each Cincinnati theater, and so on. Here we count, and complete accuracy *is* possible. The tipoff is the phrase *number of*. When a variable is expressed that way, we usually have a discrete variable.

If we think of a test as a collection of questions and of test scores as the number of items correct, we have to consider test scores as discrete values. We do often obtain scores by counting the number of correct answers; however, we usually want to consider the test scores as measures of some characteristic beyond the test itself. We are not satisfied with thinking of testee AA merely as having answered correctly 65 items on the *CAT*. Rather, we want to consider this 65 as indicating some amount of the ability that underlies the test.

All tests are merely samples of the items that might have been included. We hope that the test is a *representative sample* of this *universe* (or *population* or *domain*) of all possible items. The universe of possible items for most tests is nearly infinite, for we could not possibly write all the items that would be relevant. We find it helpful to think of any psychological or educational test as being a rather crude instrument for measuring whatever characteristic (ability, knowledge, aptitude, interest, and so on) is presumed to underlie the test. Thus, most test authorities treat test scores as continuous, and we shall do so in this book.

## The Histogram

We may show these *CAT* results graphically by marking off all possible score values (within the range of scores obtained) along a horizontal line. This horizontal line, called the *abscissa*, serves as the baseline of our graph. If we use a tiny square to represent each applicant, we will have a graph like that shown in Figure 6.1.

Since the scores are continuous, we let each of these little squares occupy the space of one full unit (or class interval). Each square occupies a space from the real lower limit to the real upper limit. AA's score was 65, and the square is placed so that it extends to the real limits of the class interval, thereby having half of its area above and half below the midpoint of the interval (65.0).

We can tell the number of cases (i.e., the *frequency*) in any interval by counting the number of squares above it or, even more simply, by reading the number on the *ordinate* (the vertical axis) of the graph at a height level with the top of the column. This type of graph is called a *histogram*.

When we draw a graph to show a set of scores, we ordinarily make no effort to retain the identity of the individuals. Usually we are less interested in knowing AA's score or AB's score than we are in portraying the general nature of the scores made by the group. We are interested in general characteristics, such as the shape of the distribution, the scores obtained most frequently, and the range in scores. Ordinarily, therefore, we would be more likely to draw the histogram in one of the ways shown in Figure 6.2.

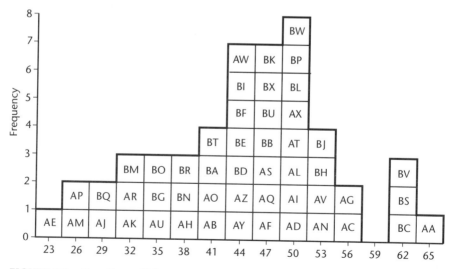

*FIGURE 6.1*    **Raw Score Values on the *Cooking Arts Test*.**

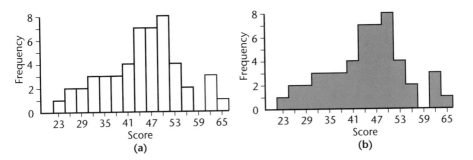

**FIGURE 6.2**  **Histograms of the Raw Score Values on the *Cooking Arts Test*.**

Here we have no need for individual squares; instead, we draw columns (each the same width) to the height required to show the appropriate frequency.

### Frequency Polygon

Another type of graph that may be used for the same purpose is the *frequency polygon*. A dot is placed above the midpoint of each score value (or each class interval) at a height corresponding to the number of people making that score (or in that class interval). Each of these dots is connected with the two adjacent dots by straight lines. In addition, the distribution is extended one unit (that is, either one score value or one class interval) beyond the highest and lowest scores obtained. This means that there will be lines to the baseline at each extreme, thereby completing the figure and making our graph a *polygon* (a many-sided figure).

Figure 6.3 is a frequency polygon showing the test scores of the fifty Culinary Crafts Company applicants; we have used class intervals that are three score values wide and show the same information displayed in Figures 6.1 and 6.2.

It can be shown mathematically that a histogram and a frequency polygon showing the same data and drawn to the same scale are identical in area. This is important, for *area is proportional to frequency of cases.*

## DESCRIPTIVE STATISTICS

After a little practice, we can learn a great deal from a graph; however, descriptive statistics provide a more precise means for summarizing and describing a set of scores. Descriptive statistics includes *measures of position*

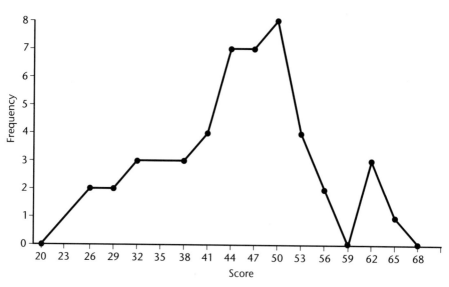

*FIGURE 6.3*   **Frequency Polygon.**

(including *central tendency*), *measures of variability*, and *measures* of *covariability*.

## Measures of Position (Other than Central Tendency)

Measures of position are numbers that tell us where a specified person or a particular score value stands within a set of scores. In a graph, *any measure of position is located as a point on the baseline.*

### 1. Rank

*Rank* is the simplest description of position—first for the best (or highest), second for the next best, third for the next, and so forth, on to the last. Its assets are its familiarity and its simplicity; however, its interpretation is so dependent on the size of the group that it is actually less useful than one might think. We never use it formally in describing test results.

### 2. Percentile rank

*Percentile rank* is a better position indicator because it makes allowance for differences in the size of the group. Percentile rank is a statement of a person's relative position within a defined group; thus a percentile rank of 30 indicates a score that is as high as or higher than the scores made by 30 percent of the people in that particular group. Percentile ranks are widely used as a type of test score and will be considered in detail in Chapter 8.

## Measures of Central Tendency (Averages)

A *measure of central tendency* is designed to give us a single value that is most characteristic of a set of scores. Three such measures are fairly common in testing: the mean, the median, and the mode. Each of these may be located as a point along the abscissa (baseline) of a graph.

### 1. Mean

The most common measure of position and of central tendency is the *arithmetic mean* (usually called simply the *mean*). This is nothing more than the average we learned in elementary school. But *average* is a generic term that properly may refer to any measure of central tendency. The mean is the preferred measure for general use with test scores. Besides having certain mathematical advantages, the mean is widely understood and easy to compute. We use the mean unless there is good reason to prefer some other statistic.

In grade school we learned to find the mean by adding up all the scores and dividing by the number of scores. Stated as a formula, this becomes:

$$\bar{X} = \frac{\Sigma X}{N}$$

where
$\bar{X}$ = the mean of Test $X$
$\Sigma$ = "add the values of"
$X$ = raw score on Test $X$
$N$ = number of cases (number of persons for whom we have scores)

### 2. Median

With income data, we are likely to have one very high salary (or a few very high salaries) and many more lower salaries; in other words, we say that income data are usually *positively skewed*, having many low values and few high values. The result is that the mean tends to exaggerate the salaries (i.e., the mean is pulled toward the extreme values), and the median becomes the preferred measure. The *median* is that value above which fall 50 percent of the cases and below which fall 50 percent of the cases; thus it is less likely to be drawn in the direction of the extreme cases. This same shape of distribution, shown in Figure 6.4(a), is also found when a test is difficult or when the examinees are not well prepared.

The distribution shown in Figure 6.4(b) is *negatively skewed*, the sort of distribution we are likely to get when a test is much too easy for the group tested. The mean gives us an erroneous impression of central tendency whenever a distribution is *badly* skewed, and in such cases the median becomes the preferred measure.

The median is also preferred when a distribution is *truncated* (cut off in some way so that there can be no cases beyond a certain point). In Figure

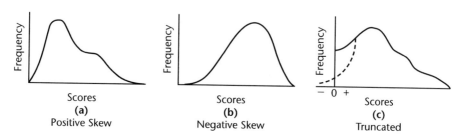

FIGURE 6.4  Three Nonsymmetrical Distributions.

6.4(c), the distribution is truncated, perhaps because of a very difficult test on which zero was the lowest score assigned; the dotted line suggests the distribution we might have obtained if the scoring had permitted the assignment of negative scores.

Since the median is the fiftieth percentile (also the second quartile and the fifth decile), it is the logical measure of central tendency to use whenever percentile ranks are being used. For computation, see percentiles (pages 102–106).

## 3. Mode

The third type of average used with test scores is the *mode*. The mode is the most commonly obtained score or the midpoint of the class interval having the highest frequency.

The mode is rarely usable in connection with further computations. It is very easily found, however, and we can use it as a quick (and rough) approximation of central tendency. If a distribution of scores is graphed, the mode is that value (on the baseline) above which the curve is at its highest point. As shown in Figure 6.5, sometimes there are two modes (*bimodal*) or even more modes (*multi-modal*) to a distribution. Graphs (c) and (d) in Figure 6.5 are both bimodal even though the peaks in (d) are not exactly of equal height.

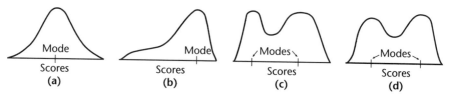

FIGURE 6.5  The Mode.

## Comparison of the Central Tendency Measures

Let's review briefly. The mean is the best measure of central tendency in most testing situations. We use it unless there is some good reason for not doing so. It is widely understood and fairly easy to compute. It fits logically and mathematically into the computation of other statistics. On the other hand, the mean should *not* be used when the distribution of scores is badly skewed or truncated, because it is not a good indicator of central tendency in such situations.

The median fits logically into the percentile scale. Its use is preferred whenever distributions are truncated or badly skewed. It involves fewer mathematical assumptions than the mean. Although it is less widely used than the mean, it is easily understood and easily computed.

The mode is less widely used than either the mean or the median. It provides a quick and easy estimate of central tendency, but it is not especially useful in connection with test scores.

There are still other measures of central tendency, but none of them is commonly used in testing. All measures of central tendency can be located as points on the abscissa of a graph.

## Measures of Variability

It is possible for two distributions of scores to have a similar (or even identical) central tendency value and yet be very different from each other. The scores in one distribution, for example, may be spread over a far greater range of values than those in the other distribution. These statistics tell us how much variability (or dispersion) there is in a distribution; that is, they tell us how scattered the scores are. In graphs, all variability measures can be shown as distances along the baseline.

### 1. Range

The *range* is familiar to all of us; it represents the difference between the highest and lowest scores. The range is easily found and easily understood, but it is valuable only as a rough indication of variability. It is the least stable measure of variability, depending entirely on the two most extreme (and, therefore, least typical) scores. It is less useful in connection with other statistics than other measures of variability are.

### 2. Semi-interquartile range

This statistic defines itself: *semi* (half) *inter* (between) *quartile* (one of three points dividing the distribution into four groups of equal size) *range* (difference or distance). The statistic equals one-half the distance between the extreme quartiles, $Q_3$ (seventy-fifth percentile) and $Q_1$ (twenty-fifth percentile).

We use the semi-interquartile range (or *quartile deviation*) as a measure of dispersion whenever we use the median as the measure of central tendency. It is preferred to other measures when a distribution of scores is truncated or badly skewed. The formula for the semi-interquartile range is:

$$Q = \frac{Q_3 - Q_1}{2}$$

where

    $Q$ = semi-interquartile range
    $Q_3$ = third quartile, the seventy-fifth percentile ($P_{75}$)
    $Q_1$ = first quartile, the twenty-fifth percentile ($P_{25}$)

(See pages 102–106 for computation of the median and all percentiles.)

## 3. Average deviation (mean deviation)

Another statistic that has been used to express variability is the *average deviation* or *mean deviation*. Its chief advantage is the simplicity of its rationale, for it is simply the mean *absolute* amount by which scores differ from the mean of the distribution of scores; however, this statistic is seldom used today. We mention it here only because there are occasional references to it in testing literature.

## 4. The standard deviation

Although its rationale is less obvious than that for other measures of variability, the *standard deviation* is the best such measure. It is the most dependable measure of variability, for it varies less than other measures from one sample to the next. It fits mathematically with other statistics. It is widely accepted as the best measure of variability and is of special value to test users because it is the basis for (1) standard scores; (2) a way of expressing the reliability of a test score; (3) a way of indicating the accuracy of values predicted from a correlation coefficient; and (4) a common statistical test of significance. *This statistic is one that every test user should know thoroughly.*

The standard deviation is equal to the square root of the mean of the squared deviations from the distribution's mean. Although more efficient computational formulas for the standard deviation exist, the following formula is descriptive:

$$s_x = \sqrt{\frac{\Sigma (X - \bar{X})^2}{N}}$$

where

    $s_x$ = standard deviation of Test $X$
    $\sqrt{\ }$ = "take the square root of"       $\bar{X}$ = mean of Test $X$
    $\Sigma$ = "add the values of"           $N$ = number of persons whose
    $X$ = raw score on Test $X$             scores are involved

What does the standard deviation mean? As a measure of variability, it can be expressed as a distance along the baseline of a graph. The standard deviation is often used as a unit in expressing the difference between two specified score values; differences expressed in this fashion are more comparable from one distribution to another than they would be if they were expressed as raw scores.

The standard deviation is also frequently used in making interpretations from the normal curve (described later in this chapter). In a normal distribution, 34.13 percent of the area under the curve lies between the mean and a point that is one standard deviation away from it; 68.26 percent of the area lies between a point that is one standard deviation below the mean and a point one standard deviation above the mean. In nonnormal distributions (and perfect normality is never achieved), the figure will not be exactly 68.26 percent, but it will be approximately that percentage. In other words, about two-thirds of the area (and two-thirds of the cases, for area represents number of persons) will fall within one standard deviation of the mean. In most distributions; approximately one-third of the cases will be more than one standard deviation away from the mean (either below or above).

## 5. Probable error (PE)

The *probable error* is rarely (if ever) used today, but it is mentioned frequently in older testing literature. It is found by multiplying the standard deviation by the constant value 0.6745; that is, $PE_x = 0.6745s_x$. Back when few people understood even basic statistics, writers used the PE to determine the points ($\pm 1$ *PE* from the mean) between which fall 50 percent of the cases and beyond which fall 50 percent of the cases in a normal distribution.

The probable error has only this explanatory use. The PE does not combine with other measures—as does the standard deviation—and the standard deviation must be computed before the PE can be found. The PE? Forget it!

## Measures of Covariability

Measures of *covariability* tell us the extent of the relationship between two tests (or other variables). There is a wide variety of correlation methods, but we shall consider only one of them here: the *Pearson product-moment correlation coefficient.*

Correlation expresses the degree of relationship between two (or, in specialized techniques, even more) variables. A correlation coefficient is an index number stating the degree of that relationship; it may take any value from 0.00 (no relationship) to +1.00 (perfect positive correlation) or −1.00 (perfect negative correlation). Let us take three extreme (and impractical) examples to illustrate correlation.

In Figure 6.6(a) we see a *perfect positive* correlation. Ten students have taken a math test. Their scores are shown as Number Right across the abscissa and as Percent Right along the ordinate. Each dot in this *scatter diagram* represents one student's score according to both Number Right and Percent Right. Since there is a perfect correlation, the dots fall along a straight line.

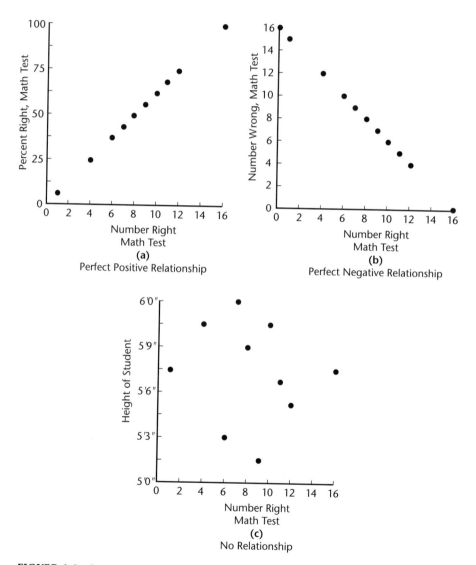

FIGURE 6.6    **Scatter Diagrams Showing Different Relationships between Two Variables.**

Since the correlation is positive, the dots proceed from lower left to upper right.

In Figure 6.6(b) we see a *perfect negative* correlation. Here we have the same ten students with their test scores as Number Right (across the abscissa) and Number Wrong (along the ordinate). The dots fall along a straight line, but proceed from upper left to lower right, as is characteristic of negative correlations.

There is no regular order to the dots in Figure 6.6(c), for this figure shows a correlation coefficient of 0.00—there is no correlation at all, either positive or negative. Once again, the Number Right is shown along the abscissa, but this time we have shown Height of Student along the ordinate. Apparently, there is no tendency for math scores on this test and heights to be related.

We never encounter a perfect correlation in actual practice. Only rarely are we likely to encounter any correlation coefficients above 0.90 except as reliability coefficients (see Reliability in Chapter 2). Validity coefficients (see Validity in Chapter 2) are much more likely to run between about 0.20 and 0.60, depending upon the test, the criterion, and the variability in scores within the group tested.

Figure 6.7 shows a correlation coefficient of approximately 0.50. This is the sort of scatter diagram we might reasonably expect to find for the correlation between a test and its criterion; in fact, such a correlation may be a reasonably good validity coefficient. Note, however, that we would not be able

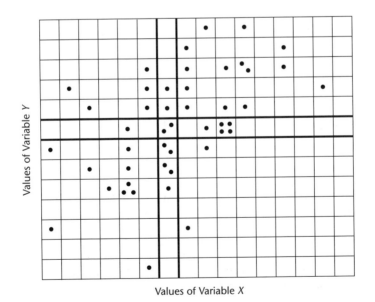

Values of Variable *X*

*FIGURE 6.7*    **Scatter Diagram Showing Correlation Coefficient of Approximately +0.50 between Variable *X* and Variable *Y*.**

to predict specific criterion values very efficiently from the test scores. If we could, there would be very little variation in scores within any one of the columns; or, stated differently, all scores in any column would tend to be very close together.

Although the correlation coefficient states the extent to which values of one variable tend to change systematically with changes in value of a second variable, correlation is **not** evidence of causation. Two variables may be related without either one causing change in the other.

Among elementary school pupils, there is a positive correlation between length of index finger and mental age. In other words, the longer the index finger, the higher the mental age. Before you start using length of index finger as a test of intelligence (or begin to stretch your child's finger), wait a minute! Do you suppose that higher intelligence causes the longer finger, or vice versa? Neither, of course. Among elementary school children, higher chronological ages result both in higher mental ages and in longer fingers.

As mentioned earlier, we shall consider here only the Pearson product-moment correlation coefficient (r). The formula is given here only for the sake of illustration; easier formulas for computation exist.

$$r_{xy} = \frac{\Sigma(X - \bar{X})(Y - \bar{Y})}{N s_x s_y}$$

where

$r_{xy}$ = product-moment correlation coefficient
$\Sigma$ = "add the values of"
$X$ = raw score on variable $X$
$\bar{X}$ = mean of variable $X$
$Y$ = raw score on variable $Y$
$\bar{Y}$ = mean of variable $Y$
$N$ = number of pairs of scores
$s_x$ = standard deviation of variable $X$
$s_y$ = standard deviation of variable $Y$

Correlation methods demand that we have a pair of scores for each individual.

We want to find a validity coefficient for the hypothetical *Industrial Index* by correlating its scores with criterion values (number of units produced during a four-hour period of work). We have test scores for seventy-nine people and criterion information on seventy-four people. The greatest number on whom we could possibly compute our correlation coefficient would be seventy-four; however, if some of the seventy-four people did not take the test, we will have an even smaller number with which to work.

The Pearson product-moment correlation coefficient assumes that each of the two variables is continuous and drawn from a normally distributed population.

Correlation coefficients are widely used in testing to express validity (where test scores are correlated with criterion values) and reliability (where two sets of scores for the same test are correlated).

## THE NORMAL PROBABILITY CURVE

So far we have been discussing *obtained* distributions of test scores. Now it is time to consider a *theoretical* distribution: the *normal probability distribution*, the graphic representation of which is known to us as the *normal curve* (see Figure 6.8). We will never obtain a distribution exactly like it, for it is based on an infinite number of observations that vary by pure chance. Nevertheless, many human characteristics do seem to be distributed in much this way, and most tests yield distributions that approximate this model when they are given to large numbers of people.

When our results are not grossly asymmetrical, we find it convenient to treat variables as if they were normally distributed because *all* properties of this mathematical model are known. If different obtained distributions approach this model, we have a better basis for comparisons than we otherwise would have.

The normal curve is important, then, because (1) it is a mathematical model whose properties are known completely; (2) it is a model that is approached by the distributions of many human characteristics and most test scores; (3) it is relevant to an understanding of certain inferential statistics; and (4) it gives a basis for understanding the relationship between different types of test scores.

### Points to Know

Chart 6.1 and Figure 6.8 provide a summary of information about the normal probability curve that every test user should know. These points are worth remembering—even if we have to memorize them!

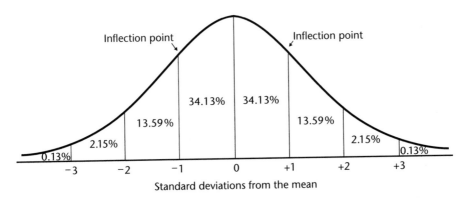

**FIGURE 6.8   The Normal Probability Curve.**

*CHART 6.1*

In the normal probability curve:

1. The curve is bilaterally symmetrical; that is, the left and right halves are mirror images of each other. (Therefore the mean and median have the same value.)
2. The curve is highest in the middle of the distribution. (Therefore the mode is equal to the mean and the median.)
3. The limits of the curve are plus and minus infinity. (Therefore the tails of the curve will never quite touch the baseline.)
4. The shape of the curve changes from convex to concave at points one standard deviation above and one below the mean.
5. About 34% (34.13%) of the total area under the curve lies between the mean and a point one standard deviation away. (Since area represents number of cases, about 34% of the examinees have scores that fall between the mean and a point one standard deviation away.)
6. Nearly 48% (47.72%) of the area (nearly 48% of the cases) lies between the mean and a point two standard deviations away.
7. Nearly 49.9% (49.87%) of the area (and the cases) lies between the mean and a point three standard deviations away.
8. About 68% (68.26%) of the area (and the cases) lies within one standard deviation (plus and minus) of the mean. (This was found by doubling the 34% in item 5, above. In the same way, the percentages in items 6 and 7 may be doubled to find the percentage of area or cases lying within two and three standard deviations of the mean, respectively.)
9. A known mathematical formula describes the curve exactly.
10. Tables exist giving all sorts of information: height of the ordinate at any distance (in standard-deviation units) from the mean, percentage of total area between any two points, etc.

## INFERENTIAL STATISTICS

*Inferential statistics* (sometimes called *sampling* statistics or *probability* statistics) tell us how much confidence may be placed in our *descriptive* statistics. Whereas descriptive statistics are values used to summarize a set of values, inferential statistics are used to answer the question "So what?" about descriptive statistics. They can be used to tell whether a descriptive statistic based on only a sample of cases is likely to be a close estimate of the value we would find for the entire population, whether the observed difference between means for two groups is probably due to something other than mere chance, and so on.

## Standard Errors

Although we won't give a detailed treatment of inferential statistics here, we must develop one concept: the standard error (especially the standard error of measurement).

Every descriptive statistic has its own standard error. A *standard error* is an estimate of the standard deviation of a distribution of like statistics; it expresses how much variation we might expect if we were to compute the same statistic on other groups similar to the one with which we are working.

Although the formulas for standard error vary according to the statistic, most standard errors become smaller (which is what we want) when the number of cases is large and when there is little variability in the original set of scores (or a high correlation between sets of scores).

### 1. Standard error of measurement ($SE_{meas}$)

The *standard error of measurement* ($SE_{meas}$) indicates how much a person's score might vary if the person were examined repeatedly, using the same test (assuming that no learning occurs). The standard error of measurement is one way of expressing a test's reliability. As test users, we do not have to compute this statistic ourselves—unless, perhaps, we want to verify that the $SE_{meas}$ for our group is comparable to that reported by the test publisher.

According to measurement theory, when one person takes the same test an infinite (or very large) number of times, the result will be a distribution of obtained scores that (1) is normal in shape; (2) has a mean equal to the person's (hypothetical) true score; and (3) has a standard deviation that is estimated by the standard error of measurement.

But in any practical situation, we have only one obtained score for a person. We may think of that score as being an estimate of the true score (even though the true score is never determinable). We can now answer such a question as, *How much is this person's score likely to differ from the true score?*

We answer the question by using our knowledge of the person's obtained score, the normal curve, and the size of the standard error of measurement, found from this formula:

$$SE_{meas} = s_x \sqrt{1 - r_{xx}}$$

where

$SE_{meas}$ = standard error of measurement
$s_x$ = standard deviation of test $X$
$\sqrt{\phantom{x}}$ = "take the square root of"
$r_{xx}$ = a reliability coefficient for test $X$

We know that about 68 percent of all cases lie between points 1 standard deviation above and 1 standard deviation below the mean. It follows that the probability is 0.68 that our one obtained score is no more than $\pm 1\ SE_{meas}$ away from the true score (that is, the mean of the theoretical distribution of scores). Similarly, the probability is 0.95 that the obtained score is no further than ±1.96 $SE_{meas}$ from that mean.

When we focus our interest on a *range* of score values within which the true score is most likely to be, we are creating a *confidence interval*; the score values at the two extremes are *confidence limits*. Thus, the 95 percent confidence interval extends from 1.96 $SE_{meas}$ above to 1.96 $SE_{meas}$ below the obtained score; the score values at +1.96 $SE_{meas}$ and at −1.96 $SE_{meas}$ are the 95 percent confidence limits.

Following this line of reasoning, we can set up whatever confidence limits seem reasonable. If we want to be extremely certain of the value of any score that we attribute to a counselee, we may use the 99 percent confidence limits; however, very often we are more interested in suggestions that may be gained from the various tests we've had the counselee take. In such instances, I have found it helpful to use something like a 90 percent confidence interval. This, it seems to me, is a good compromise between being too stringent and too loose. (Actually, I sometimes use ±1.6 $SE_{meas}$ instead of ±1.65 $SE_{meas}$ to make the multiplication easier.)

Let's take an example:

Mickey makes a score of 73 on an aptitude test. How close is this to her true score? We can't tell exactly, but we can gain some information. First, Mickey's obtained score (the only one we have) of 73 is the best estimate of her true score. Second, through the use of confidence limits, we can state the probability of the true score's being within any given distance from that obtained score.

Thus, if we use the 90 percent confidence interval with Mickey's score of 73, we can say that we are about 90 percent certain that her true score falls within the interval 73 ± 1.6 $SE_{meas}$. Assume that the test has a standard error of measurement of 2.5. We multiply: 1.6 × 2.5 = 4.0. Thus, the confidence interval would be 73 ± 4, or 69 to 77. We can have reasonable confidence that Mickey's true score falls within that interval.

The standard error of measurement is extremely important for test users. If we assume that a person's obtained score is necessarily her or his true score, we will make all kinds of misinterpretations.

Willie and Wallie Wendy are sisters. Willie's IQ, found on a group test taken in the second grade, was 108. Wallie's IQ, found on the same test when she was in the second grade, was 111. Willie's score was interpreted as *average*, but Wallie's score was described as *above average*. According to many IQ classifications, we might very well describe these two IQs in this fashion. We should note, however, that no test scores are perfect, and that it is entirely possible that the true scores of Willie and Wallie on this test would place them in the reverse order.

Those of us who teach know the difficulty we often have in deciding exactly where to draw the line between **A** and **B** grades, **B** and **C** grades, and so on. It is probable that true appraisals (if available) would reverse the grades of many borderline students. This same situation exists with every type of score.

## 2. Errors, not necessarily mistakes

When we speak of error here, we are speaking of the error that is inherent in any measurement. It is something with which we must cope whenever we are dealing with a continuous variable. Mistakes can be guarded against. But the error of measurement we are considering here is always with us.

We cannot eliminate measurement error, but we can estimate how much error is present. We can eliminate mistakes, but we cannot estimate their extent when they are present.

Because of certain similarities, the standard error of *measurement* is often confused with the standard error of *estimate*, the only other standard error that we'll mention.

## 3. Standard error of estimate ($SE_{yx}$)

The purpose of the *standard error of estimate* is to indicate how well test scores predict criterion values. Correlation coefficients give us the basis for predicting values of a criterion from our knowledge of obtained test scores. The $SE_{yx}$ shows how much our obtained criterion values are likely to differ from those predicted. With a perfect correlation (±1.00), we can predict perfectly; the $SE_{yx}$ will equal 0.00, for there will be no difference between predicted and obtained criterion values. With no correlation between the test and the criterion, we can assume that everyone will fall at the mean on the criterion, and we will be less wrong in making this assumption than we would be in making any other sort of prediction. But the $SE_{yx}$ now will be as large as the standard deviation.

Most $SE_{yx}$, of course, fall between these two extremes. (This concept is developed thoroughly in statistics texts, and I'll make no effort to do so here.)

We find that we need very high correlations in order to predict *specific* values with much accuracy; however, we can make *general* predictions very effectively with the modest-sized validity coefficients that we typically find in real-life situations. Consider the following example, adapted from The Psychological Corporation's *Test Service Bulletin No. 45*:

> In a given company, seventy-four stenographers were given The Psychological Corporation's *Short Employment Tests* (*SET*). Each stenographer was rated by a supervisor as low, average, or high in ability. The validity coefficient (based on these ratings) was just 0.38, so there would be little predictive efficiency, according to the standard error of estimate.

Let us see what happens if we try to predict which employees will fall into which criterion categories instead of the specific criterion values we were concerned with in earlier examples. Table 6.3 shows for each criterion category the percentage of stenographers in each third on the Clerical part of the *SET.* The late Alexander Wesman, author of the *Bulletin,* states:

> By chance alone, the percent of upper, middle, and low scorers in each of the rated groups would be the same—in this case, 33-1/3%. The boldface numbers in the table would consist of nine 33s. Note how closely this expected percent is approximated for those ranked average in proficiency, and for those in the middle third on test score; the percentages in the middle row and those in the middle column run between 28 and 36. Note also that at the extremes—the four corner numbers—the prediction picture is more promising. Among those rated low, there are almost three times as many people from the lowest third on the test as there are from the top third. Among those rated high, the percent from the top third on the test is almost two and one-half times as great as the percent from the bottom third. The personnel man would do well to be guided by these data in selecting future stenographers, even though the validity coefficient is just 0.38.

> The data in the above example are based on relatively small numbers of cases (which is typically true of practical test situations) and the percents found in each category are consequently somewhat unstable. The validity coefficients based on groups of such sizes are, of course, also less stable than coefficients based on large numbers of cases. The wise test user will make several validity studies using successive groups. Having done so, he may take an average of the validity coefficients from these studies as being a more dependable estimate of the validity of the test in his situation.[1]

## EXPECTANCY TABLES

Table 6.3 is an *expectancy table,* that is, a table showing the relationship between test-score intervals and criterion categories. Typically, intervals of test scores are shown at the left of the table, with the number of intervals depending partly on the number of cases involved and partly on the degree of differentiation desired for the situation. Criterion categories are usually shown across the top of the table, with the number of categories here also depending on the number of cases and on the degree of differentiation desired.

Into the individual cells of the table are placed either the number of cases or the percentage of cases that fall into that score interval and criterion category; most people prefer to use percentages, feeling that they are easier to interpret.

Although not too widely used in test interpretation, the expectancy table is an excellent device to use when communicating test results to laypersons. It is easy to understand and to explain to others. It directs attention to the pur-

---

[1]The Psychological Corporation, *Test Service Bulletin No. 45* (1953).

*TABLE 6.3*    Percentage of Stenographers in Each Third on *SET*-Clerical
Who Earned Various Proficiency Ratings*

|  | *Proficiency Rating* | | |
|---|---|---|---|
| *SET-Clerical Test Score* | *Low* | *Average* | *High* |
| Upper Third | 18 | 33 | 50 |
| Middle Third | 29 | 36 | 28 |
| Lower Third | 53 | 31 | 22 |
| Total Percentage | 100 | 100 | 100 |
| Number of Stenographers | 17 | 39 | 18 |

* Adapted from The Psychological Corporation's *Test Service Bulletin No. 45*, "Better than Chance"
(1953). (Used with permission.)

pose of testing by comparing test scores with criterion performance. (Note
also the similarity to Norms in Chapter 7.)

Furthermore, the expectancy table is an aid in test interpretation that
shows a realistic outlook so far as criterion results are concerned. A common
misinterpretation of test scores goes something like this: "This score means
that you will fail in college." No test score (except, perhaps, the final examination in some course) means any such thing. The expectancy table encourages different kinds of interpretation: "In the past, students with scores like
yours have seldom succeeded at our college; in fact, only two students in ten
have had satisfactory averages at the end of their first year." The latter type of
interpretation can be supported; the former cannot.

Wesman has pointed out that the same general principle can be extended to two (or even more) predictor variables. (See The Psychological
Corporation's *Test Service Bulletin No. 56*, 1966.)

When interpreting the results of an expectancy table, we should keep
these points in mind:

1. We need to be certain that we are using the same test (including the
   same form, level, edition, etc.).
2. The table is based on results that have been found in the past; it may
   or may not be relevant to the present group (or individual).
3. If the table is based on the performance of people from another office
   (company, school, college), it may (or may not) apply to ours.
4. We can have more confidence in expectancy tables that are based on
   large numbers of scores. (Percentages sometimes disguise—and
   overemphasize—small numbers.)
5. Even with no special training in testing or statistics, we can make

expectancy tables of our own very easily. (Several issues of The Psychological Corporation's *Test Service Bulletin* contain excellent suggestions written by the late Alexander G. Wesman; see especially *Bulletins Nos. 38* and *56*.)

6. An expectancy table may be used to spot individuals (or subgroups) that do not perform as we would expect; when we note instances in which predictions miss, we may check back to discover possible reasons for the failure.

7. In a sense, we may think of an expectancy table as a set of norms in which one's test score is compared directly with the performance of others who have made that same score.

8. The use of a double-entry expectancy table permits the simultaneous display of relationships among two predictor variables and a criterion.

## AN OMISSION AND AN EXPLANATION

There are many more inferential statistics that well-trained test users should know if they are to read the testing literature or conduct research with tests. They should know that there are standard errors of differences, statistical tests of significance, and the like. But such topics are not essential to a *basic* understanding of psychological and educational test scores, and I have chosen to omit them for that reason.

Some readers may be surprised that I included expectancy tables in this chapter on statistics. I placed the topic here because a logical basis for expectancy tables had been developed in the brief discussion of the standard error of estimate.

# Information About Tests

Where can we go to get information about tests?

## TEST CATALOGS

We can get some basic information from test catalogs, but a catalog simply lists the tests and test-related items that a company offers for sale. The amount of detail varies considerably with the publisher. Some companies issue fancy, thick, large-page catalogs in full color. Others publish modest little leaflets. Whatever its appearance, the catalog should contain at least the following information for each test listed:

1. Title of test, including designation of form(s) available.
2. Name(s) of author(s).
3. Age/level of persons for whom the test is appropriate.
4. Titles of the areas for which different scores are obtained—for example, the various subject matters in an achievement battery.
5. Eligibility for purchase and use. [The American Psychological Association suggests a classification of A, B, or C. Level A tests are those

having no specific requirements beyond an ability to read and follow directions (for example, simple paper-and-pencil tests of proficiency and achievement); Level B tests require some training in testing (such as simple adjustment or interest inventories, paper-and-pencil intelligence and aptitude tests, etc.); and Level C tests require extensive relevant training (such as individual tests of intelligence or personality).]

6. Length of time required for administration and scoring.
7. Availability of (or necessity for using) a special scoring service. Some tests cannot be scored locally.
8. The formats in which the test, answer sheets, and other test-related materials are available. Some tests may be purchased in either consumable or reusable test booklet forms and may be used with several different types of answer sheet that may be hand scored or machine scored. Some tests are available for computer administration and/or scoring and interpretation.
9. Need for special equipment. Individual tests, for example, almost always require a special kit of equipment.
10. Prices, instructions for ordering, etc.

Many catalogs also include pictures of the test. This feature is especially useful when the test involves special equipment.

In short, the catalog is the publication that a publisher uses to tell people the products and services the company has for sale. The test publisher has an obligation to describe these products and services briefly and accurately. The publisher has no obligation to give an extended and detailed description of each test and how it can be used. Such material belongs in the manual.

## TEST PUBLISHERS

Test publishers are unique people: They must adhere to professional ethics while competing actively in the business world. With more than one million tests being used each school day in American schools alone, testing is big business!

But, competitive as test publishing is, the publishers are expected to adhere to a code of professional ethics. And most publishers do. They are expected, for example, to accept orders only from qualified purchasers. No law prohibits—or even restricts—the sale of the *Thematic Apperception Test* or the *California Psychological Inventory* or the *Kaufman Assessment Battery for Children*, but the publishers will sell them only to qualified professionals. The integrity of all tests depends on the integrity of the people who publish and sell them. Most publishers prove worthy of that trust. In fact, reputable publishers will even recommend the products of other publishers when appropriate; their professional and sales personnel typically are excellent sources of information about tests.

## TEST MANUALS

Once upon a time . . . the test publisher issued a manual and that was that! The manual was a tiny leaflet that included some directions for administering and scoring the test, together with a set of norms. And that single set of norms might be based on just 100 or 200 people, with no real clue given as to *who* they might be. The manual, of course, was issued free with any order for the test.

But those days are long past! Test publishers are sophisticated enough to know that a good test manual must contain much more information than that. Further, and more important, test *users* realize that more information is needed. Manuals today often run to more than one hundred pages, and are not giveaway items.

Progress certainly has been made, but not without creating new problems. There are complete manuals (or handbooks), manuals for administration and scoring, manuals for interpretation, technical manuals and supplements, and so on. The amount of information available on the best-selling tests is truly impressive.

There are some tests for which short manuals may be sufficient, but widely used tests often demand much more.

Indeed, a good manual is likely to be an impressive book, full of tables, statistical formulas, and technical data. It's so imposing, in fact, that it is likely to alarm the new test user. Thus, the paradox: The better a publisher succeeds in preparing a manual that is reasonably complete, the more overwhelming it may seem. A good manual should include at least the following, in addition to full identification of the test and its authors:

1. Rationale: what the test is all about
2. Description of the test
3. Purposes for which the test seems appropriate
4. Development of the test and test items
5. Directions for administration
6. Directions for scoring
7. Reliability data
8. Validity data
9. Norms tables
10. Interpretation of the test
11. Profiles
12. References

With some tests there is need for additional sorts of information. For an achievement test, the manual may need to include an explanation of the importance of some of the items and perhaps item analysis data. For an aptitude battery, it may require information about the intercorrelations of the several tests in the battery. A test that is available in alternate or multiple forms requires evidence that the forms yield similar results.

## Rationale

Good test manuals contain a statement of the orientation of the test author. What is the author trying to accomplish? With some tests, there is little need for a detailed statement; one sentence may be enough: "The *Wesman Personnel Classification Test* (*PCT*) measures the two most generally useful aspects of mental ability—verbal reasoning and numerical ability," according to The Psychological Corporation's manual for the *PCT*. On the other hand, the same publisher devotes several pages to "The Rationale of the Children's Scale" in its manual for the *Wechsler Intelligence Scale for Children—Revised*; even then, it is noted that further details on the late David Wechsler's views on the nature of intelligence are found among Wechsler's other publications.

If a test differs in major ways from other tests, the author and publisher need to explain what is new and different. If the test is for a familiar and common use (such as the selection of clerical employees), there is less need for an extensive statement.

## Descriptions of the Test

Here, too, the amount of detail needed depends on a variety of factors, such as familiarity or novelty of the variables, number of variables reported, and so on. On typical-performance tests, the descriptions are usually brief paragraphs explaining what each variable means. Obviously there is less need for detailed descriptions of the test variables if there has been an extensive coverage elsewhere in the manual.

## Purposes of the Test

Here again, how much needs to be said about the purposes for which the test may be used depends on the test and on how much of the information has been stated elsewhere in the manual. Regardless of how the information is labeled, the manual should contain somewhere a clear statement of the purposes the publisher believes that the test will fulfill.

## Development of the Test

Test publishers vary widely in the attention they give to explaining the research underlying the test. Some are commendable; some are not. The manuals for most of the better-known achievement batteries contain comprehensive and detailed statements of development. Usually publishers are extremely careful to describe the research evidence that makes the current edition comparable to previous editions. Also, they give full details about the comparability of any alternate forms.

Regardless of the type of test, the user should expect suitable details of the research involved in its development. This is especially true where there is little evidence of criterion-related validity.

## Directions for Administration

Some publishers are a bit careless about the directions for administration. They've been in testing for so long that they forget that there are always newcomers to testing. You and the test publisher and I may know that we need to plan ahead of time whenever we're giving a test—plan to make certain that we have all the necessary materials, that we have reserved the right room for the right time, that all clearances have been provided by school or plant officials, and that all examinees know where they are to be, when, and for what purpose. *We* may know, but there are newcomers who need to be told. The thoughtful publisher remembers them and includes a section labeled "Preparing for the Test," "General Directions," or something similar.

General instructions for test administration are also needed in manuals for individual tests, but the emphasis there characteristically is on the need for establishing and maintaining rapport (a good testing relationship with the examinee), details of test administration, and the like.

There are now so many different ways of scoring tests that there may be (as we noted earlier) several different types of answer sheets on which the test may be taken. When options exist, the examiner needs to note carefully whether there are different directions to be followed for each type of answer sheet. There should be—and the differences may be more important than mere differences in how to make marks on the answer sheets.

If, for example, any parts of a test are timed, which type of answer sheet is used may make a considerable difference; this is most true when the test is genuinely speeded (long enough so that a substantial number of the examinees will not finish). If there are truly no differences in results, the manual should cite the experimental results to justify the interchangeable answer sheets.

## Directions for Scoring

If there are different types of answer sheets that may be used, the manual must explain the procedure for handling each one. As noted above, it is sometimes possible to hand-score tests even when machine-scorable answer sheets have been used. The manual should explain this, too.

Because of the increasing usage of commercial scoring services, the manual should indicate the availability of such scoring services, and should indicate, whenever applicable, the procedures to follow in preparing and shipping answer sheets to such service centers.

## Reliability Data

Reliability is such a complex topic that no manual can dismiss it with a statement such as: "The reliability of the test is 0.89." A good manual considers the following questions (and many others): What type of reliability? What sort of group? Why are these estimates of reliability appropriate? One manual for the *Differential Aptitude Tests* spends about ten pages on the discussion of reliability. The authors list reliability coefficients separately by sex and by grade, for each form, and for each of the tests in the battery. There are split-half coefficients, test-retest coefficients, and alternate-form coefficients. In addition, standard errors of measurement are given for each sex and each grade for each of the tests.

## Validity Data

When the test is a simple, job-oriented aptitude test, the statement of validity can be fairly straightforward. The manual can state criterion-related validity coefficients, both predictive and concurrent, for various groups. These, when well and appropriately accomplished, may be sufficient for such tests.

With other tests, there is greater need for more consideration of validity data. Let's take a look at the common achievement battery. There is no good criterion; the standardized tests should do a better job than informal, teacher-made tests, and there is little likelihood that the standardized tests were designed to parallel exactly the teacher-made tests, anyway. Part of the validity data may be correlation coefficients between the achievement tests and corresponding course achievement, but more is needed. With achievement tests, publishers tend to lean heavily on evidence of content validity, that is, evidence of agreement between the content of test items and the content of courses and textbooks that should be relevant.

Another type of evidence of validity that is found in many manuals is correlations with other tests. This sort of evidence, although rarely sufficient, often is valuable supplementary evidence. After all, if the only evidence of validity is that the test relates to some other test, what are we to infer? Is the other test sufficiently valid that we may accept it immediately? Then why not use that other test?

Correlations with other tests, as used with the *Differential Aptitude Tests* (*DAT*), can be of great help in deciding whether another test is sufficiently different to justify our using both of them or whether it would be sufficient to use just one. Such correlations are also helpful in determining the exact nature of the test variable. A recent edition of the manual for the *DAT* contains eight pages of correlations with other tests. To be maximally informative, of course, these other-test correlation coefficients must be given for the tests of various publishers, not just those of this test's publisher.

Construct validity data may take almost any form. Inasmuch as personality and intelligence tests do not adapt well to criterion-related validity, evidence must usually be sought through construct validity. What group differences are likely if the test has good validity? What other variables can give evidence of the test's validity?

Differences between age groups and the like are commonly used as evidence of validity of tests for school use. Similar reasoning can be used with occupational groups, as has been done by The Psychological Corporation with the *Wesman Personnel Classification Test*. The logic is that if the test possesses high validity, there should be reasonable order to the means for the various occupations. The data in Table 7.1 suggest that the *PCT* may have validity for use in personnel selection.

Validity is the most important attribute of a test. The manual must cite appropriate evidence that the test possesses some sort of validity. It is the test user's responsibility to evaluate the evidence that is presented, and to evaluate it in view of the use that is to be made of the test. Remember: A test may have high validity for one purpose but have little or no validity for some other purpose.

## Norms and Norms Tables

Norms are vital to an understanding of test results, for they provide us with the standards against which to compare test performance. Most test manuals

*TABLE 7.1\**

| Occupational Group | Mean Score | | |
| --- | --- | --- | --- |
| | Verbal | Numerical | Total |
| Chain-store clerks | 12.0 | 6.4 | 18.4 |
| Production workers | 17.1 | 8.2 | 25.3 |
| Female clerical employees | 23.0 | 8.9 | 31.9 |
| U.S. Air Force captains | 23.9 | 11.2 | 35.2 |
| Executive trainee applicants | 27.1 | 14.5 | 41.6 |
| Technical sales applicants | 29.4 | 14.7 | 44.1 |

\*Data extracted from Table 3, *Wesman Personnel Classification Test Manual*. The original table lists twenty-four different occupational groups, together with the number of cases involved in each and the standard deviation for each. Copyright © 1946, 1965 by The Psychological Corporation. Reproduced by permission. All rights reserved.

contain several sets of norms, and it is important for the test user to select the set that is most appropriate. As we shall see, an individual's score may show a person as either doing well or doing poorly, depending on the group with which he or she is compared. Mitzi may have made the lowest score of all the fifth graders in her Executive Heights School, but the same score might have placed her in the highest quarter of her class if she had been attending the Bottoms District School or the Jelly Junction School. As we shall note from time to time, we may very well find it useful to use more than one norms group (especially in educational or vocational counseling).

### The norm

The simplest statement of norms is given by the *norm*. This is nothing more than the average (either mean or median) score for some specified group. *Norm*, in fact, is used occasionally as a synonym for *average*. The norm is also sometimes used in place of more complete norms if the available scores are inadequate, inappropriate, or suspect for some reason. On a new test, for example, scores may be available initially on very few people.

A set of norms for a test consists of a table giving corresponding values of raw scores and derived scores. Derived scores are intended to make test interpretation easier and more meaningful than is possible with raw scores alone.

Norms are frequently designated according to the type of score involved; we may, for example, read of percentile norms, grade-equivalent norms, and so on. Because of the large number of different types of derived score in common use, I have devoted an entire chapter (Chapter 8) to discussing them.

### Norms tables

A good *norms table* should include a derived-score equivalent for each raw score that can be made. The table should include a full description of the group on which it is based. It may present one or several types of derived score, for one or several groups, for one or more tests. An incomplete norms table can be confusing to the test user.

**Simple norms tables.**   The simplest norms tables consist of two columns, one containing raw-score values and the other containing corresponding derived-score values. Table 7.2 illustrates such a table with hypothetical results presumed to be based on a national sample of laboratory technicians.

Note that the group is described in some detail. The test manual should list the laboratories that contributed data (or should note that the list is available upon request). In this example, we might still ask questions about the educational background and work experience of the examinees, for these factors could influence our interpretation. Of course, if the *TAPT* is to be useful for individual decisions, it will have to be much longer.

TABLE 7.2   Example of Simple Norms Table (Percentile Norms for the Hypothetical *Technician's Aptitude and Proficiency Test*)*

| Raw Score | Percentile | Raw Score | Percentile | Raw Score | Percentile | Raw Score | Percentile |
|---|---|---|---|---|---|---|---|
| 11 | 98 | 8 | 75 | 5 | 34 | 2 | 10 |
| 10 | 96 | 7 | 62 | 4 | 23 | 1 | 4 |
| 9 | 85 | 6 | 48 | 3 | 18 | 0 | 1 |

*Hypothetical data. Presumably based on 6,245 laboratory technicians tested last year at 450 hospital laboratories and 785 industrial and commercial laboratories in 39 states. (The complete list of participating laboratories should be included in the manual or made available upon request.)

**Multiple-group norms tables.**   Very often a single norms table is constructed to show results for several different groups. Besides the obvious economy in printing, this practice permits the immediate comparison of a person's raw score with as many of these groups as we wish. Table 7.3 illustrates such a table with data drawn from Project TALENT; it is based on a 4 percent random sample of the approximately 440,000 high school students tested in 1960 as part of that research study. The test mentioned here is the *Information Test— Aeronautics and Space*. Here again there are so few items that we would need to be cautious in interpreting individual scores. The chance passing of one more item or chance failing of one more item makes a great apparent difference in performance.

> Pauline, a ninth-grade girl, had a raw score of 3; this gives her a percentile rank of 65 when compared with other ninth-grade girls. Pauline knows very little about aeronautics and space, and she might easily have missed one more item; that would have placed her at the fortieth percentile. On the other hand, if she had happened to guess correctly on one or two more items, she would have had a percentile rank of 83 or 93.

With very short tests such as the two illustrated in Tables 7.2 and 7.3, reliability is likely to be extremely low, especially when the items are so difficult that lucky guesses become important in determining one's score. We would need to be very careful in making any interpretations of individual test scores here except for students who are clearly at one extreme or the other.

We can rely on group differences to a far greater extent. We often can have confidence in group differences in test performance even when test reliability is too low to permit much confidence in individual scores. In this example, there is no level at which youngsters have achieved better than those in a higher grade. Nor is there any level at which the girls have outscored boys.

**Multiple-score norms tables.**   Sometimes a norms table includes derived scores for each of several tests (or subtests). For obvious reasons, this should never be done unless the same norms group is used for each test. Sometimes

TABLE 7.3    Example of Multiple-Group Norms Table (Percentile Norms for the *Information Test—Aeronautics and Space* of the Project TALENT Test Battery)*

| Raw Score | Percentile Score | | | | | | | |
|---|---|---|---|---|---|---|---|---|
| | Grade 9 | | Grade 10 | | Grade 11 | | Grade 12 | |
| | Boy | Girl | Boy | Girl | Boy | Girl | Boy | Girl |
| 10 | 99+ | 99+ | 99 | 99+ | 99 | 99+ | 98 | 99+ |
| 9 | 97 | 99+ | 96 | 99+ | 96 | 99+ | 92 | 99 |
| 8 | 92 | 99+ | 91 | 99+ | 89 | 99+ | 84 | 99 |
| 7 | 86 | 99 | 83 | 99 | 80 | 99 | 75 | 98 |
| 6 | 78 | 97 | 73 | 96 | 69 | 96 | 63 | 95 |
| 5 | 66 | 93 | 62 | 92 | 55 | 91 | 51 | 89 |
| 4 | 52 | 83 | 47 | 81 | 41 | 79 | 36 | 77 |
| 3 | 36 | 65 | 31 | 62 | 26 | 61 | 22 | 59 |
| 2 | 20 | 40 | 16 | 40 | 14 | 38 | 11 | 38 |
| 1 | 8 | 18 | 6 | 18 | 5 | 16 | 4 | 16 |
| 0 | 2 | 4 | 1 | 4 | 1 | 4 | 1 | 3 |

*Based on a 4 percent random sample of the approximately 440,000 high school students in 50 states tested in 1960 as part of the Project TALENT study directed by John C. Flanagan. Reprinted from *Project TALENT Counselors' Technical Manual for Interpreting Test Scores*, University of Pittsburgh (1961). (Used with permission.)

scaled scores are used instead of raw scores, especially when some of the sub-tests have many more items than do others.

**Abbreviated norms tables.**   An occasional norms table includes only every other raw-score value (or, perhaps, every fifth raw-score value), forcing the test user to interpolate whenever he or she has raw-score values that are not on the table. Such a table saves money in printing, but it encourages mistakes and costs the test user additional time and trouble. In my opinion, abbreviated tables should rarely, if ever, be used.

**Condensed norms tables.**   Very similar to the abbreviated table is the condensed table, where selected percentile (or other) values are given, and the corresponding raw scores shown. This style of table is still used, especially when the publisher wishes to present a large amount of data in a single table for comparison purposes.

### Expectancy tables and charts

At this point we need to mention expectancy tables and charts once again (see pages 68–70 in Chapter 6 for a more complete discussion). They differ from norms tables in one important characteristic: Whereas norms tables state derived-score values corresponding to each raw score, expectancy tables show *criterion performance* for each *interval* of raw scores. In all other respects, expectancy tables are the same as norms tables. We reemphasize here that expectancy tables, like norms tables, state the results found for some specified group. When interpreting anyone's score through the use of either an expectancy table or a norms table, we must consider whether our group and our situation are comparable.

### Articulation of norms

A specified test may vary in edition, form, level, or any combination of these. *Edition* usually refers to the *date* of publication (1997 edition) or to the *number* of editions published (for example, the sixth edition). Different editions may be needed to keep test content up to date. *Form* usually refers to an equivalent version; that is, different forms will contain different items, but will be similar in content and difficulty. Different forms may be needed to ensure test security; that is, to minimize the likelihood of test items leaking out to examinees. Equivalent forms are frequently useful when it is necessary to retest a person. Different form designations may also be given when item content is identical, but scoring method is different (for example, hand-scored versus machine-scored).

*Level* usually refers to the age or grade placement of those for whom a specified version of the test is intended. Different levels may be needed to make subject content and item difficulty appropriate for the examinees. From three to eight levels sometimes are used to cover the range of school grades. Some tests have some overlapping items for adjacent levels.

Some excellent tests exist in only a single edition, form, and level. The need for multiple versions of a test becomes greater as the test is used more widely. Thus, the need is greatest, especially for different levels, with tests designed for wide-scale administration throughout whole school systems.

With few exceptions, new editions are intended to replace and improve upon earlier editions. There may or may not be a desire to make results from two editions directly comparable. It is nearly always important, however, to make different forms and levels yield somewhat comparable results; the aim is to achieve articulated (neatly jointed) norms. All major publishers of tests for schools are aware of this need for articulation, and all take steps toward ensuring comparability. The exact procedures followed differ, and some publishers are more successful than others.

People who use tests should check the manual carefully for evidence of articulation studies to see how comparable are the test scores from different forms and levels. This information may be found under such headings as "Articulation," "Interlocking Studies," and "Overlapping Norms." It is more difficult to obtain reliable information about the comparability of scores on tests from different publishers, but data from Project TALENT, directed by John C. Flanagan, of the American Institutes for Research, have been used for more than thirty years by some publishers in an attempt to fulfill this need for anchoring norms.

### Norms groups

I cannot emphasize too strongly the tremendous importance of the norms group. Regardless of the type of norms, we are dealing with results that are based on some group of people. But it makes a great deal of difference *which* group of people. Consider the hypothetical example of Alan Alexakis.

Alan Alexakis, a graduate assistant in philosophy at Athol University, answered 210 words correctly on the hypothetical *Orange Omnibus Test* of 300 items. His raw score of 210 on the *OOT* means that he did as well as or better than:

99 percent of the seventh-grade pupils in the Malone Public Schools
92 percent of the Athol High School seniors
91 percent of the high school graduates in Worcester Academy
85 percent of the entering freshmen at Patricia Junior College
70 percent of the philosophy majors at Lamia College
55 percent of the graduating seniors at University of Thessaloniki
40 percent of the graduate assistants at American College of Athens
15 percent of the English professors at University College London

Although Alan's absolute performance (210 items answered correctly) remains unchanged, our impression of how well he has done will differ markedly as we change norms groups.

This illustration is extreme. Under no normal circumstances would we compare a graduate assistant's score with those of seventh-grade pupils. However, results every bit as far-fetched as these can be obtained in real-life situations—and results nearly as far-fetched often do occur.

Even professional measurements people occasionally are misled when they try to understand differences in norms groups, as in the following situation:

> Two tests (scholastic aptitude and reading comprehension) published by the same highly reputable testing firm were once commonly used together in college admissions batteries. At most colleges, students tended to stand relatively higher on the scholastic aptitude test than on the reading comprehension test. The norms most commonly used were national norms prepared by the publisher and based on thousands of cases from colleges in all sections of the country. The norms could be trusted. Or could they?

> The norms should not have been accepted so readily, for more select colleges (with higher admissions standards) had been used unintentionally in establishing the reading test norms. The net result was that most students who took both tests seemed to do less well in reading comprehension than in scholastic aptitude.

Before this difference in norms groups was generally recognized, interoffice memoranda had been exchanged at many colleges, asking why their students were so deficient in reading ability!

The same sort of difficulty is encountered frequently in school testing, especially when we use tests from different publishers. The following situation shows what may happen in real-life school settings when different achievement batteries are used at different grade levels.

> Winifred Winchester's pupils are tested on the *AAB* at the end of the fifth grade; their mean grade-placement score is 5.4 (which is about one-half grade below the expected norm for her class). The same pupils had taken the *BAB* at the end of the fourth grade and had earned a mean grade-placement score of 5.1 (very slightly above the norm at that time). It looks as if Ms. Winchester has not taught her class much, especially when these pupils take the *BAB* again at the end of the sixth grade and obtain a mean grade-placement score of 7.2 (once again slightly above the norm for their actual grade placement).

Ms. Winchester is a victim of circumstances. If her pupils had taken the *AAB* at the end of the fourth grade and the *BAB* at the end of the fifth grade, they would have shown great apparent improvement during their year with her.

This same sort of situation occurs in industrial settings when test-naive personnel workers fail to consider the differences in norms groups from test to test. "After all," they may reason, "Test *Y* and Test *Z* were both standardized on mechanical employees." And such personnel workers may ignore the fact that the "mechanical employees" used for the Test $Y$ norms were engineering technicians, whereas those used for the Test $Z$ norms were machine wipers and machine-shop porters.

The list of possible mistaken inferences could be extended almost infinitely. The point we must remember is: Be sure to understand the nature of the norms groups.

### Which norms to use

Most test manuals include several norms tables. Which should we use? The obvious general answer is that we should use whichever norms are most appropriate for the individual examinee and the situation involved.

We seldom have much difficulty in selecting an appropriate set of norms to use when the test is a maximum-performance test designed for routine school use. With tests that are not commonly given to all pupils in a school (for example, specific aptitude tests) or tests designed primarily for out-of-school use, our selection can be much more difficult. For a clerical aptitude test, we may have to decide whether Stephanie should be compared with 225 clerk-typists employed by a large insurance company, 456 applicants for clerical positions with four midwestern companies, or 839 eleventh-grade students in a secretarial sequence. The same problem exists with many tests.

In guidance settings we often decide to use several different norms groups:

> Maria Malone has taken an art aptitude test. Her score would place her very high among nonart students and adults, high average among first-year students at an art academy, and low average among employed fashion designers. All of this information may be helpful to Maria in deciding whether to strive for a career in art, whether to attend an art academy, or whatever.

### Local norms

Local norms are sometimes better than national norms. Developing our own local norms is not too difficult. We keep a careful record of the test scores made by some defined group (all applicants for some sort of position, all bookkeepers currently employed by our company, or all fourth-grade pupils in our school district) until a satisfactory number has been acquired. We arrange the scores in a frequency distribution and assign appropriate derived scores (see Chapter 8).

Circumstances help us to decide whether we should be satisfied with available national norms or whether we should develop our own. In the first place, we have no choice unless we are using the same test on a fair number of people. If we use a particular test on only an occasional individual, we will have to depend on national norms because we will not have enough of our own examinees to do much good.

If national norms are suitable, we have no problem. We can use them without difficulty if we want to. Yet even when the national norms are not especially appropriate, we may prefer to use them rather than to develop our own if it seems that there is nothing to be gained by developing our own. On an interest inventory used for guidance purposes, for example, it would make little sense to compare an individual's score only with the scores of other local people.

On the other hand, even though there are adequate national norms, there may be situations in which we would like to be able to compare individuals with only other local people. We may be much more interested in knowing how well Jane compares with other local applicants than in knowing how well she has done when compared with some national normative group.

### Unisex or separate sexes

Traditionally, many tests have had separate norms for each sex. But there has been increased demand from women's groups for unisex norms. There are good reasons for each practice.

Where there are noticeable score differences between females and males, separate sex norms obviously are more descriptive of the test performances of each sex. On the other hand, one can argue that separate sex norms reinforce differences and tend to perpetuate any biases that may exist.

Which is better? Test users must make their own decisions.

### Assorted tests and integrated batteries

Tremendous strides have been made in psychological and educational testing during recent years. Modern-day standardized testing is not very old. Binet and Simon gave us the first acceptable intelligence test as recently as 1905. The first group intelligence test and the first personality inventory appeared during World War I. With the exception of a few standardized achievement test batteries that emerged during the late 1920s and 1930s, almost all tests published prior to World War II were separate tests. Each new test was developed independently of every other, and very little effort was made to equate norms groups. Inevitably the test user would find results that looked like these for Zoe Zyman:

Percentile rank of 96 on reading speed; compared with high school students

Percentile rank of 77 on reading comprehension; compared with college freshmen

IQ of 119 on an intelligence test

IQ of 131 on another intelligence test

Standard score of 59 on clerical aptitude; compared with data processing clerks

Stanine of 8 on mechanical aptitude

Under such conditions, even skilled counselors had difficulty making much sense of the results. Because each test had been developed independently by different authors, usually to meet some important needs of their own, no one could safely compare the scores on one test with the scores on another.

The situation has improved markedly since World War II. Several major publishers now have multiple-aptitude test batteries on which all of the tests have been standardized on the same group and all of the norms are based on the same group. With integrated batteries such as these, we can now compare the various scores made by the same person. Has Ketya done better on clerical aptitude than on reading comprehension? Better on reading speed than on mechanical aptitude? The use of tests in guidance demands answers to such questions, and with integrated test batteries we can begin to find answers.

There are still many tests that are not part of any integrated test battery. Probably there always will be. If we are concerned with selecting people (whether for employment or for training), we want to use the test (or tests) that will do the best job for us; there is no reason for us to consider whether a test is part of an integrated battery. An integrated battery of tests is most important in guidance and in differential placement, where the use of the common norms group is valuable in making comparisons of a person's relative ability within the various test areas.

It is impossible to exaggerate the value of good norms tables. The skillful test user needs to develop competence in studying the data in the manual.

## Interpretation of the Test

Although significant technical improvements have been made in tests, I believe that the increased attention being paid to test interpretation is the greatest improvement in test manuals during the past quarter century. More and more, the publishers are recognizing the importance of suggesting how test users can get the most meaning out of their test results.

Test catalogs of several publishers mention special interpretation aids. Until a few years ago, several publishers had useful leaflets that were available free or for minimal charge; however, these seem to have disappeared—apparently victims of the cost of printing.

Most manuals have at least a few paragraphs illustrating how meaning can be derived from the results of the test; however, it is important to remember that illustrative examples do not establish the validity of a test. Even very poor tests can be right occasionally! The proper role and function of the interpretive material is to suggest ways for using the test, not to establish the test's validity.

## Profiles

A good manual contains a complete description of any profile that may be generated for a multiscore test or test battery. Chapter 9 is devoted to a more complete discussion of profiles than is possible before we have considered the various types of score (the topic of the next chapter).

## References

Almost all manuals include some bibliographic entries describing the research performed in developing the test. Some bibliographies are extensive; some are not. The *Eleventh Mental Measurements Yearbook* is probably the best single reference for research performed with psychological and educational tests; earlier *Mental Measurements Yearbooks* may also be helpful.

Measurement textbooks in both education and psychology contain a great deal of interesting material. In my teaching, I have used many different books—almost all of them excellent. Without meaning to deprecate any of my fellow psychologist-author colleagues, I have generally found Anne Anastasi's *Psychological Testing* most generally useful. Her text is highly accurate. It tends to be somewhat encyclopedic, which makes it continue to be useful long after my students have completed the course.

## DON'T OVERLOOK YOUR PERSONAL COMPUTER

For the person who wants to learn more about the use of tests, especially the use of tests in school, the personal computer can be of great help. Check into America Online, for example. You may be surprised how much you can learn—both stuff that's theoretical and stuff that's very practical.

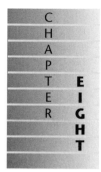

# *Derived Scores*

There are two reasons for using derived scores (rather than raw scores): (1) to make scores from different tests more comparable by expressing them in the same metric and (2) to let us make more meaningful interpretations of test results.

We must have accurate raw scores in order to get accurate derived scores. No amount of statistical manipulation can make up for the use of a poor test or for mistakes in scoring. Nor do derived scores do anything to reduce measurement error.

## A CLASSIFICATION SCHEME

Chart 8.1 shows an original classification of the various types of score that may be used to report test results; it has become widely used since I first introduced it nearly fifty years ago. This same information is shown in graphic form in Chart 8.2 in the belief that some testers will find it easier to appreciate the interrelationships among the score types. I hope that all readers will commit to memory the score forms represented by **Type I, Type II A, B, C, D,** and **Type III.** Knowing the basic skeleton of the outline will make the subtypes much easier to understand.

There are three principal bases for expressing test results: (1) comparison with an "absolute standard," or content difficulty, (2) inter-individual comparisons, and (3) intra-individual comparisons. My system centers on these three bases and a fourth (assorted) category.

In a normal distribution (see Chapter 6, pages 63–64), Type II A and Type II B scores are interrelated. Also, as shown in Figure 8.1 of Chart 8.3 (pages 92–93), we can make transformations from one kind of score to another very easily if we assume a normal distribution based on the same group of individuals. Under these two assumptions, normality and same group, the relationships shown in Figure 8.1 will always exist. When different groups are involved, we cannot make any direct comparisons; when the set of scores cannot be assumed to be distributed normally, we find that some of the relationships are changed while others remain unchanged.

> A certain test is given locally and is found to have a mean of 300 and a standard deviation of 40. We notice that the distribution of scores seems to resemble the normal probability curve. If we are willing to treat our set of scores as being normal, what can we say about the scores? Let us take a couple of cases and see.
>
> Bob has a raw score of 300. This would give him a $z$-score of 0.00, a $T$-score of 50, a stanine of 5, a percentile rank of 50, and so on.
>
> Patricia has a raw score of 320. This would give her a $z$-score of 0.5, a $T$-score of 55, a stanine of 6, a percentile rank of 69, and so on.

Figure 8.1 has been drawn with several baselines. Each of these can be used equally well as the graph's abscissa. To change from one type of score to another, we merely move vertically to another line.

Figure 8.2 of Chart 8.3 shows some of these same types of score in a badly skewed distribution. The sole purpose of this figure is to indicate which scores change in their relationship to others. Somewhat less detail has been shown here, for this distribution is not subject to generalization as is the distribution in Figure 8.1. Note that $z$- and $T$-scores do not change in their relationship to each other, nor would their relationship to raw scores change. Normalized standard scores and percentiles maintain a constant relationship to each other, but they do not relate to $z$- and $T$-scores (or to raw scores) in the same manner as in the normal distribution.

## Discussion of the Classification Scheme

Type I scores are the most familiar, for they are commonly used in reporting the results of classroom tests. These scores are unique in that they consider only the specified individual's performance; the performance of all other examinees is ignored in assigning the score. In a sense, Type I scores compare each examinee individually against an absolute standard of perfection (i.e., a perfect score on the test). This absolute-standard reasoning is attractive at first glance; however, thoughtful testers soon realize that the individual's score

CHART 8.1    Lyman's Classification of Different Types of Test Score

---

I.  **Comparison with "Absolute Standard"; Content Difficulty**
    A.  Percentage correct scores
    B.  Letter grades (sometimes)

II. **Inter-Individual Comparison**
    A.  Considering mean and standard deviation (linear standard scores)
        1.  z-scores
        2.  T-scores
        3.  AGCT-scores
        4.  CEEB-scores
        5.  Deviation IQs (sometimes)
            (a)  Wechsler IQs
            (b)  Stanford-Binet IQs
    B.  Considering rank within groups
        1.  Ranks
        2.  Percentile ranks and percentile bands
        3.  Letter grades (sometimes)
        4.  Decile ranks
        5.  Normalized standard scores (area transformations)
            (a)  T-scaled scores
            (b)  Stanine scores
            (c)  C-scaled scores
            (d)  Sten scores
            (e)  Deviation IQs (sometimes)
                (1)  Wechsler subtests
            (f)  ITED-scores
            (g)  Standard Age Scores
            (h)  Normal curve equivalents
    C.  Considering range of scores in a group
        1.  Percent placement
    D.  Considering status of those obtaining same score
        1.  Age scores
            (a)  Mental ages
            (b)  Educational ages, etc.
        2.  Grade-placement scores

III. **Intra-Individual Comparison**
    A.  Ratio IQs
    B.  Intellectual Status Index
    C.  Educational Quotients
    D.  Accomplishment Quotients

IV. **Assorted Arbitrary Bases**
    A.  Nonmeaningful scaled scores
    B.  Long-range equi-unit scales
    C.  Deviation IQs (Otis-style)

**CHART 8.2    Relationships Among Different Types of Score in Lyman's Classification**

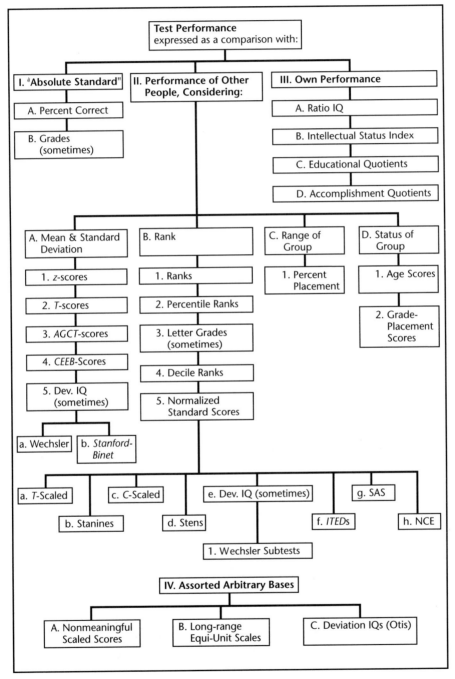

**CHART 8.3**

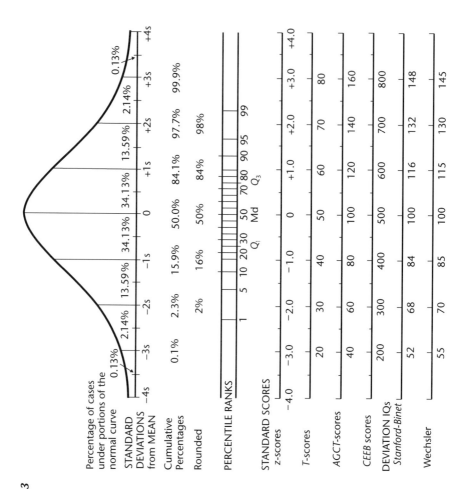

| | | | | | | | | | |
|---|---|---|---|---|---|---|---|---|---|
| **Percentage of cases under portions of the normal curve** | 0.13% | 2.14% | 13.59% | 34.13% | 34.13% | 13.59% | 2.14% | 0.13% | |
| **STANDARD DEVIATIONS from MEAN** | −4s | −3s | −2s | −1s | 0 | +1s | +2s | +3s | +4s |
| **Cumulative Percentages** | 0.1% | | 2.3% | 15.9% | 50.0% | 84.1% | 97.7% | 99.9% | |
| **Rounded** | | | 2% | 16% | 50% | 84% | 98% | | |

**PERCENTILE RANKS**   1   5   10   20 30   50   70 80   90 95   99
   Q₁   Md   Q₃

**STANDARD SCORES**

| | | | | | | | | | |
|---|---|---|---|---|---|---|---|---|---|
| **z-scores** | −4.0 | −3.0 | −2.0 | −1.0 | 0 | +1.0 | +2.0 | +3.0 | +4.0 |
| **T-scores** | | 20 | 30 | 40 | 50 | 60 | 70 | 80 | |
| **AGCT-scores** | | 40 | 60 | 80 | 100 | 120 | 140 | 160 | |
| **CEEB scores** | | 200 | 300 | 400 | 500 | 600 | 700 | 800 | |
| **DEVIATION IQs** *Stanford-Binet* | | 52 | 68 | 84 | 100 | 116 | 132 | 148 | |
| **Wechsler** | | 55 | 70 | 85 | 100 | 115 | 130 | 145 | |

**CHART 8.3**

| ITED scores | 0 | 5 | 10 | 15 | 20 | 25 | 30 |
|---|---|---|---|---|---|---|---|
| Standard Age Scores | 52 | 68 | 84 | 100 | 116 | 132 | 148 |

| STANINES | 1 | 2 | 3 | 4 | 5 | 6 | 7 | 8 | 9 | |
|---|---|---|---|---|---|---|---|---|---|---|
| Percent in stanine | 4% | 7% | 12% | 17% | 20% | 17% | 12% | 7% | 4% | |
| C-SCORES | 0 | 1 | 2 | 3 | 4 | 5 | 6 | 7 | 8 | 9 | 10 |
| Percent in C-score | 1% | 3% | 7% | 12% | 17% | 20% | 17% | 12% | 7% | 3% | 1% |
| STENS | | 1 | 2 | 3 | 4 | 5 | 6 | 7 | 8 | 9 | 10 |
| Percent in sten | | 2% | 5% | 9% | 15% | 19% | 19% | 15% | 9% | 5% | 2% |

**FIGURE 8.1** Relationships of Selected Scores in a Normal Distribution. Adapted from The Psychological Corporation Test Service Bulletin No. 48 (1964). (Used with permission.)

| STANDARD DEVIATIONS from MEAN | -2s | -1s | 0 | +1s | +2s | +3s | +4s |
|---|---|---|---|---|---|---|---|
| PERCENTILE RANKS | 1 | 25 | 50 | 75 | | 99 | |
| T-score | 30 | 40 | 50 | 60 | 70 | 80 | 90 |
| T-scaled score | 27 | 43 | 50 | 57 | | 73 | |

**FIGURE 8.2** A Positively Skewed Distribution.

may depend more on the difficulty of the tasks presented by the test items than on the individual's ability. Type I scores usually are not suited for use with standardized tests. When test scores are based on each person's own absolute level of performance, we have no way of illustrating the scores in a generalized fashion. (In other words, the mean and standard deviation are likely to differ for each administration of the test, and we have no typical distribution to illustrate.) Type I scores are never used with typical-performance tests; they are used with criterion-referenced achievement tests.

With Type II A scores, we can show how scores are likely to be distributed for any group. Type II A scores are known as linear standard scores. They always reflect the original distribution of raw scores; that is, if we were to draw separate graphs of the distribution of raw scores and the distribution of their standard-score equivalents, the two graphs would have identical shapes, and it would be possible to switch accurately from raw scores to standard scores and back again. Type II A scores can be used with any sort of test.

With Type II B scores, we lose information about the shape of the distribution of raw scores unless the original distribution was normal (and of course it can never be perfectly normal). With nonnormal distributions, we lose information that we would need in order to re-create the shape of the raw-score distribution; for example, when we use ranks, we lose all information as to how far apart the scores of any two examinees are. Even with Type II B scores, however, we can generalize the score systems to show what relationships always exist within a normal distribution. Type II B scores can be used with any sort of test.

Type II C scores, dependent on the two most extreme scores earned by members of a group, are more suited for use with informal than with standardized tests. They are more a curiosity than a useful metric. These scores can never be generalized.

With Type II D scores, the values expressed are averages of groups differing in age or in grade placement. It is impossible to generalize these scores, for they are specific to each test and group. Type II D scores can be used only with achievement or intelligence tests.

Type III scores are based on intra-individual comparisons, and there is no reason to expect that such scores can be generalized; therefore, we cannot show how such scores are distributed except for a specified test and group. Type III scores can be used only with achievement or intelligence tests.

Type IV scores do not fit readily into this classification scheme. They are an assortment primarily of scaled scores with more or less arbitrary values that are not intended for interpretation in themselves—that is, they are a sort of intermediate score, and some other type of derived score is ordinarily provided for purposes of interpretation.

Still another aid to understanding the similarities and differences among these scores is to be found in the Conversion Table for Derived Scores starting on page 177. This table shows comparable values of several commonly used derived-score systems. Note carefully the directions for using the Conversion Table (page 176).

## THE SCORES

The reader of this book should have at least a basic understanding of the mean, median, standard deviation, range, and the normal probability curve. These concepts, developed in Chapter 6, should be reviewed by the reader who feels uncertain about their meaning and use.

## TYPE I: COMPARISON WITH AN "ABSOLUTE STANDARD," OR CONTENT DIFFICULTY

Type I scores are suited only for maximum-performance tests and are rarely used except as scores on classroom achievement tests. One's performance on any maximum-performance test is determined in part by knowledge and skill and in part by motivation; these elements are common in determining any person's level of performance. The only other important determinants of a person's Type I score are measurement error and the difficulty of the test content, for the person's performance is being compared with perfection (that is, with the maximum possible score on the test). The scores of other examinees play no part in determining the score of any given examinee. Type I scores can be used with criterion-referenced tests.

### Type I A: Percentage Correct

The percentage-correct score often is used to report the results of classroom achievement tests, but is almost never used with any other type of test. It compares an examinee's score with the maximum possible score, and it may be thought of as one's score per 100 items.

*Formula:*

$$\%_c = 100R/T$$

where
    $\%_c$ = percentage-correct score
    $R$ = number of right answers (items answered correctly)
    $T$ = total number of items on test

*Example:* Helen Hill answers correctly 44 items on a 50-item test. Her percentage-correct score is 88 (100 × 44/50 = 88).

Percentage-correct scores are the only derived scores (except for Type I B, letter grades) that tell us anything about an examinee's knowledge of test content per se. We can understand their natural appeal to the schoolteacher who wants to consider what students achieve according to predetermined standards of quality. On the other hand, most teachers realize that these pre-determined levels of quality are not so objective and unchanging as might be desired, for the apparent achievement level of students can be altered tremendously by writing either easier or harder test questions covering the same subject-matter unit. Many experienced teachers use a $J$ factor to "jack up" scores (by adding a few points to everyone's score) when scores have been very low. Over the years, many teachers have come to believe that it may be more meaningful to base test scores on a system in which a student's performance is considered in comparison with others.

*Do not confuse percentage-correct scores with percentile ranks.*

## Type I B: Letter Grades (Sometimes)

The basis for the assignment of letter grades at most schools and colleges is stated in terms of percentage-correct scores. Thus, letter grades are one of our most common types of score. Although they may be determined on some comparative basis (Type II B 3), letter grades are most often Type I. Often the grading system of a school or college will state something like the following: A for 91–100; B for 81–90, etc., where the numbers refer to average percentage correct on classroom tests. Some teachers have absolute faith in such a system.

The basic rationale, advantages, and limitations of these letter grades are the same as those for percentage-correct scores. The only important difference between these scores is that letter grades are expressed in coarser units. Because of this, letter grades cannot reflect small differences in ability; but, by the same token, they are not likely to differ greatly from hypothetical true scores. Note, however, that even a single unit of change is relatively large.

Type I letter grades are found by either of two methods: (1) direct grading according to judged quality (as is often done in grading essays), or (2) conversion from percentage-correct scores to letter grades following a predetermined schedule, as in the school and college grading system mentioned above.

When letter grades are assigned with strict adherence to quality standards (without any consideration of relative performance within the group), they are determined more by test difficulty than by anything else.

"Don't take 'Introductory' from Jones," I heard a student say the other day. "He doesn't know that the letter A exists." I have known such teachers; haven't you? Two teachers of the same subject may differ greatly in the number of As, Fs, etc., given to students. Research shows that grading changes over time, too; average college grades today are higher than those of a generation ago (a process known as *grade inflation*).

No type of score is perfect. But Type I letter grades are worse than most others because they rely more on test difficulty than on their apparent basis, true quality of performance. Compare with Type II B 3 letter grades.

## TYPE II: INTER-INDIVIDUAL COMPARISONS

Type II scores are commonly used with standardized tests. Almost all standardized tests use some version of Type II A, B, or D scores in their norms tables. Types II A and II B may be used with either typical-performance or maximum-performance tests.

Type II scores are relatively independent of content difficulty, for they base an examinee's score on the performance of other people in a comparative (or normative) group. If the test content is inherently difficult, any given person's raw score is likely to be lower than on an easier test; however, this difficulty of content will also influence the scores of the other examinees. Thus it is sometimes possible to use the same test for individuals (and for groups) ranging widely in level of ability. It also permits the test constructor to aim for test items of about 50 percent difficulty, the best difficulty level (from a measurement point of view) because it permits the largest number of inter-individual discriminations. On the other hand, all Type II scores are influenced by the level of the comparison group. For example, I will score higher when compared with college freshmen than when compared with university professors. (Note the example on page 82.)

### Type II A: Inter-Individual Comparison Considering Mean and Standard Deviation

In Type II A scores, inter-individual comparison is expressed as the number of standard deviations between any given score and the mean. As with all Type II scores, a change in norms group will influence the level of score.

All Type II A scores are linear standard scores. They are called standard because they are based on the standard deviation; we shall see shortly why they are linear. They may be viewed as statements of standard-deviation distance from the mean or as scores that have been given a substitute mean and standard deviation. All Type II A scores have properties that make them more valuable in research than most other derived scores: (1) for every test and group, each Type II A score gives the same mean and standard deviation; (2) these scores retain the shape of the raw-score distribution, changing only the metric or the calibration numbers; (3) they permit intergroup or intertest comparisons that are not possible with most other types of score; and (4) they can be treated mathematically (for example, averaged) in ways that some other scores cannot be.

## 1. z-score

The basic standard score is z. All other linear standard scores may be found directly from it. It tells in simple terms the difference (or distance) between a stated group's mean and any specified raw score value.

*Formula:*

$$z = \frac{X - \bar{X}}{s}$$

where

$X$ = a specified raw score
$\bar{X}$ = mean raw score for some group
$s$ = standard deviation of that same group

Thus, if a z-score is found for each examinee in the group, the mean z-score will be 0.00 and the standard deviation of the z-scores will be 1.00.

*Example:* Joanna Jansen had a score of 49. She is to be compared with other local examinees; the mean and standard deviation of this group are 40 and 6, respectively. Joanna's z-score = (49 – 40)/6 = 9/6 = 1.5. Joanna's score is 1.5 standard deviations above the mean. (Assuming a normal distribution, we find that she did as well as or better than about 93 percent of this group.)

Although z-scores have distinct advantages for the research worker, they are not too handy for the test user, except as a step in computing other types of linear standard score. About one-half of all z-scores are negative, and all z-scores are expressed to one or two decimal positions. The other linear standard scores have been designed to eliminate the decimal point and obtain smaller units (by multiplying each z-score by a constant) and to eliminate the negative values (by adding a constant positive value to each score).

## 2. T-score

The T-score is one of the most common linear standard scores. Its rationale is the same as that for the z-score, except that it has a mean of 50 and a standard deviation of 10.

*Formula:*

$$T = 10z + 50$$

where

$z$ = a z-score, as defined above
10 = a multiplying constant (that is, each z-score is multiplied by 10)
50 = an additive constant (that is, 50 is added to each value of 10z)

*Example:* Joanna's z-score is 1.5; therefore, her T-score = 10(1.5) + 50 = 15 + 50 = 65. [Assuming a normal distribution, we find that she did as well as or better than about 93 percent of her comparison group. In any event (normal distribution or not), her T-score of 65 is directly under her z-score of 1.5 (see Chart 8.3).]

The T-score has much the same advantages and limitations as the z-score. It is somewhat less useful than z for certain research purposes, but it is more convenient to interpret because there are no negative values. (The probability of obtaining a value that is more than five standard deviations below the mean in a normal distribution is less than one three-millionth.) Nor do we typically use decimals with T-scores.

Unfortunately, T-scores are easily confused with certain other types of score, especially the T-scaled score (a Type II B score). These two Ts are identical in a normal distribution, but may differ considerably in a badly skewed distribution. T-scores are also often confused with percentile ranks, for they use similar numbers. The reader may wish to check these similarities and differences in Chart 8.3.

### 3. AGCT-score

This score gets its name from the *Army General Classification Test*. It is similar to z and to T, except that it has a mean of 100 and a standard deviation of 20.

*Formula:*

$$AGCT = 20z + 100$$

where

z = a z-score, as defined above; and 20 and 100 are multiplying and additive constants, respectively

*Example:* Joanna's z-score was 1.5; therefore, her AGCT-score = 20(1.5) + 100 = 30 + 100 = 130. [Assuming a normal distribution, we find that she did as well as or better than about 93 percent of her comparison group. In any event (normal distribution or not), her AGCT-score of 130 is directly under her z-score of 1.5 and her T-score of 65 (see Chart 8.3).]

As originally used, the AGCT-score was based on a large sample of soldiers who took the first military edition of the test; their mean was set at 100 and their standard deviation at 20. Subsequent editions of the test have been made to give comparable results. These scores are very similar to deviation IQs (which will be considered shortly); however, AGCTs have a standard deviation somewhat larger than that commonly used with IQs. A convenient scale, AGCT-scores are used today with the military and civilian editions of the *Army General Classification Test* and, even more commonly, with the *General Aptitude Test Battery*.

### 4. CEEB-score

This score was developed for the purpose of reporting the results of the College Entrance Examination Board tests and is used by the Educational

Testing Service as the basis for reported scores on many of its other special program tests [including the *Scholastic Aptitude Test* (now called the *Scholastic Assessment Test*), the *Graduate Record Examination*, and others]. It is similar to other linear standard scores, but has a mean of 500 and a standard deviation of 100.

*Formula:*

$$CEEB = 100z + 500$$

where

z = a z-score, as defined above; and 100 and 500 are multiplying and additive constants, respectively

*Example:* Joanna's z-score of 1.5 would be expressed on the *CEEB* scale as 650. (Her percentile rank would be 93, assuming a normal distribution. In any distribution, her *CEEB* score of 650 lies in a direct straight line below a z of 1.5, a *T* of 65, etc.)

Originally, the *CEEB* scores were set up differently each year, using the mean and standard deviation of that year's examinees. Then, for many years, they were keyed to the mean and standard deviation of 1941 examinees; however, in April 1995, the norms for the *SAT* were "recentered" so that, once again, 500 will be the mean for the current year's testing group. ETS also reports percentile ranks based on current examinees. It is *essential* that one consult the interpretive information furnished by the publisher for a full understanding of this type of score.

### 5. Deviation IQs (sometimes)

The IQ (Intelligence Quotient), suggested nearly a century ago by the German psychologist Wilhelm Stern, sounded very reasonable. Lewis Terman, at Stanford University, was the first to use it with a test (the *Stanford-Binet*) in 1916, and soon other test writers began using it. Few tests (if any) still use the *ratio IQ* (a Type III score), where IQ is based on the ratio of mental age to chronological age. One big advantage of a *deviation IQ* is that it has a common standard deviation for all ages covered by the test.

The term *deviation IQ* is used to describe three different types of score. We shall deal here with the first (and most common) meaning, a linear standard score (but see also Type II B 5 e and Type IV C). *This* deviation IQ has the same advantages and limitations as other linear standard scores except that it has a mean of 100 and a standard deviation as fixed by the test's author.

**(a) *Wechsler* IQs.**    Three popular individual tests of intelligence are the *Wechsler Preschool and Primary Scale of Intelligence—Revised* (*WPPSI-R*), the *Wechsler Intelligence Scale for Children—III* (*WISC-III*), and the *Wechsler Adult Intelligence Scale—III* (*WAIS-III*). IQs are determined in similar fashion on all three: Each test yields a Verbal IQ, a Performance IQ, and a Full Scale IQ.

Dr. Wechsler had decided in advance that he wanted his test to have a mean of 100 and a standard deviation of 15. He therefore used the formula IQ = 15z + 100. Users of the Wechsler tests, of course, need only consult the appropriate tables to find the IQ values.

**(b) 1960 *Stanford-Binet* IQs.**    Until the 1960 revision, *Stanford-Binet* (*S-B*) IQs were ratio IQs. The authors of the 1960 revision decided to adopt the deviation IQ so that the standard deviation would be constant from age to age—in spite of careful and extensive effort in preparing the previous revision (1937), standard deviations for different ages had differed by as much as eight IQ points! In the 1960 *S-B*, the IQ is a linear standard score with a mean of 100 and a standard deviation of 16.

The *Stanford-Binet* metric was changed again in 1987. The *Fourth Edition S-B* uses a Standard Age Score (Type II B 5 g); this is essentially a normalized standard score with the same characteristics ($\overline{X}$ = 100, $s$ = 16) as the 1960 *S-B*.

### Summary of linear standard scores

All linear standard scores tell us the location of an examinee's raw score in relation to the mean of some specified group and in terms of the group's standard deviation. In any distribution, normal or not, we can convert freely from raw-score values to linear-standard-score equivalents without in any way changing the shape of the original distribution. Because of these properties, we can average these scores exactly as we can raw scores; we cannot average other Type II scores.

## Type II B: Inter-Individual Comparison Considering Rank

Like Type II A scores, Type II B scores are very commonly used in reporting standardized test results. Unlike Type II A scores, they are based on the number of people with scores higher (or lower) than a specified score value. Therefore, we lose such information as distance away from the mean. On the other hand, some of these scores (especially Type II B 5) have the effect of creating a distribution that is more nearly normal than the actual distribution of obtained raw scores. As with all other scores (except Type I), values will change for different groups. Note: Because their units differ in size, Type II B scores must not be averaged.

### 1. Rank

The simplest possible statement of relative position is *rank*: first for highest or best, second for next, third for next, and so on. It has the unique disadvantage of being so completely limited by the number of cases that it is never used formally in reporting test results.

## 2. Percentile rank and percentile band

The *percentile rank* (sometimes called centile rank) is probably the score used most frequently in reporting the results of standardized tests. All things considered, it is probably the best type for general use in test interpretation; however, it does have limitations, as we shall see presently.

A *percentile* is any one of the 99 points dividing a frequency distribution into 100 groups of equal size. A percentile rank (PR) is a person's relative position within a specified group.

> We find the percentile rank of an examinee or of a given raw-score value. We find a specified percentile value by finding the equivalent raw-score value. Thus a raw score of 162 may have a percentile rank of 44; the forty-fourth percentile will be a raw score of 162.

Because of the importance of percentiles and percentile ranks, Charts 8.4(A) and 8.4(B) have been included to describe and illustrate their computation. The raw-score values used were selected deliberately so as not to conflict with the numbers used to express any common type of derived score. Here, the range in raw scores is smaller and the number of people is smaller than we would expect to find in most practical situations; this was done deliberately in order to simplify the presentation.

**Advantages and limitations of percentile ranks.**   The principal advantage of PRs lies in their ease of interpretation. Even a person who thinks of percentiles as being equally spaced (which they could not be unless the same number of persons obtained each raw score) can understand something about these scores if he or she at least knows that a PR is a statement of the percentage of cases (persons) in a given group who fall at or below a given score value.

On the other hand, we find it very easy to overemphasize differences near the median and to underestimate differences near the extremes; in Figure 8.1 of Chart 8.3 we should note the slight difference between PRs of 45 and 55 as compared with the difference between PRs of 90 and 99. And even these varying differences are altered when a distribution departs markedly from the normal probability model, as may be seen in Figure 8.2 of Chart 8.3.

**Averaging percentile ranks.**   Because interpercentile distances are not equal, we cannot average them directly (as we could Type II A scores). This point applies equally to averaging the performance of one person on two or more tests and averaging the performance of a group of people on one test.

> To find the average PR of one person on several tests, convert each PR to a z-score using the Conversion Table on pages 177–182; average the z-scores, and convert the average z to a PR. Note: This method assumes a normal distribution for each test and the same normative group for each test. Only slight errors will

be introduced if the distributions are nearly normal, but no averaging can be done if the original PRs were based on different norm groups.

To find the average PR for a group of persons on one test, average the raw scores and find the PR corresponding to this average raw score. Note that this method is one we might follow to determine how our local group compares with a national normative group. Note further that this procedure gives the PR corresponding to the average raw score. Since group averages vary less than do individual raw scores, the value found should never be thought of as the PR of the group (in comparison to other groups). This misleading sort of information can be found in some test manuals.

**More advantages and limitations.**   With percentiles, we are using a common scale of values for all distributions on all tests. Regardless of the range of raw scores, the range of PRs will be the same: 0 or 1– to 100 or 99+ (unless more than 0.5 percent of the examinees make either of the most extreme scores). On very short tests, a difference of 20 or 30 PRs may represent a difference of only one or two raw-score values.

Some publishers use PRs of 0 and 100; some do not. The following example reflects the philosophical issue:

Niko Nikam has a lower score than anyone in the normative group. A PR of 0 would certainly describe his performance. On the other hand, we like to think of a normative group as being a sample representative of a large population. If Niko is being compared with an appropriate group, he presumably belongs to the population from which the normative group was taken. It is not logical to say that he did less well than everyone in the population of which he is part. Following this line of reasoning, I prefer to use 1– instead of 0 and 99+ instead of 100.

Some readers may wonder how this issue can exist if a percentile rank, as defined above, is one of the 99 points that divide a frequency distribution into 100 groups of equal size.

Figure 8.3 gives us the answer. If we divide the ranked distribution of scores into 100 subgroups of equal size, as shown across the top of the line, there are 99 percentile points setting off the 100 subgroups. In expressing a percentile rank, however, we round to the nearest whole percentile value, as shown by the lines drawn across the bottom of the line to indicate the real limits of each percentile rank. Ninety-nine of these units leave 0.5 percent at each extreme of the distribution; it is these extremes that we call 1– and 99+.

One final disadvantage of percentile ranks is that they use a metric (or scale of numbers) that is shared with several other types of scores; some examples are percentage-correct scores, T-scores, and IQs. There is the possibility of confusion, especially with percentage-correct scores. We must remember that percentage-correct scores are based on percentage of content (items), whereas PRs are based on percentage of cases (people) in a given group.

*CHART 8.4(A)*    **Computation of Percentiles and Percentile Ranks**

| 1<br>X | 2<br>f | 3<br>cf | 4<br>$cf_{mp}$ | 5<br>$cP_{mp}$ | 6<br>PR |
|---|---|---|---|---|---|
| 225 | 1 | 50 | 49.5 | 99.0 | 99 |
| 224 | 1 | 49 | 48.5 | 97.0 | 97 |
| 223 | 2 | 48 | 47.0 | 94.0 | 94 |
| 222 | 4 | 46 | 44.0 | 88.0 | 88 |
| 221 | 2 | 42 | 41.0 | 82.0 | 82 |
| 220 | 5 | 40 | 37.5 | 75.0 | 75 |
| 219 | 6 | 35 | 32.0 | 64.0 | 64 |
| 218 | 8 | 29 | 25.0 | 50.0 | 50 |
| 217 | 5 | 21 | 18.5 | 37.0 | 37 |
| 216 | 4 | 16 | 14.0 | 28.0 | 28 |
| 215 | 4 | 12 | 10.0 | 20.0 | 20 |
| 214 | 4 | 8 | 6.0 | 12.0 | 12 |
| 213 | 3 | 4 | 2.5 | 5.0 | 5 |
| 212 | 0 | 1 | 1.0 | 2.0 | 2 |
| 211 | 1 | 1 | 0.5 | 1.0 | 1 |

where

$X$ = value of raw score
$f$ = frequency (number of examinees making this score)
$cf$ = cumulative frequency
$cf_{mp}$ = $cf$ to midpoint of score
$cP_{mp}$ = cumulative percentage to midpoint of score
$PR$ = percentile rank for the specified raw-score value

**To Find PRs for Stated Raw-Score Values**

1. List every possible raw-score value.
2. Show the frequency with which each score occurs.
3. Find the cumulative frequency up through each score by adding that score's frequency to the frequencies of all lower scores; for example, $cf$ through a score of 214 (that is, through its upper limit, 214.5): 4 + 3 + 0 + 1 = 8.
4. Find the cumulative frequency to the midpoint of each score by adding one-half of the frequency at that score to the cumulative frequency up through the next lower score; for example, $cf_{mp}$ for 212.0: ($\frac{1}{2}$ × 0) + 1 = 1.0; $cf_{mp}$ for 216.0: ($\frac{1}{2}$ × 4) + 12 = 14.0.
5. Convert to cumulative percentage by the formula $cP_{mp}$ = 100 ($cf_{mp}$)/$N$, where $cP_{mp}$ and $cf_{mp}$ are defined as above, and $N$ = number of cases; or use 100/$N$ as a constant to multiply by successive $cf_{mp}$ values, as here: 100/$N$ = 100/50 = 2.0.
6. Find percentile ranks by rounding each $cP_{mp}$ value to the nearest whole number (except use 1– for 0 and 99+ for 100).

*CHART 8.4(B)*

## To Find Raw-Score Equivalents of Percentile Values

1. Prepare columns 1–3 as in Chart 8.4(A).
2. Change from percentile to number of cases by multiplying $P_x$ by $N/100$; for example, in finding $P_{20}$, $20 \times 50/100 = 10$.
3. Count up through the number of cases found in step 2, assuming that cases are distributed evenly across each score; for example, one-third of the cases at a score lie one-third of the way between the real lower limit and the real upper limit of the score, and so on. See the examples given below.
4. The corresponding raw-score value is the desired percentile.

---

Examples:

### Find $P_{30}$, the raw-score value at or below which fall 30% of the cases:

A. 30% of 50 cases = $30 \times 50/100 = 15$; we must count up through 15 cases.
B. Find the biggest number in the *cf* column that is *not greater than* 15. This number is 12.
C. Subtract the number found in step B from the number of cases needed; $15 - 12 = 3$.
D. We need to get these three cases from those individuals at the next higher score; in other words, we need three of the four cases at the score of 216.
E. We go that fractional way through the score: ¾ (or 0.75) + 215.5 (real lower limit of score) = 216.25. $P_{30} = 216.25$.

### Find $P_{50}$ (the median):

A. 50% of 50 cases is 25.
B. We note 25 in the $cf_{mp}$ column; $P_{50}$ = midpoint of the score, 218, or 218.0.

### Find $P_{80}$, the eightieth percentile:

A. 80% of 50 cases is 40.
B. We note 40 in the *cf* column; $P_{80}$ = upper limit of the score, 220, or 220.5.

We should note that in Chart 8.4(A) we have found cumulative frequencies up to the midpoint of each raw-score value, and have translated these $cf_{mp}$ values into percentages that, rounded to whole numbers, are the percentile ranks.

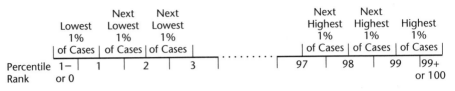

*FIGURE 8.3*   **Graphic Explanation of Percentile Ranks at Upper and Lower Extremes of a Distribution. (See further explanation in text.)**

**Summary of percentile ranks.**    Although PRs have limitations, they are very commonly used in expressing the results of standardized tests. They are reasonably easy to understand and to explain to others. Considering all their advantages and limitations, PRs are probably the best single derived score for general use in expressing test results. Consider, too, the following application.

**The percentile band.**    An interesting application of percentile ranks is found in the percentile band, developed by the Educational Testing Service and now used by several publishers. The *percentile band* is a band or range of percentile ranks. The upper limit of the ETS percentile bands corresponds to the percentile rank of a score one standard error of measurement above the obtained raw score; similarly, the lower limit is one standard error of measurement below the obtained score.

The width of the band may, of course, vary for different tests and different publishers; however, the general concept is the same. Publishers using the band approach give full information about it in their manuals. Test users wishing to make their own bands may do so—they need only a set of percentile norms, the standard error of measurement, and the directions above.

The purpose of percentile bands is to emphasize that test measurement error is present in each score. The percentile band is useful, too, in interpreting differences between different tests within the same test battery. Percentile bands combine the stated advantages of the percentile rank with an emphasis that the score should not be treated as a precise value. In addition, percentile bands seem to have the advantages of other coarse-unit scores while avoiding their principal limitation (that a single unit of change is relatively large) by centering the band on the obtained score, so that the limits of the band change only slightly for slight differences in score. This may be the most valuable single type of score for general test interpretation purposes.

### 3. Letter grades (sometimes)

As suggested earlier, letter grades may be based on comparative performance. When this is done, they are a Type II B score. A few standardized tests have used such scores, clearly indicating those values to be assigned As, those to be assigned Bs, and so on. Far more commonly, a teacher will use some inter-individual comparison in assigning course grades.

Note that it is not necessary to decide in advance how many students will receive each letter grade. "Grading on the curve" is rather old-fashioned anyway. The practice of basing letter grades on a normal curve (perhaps by giving 10 percent A, 20 percent B, 40 percent C, 20 percent D, and 10 percent F) is indefensible unless one has very large numbers of unselected students. One way of assigning grades on the basis of comparative performance that I like is as follows:

> I make no assumption about the number of students who will fail or who will get any particular grade. During the term, I give several quizzes and make certain that the standard deviation of each is about the same size (for tests "weight" themselves according to size of standard deviation). I make the standard deviation of the final examination somewhat larger than those on the quizzes. I add these raw scores and arrange the students in order of summed scores. Often the results will show several clusters of students, which suggests that they should be given the same grade. If there are students whose summed scores seem almost to "drop out" of the distribution, these may receive Fs. I will, however, consider carefully whether any of these students has shown a little promise—perhaps by great improvement on the final examination—that might justify some grade other than F. I try to be a little more generous with higher grades when my class has been better than usual. Some years my students seem less promising, and I am more cautious about assigning many high grades.

Every teacher recognizes that grades are somewhat arbitrary and subjective. I try to make the grades I assign as fair as possible, reflecting comparative performance for the most part, but with just a dash of consideration for the sort of class I have. There is one thing that each teacher must accomplish: *Make certain that your students understand how you assign grades.*

Let me know if you ever find the perfect grading system, will you? And thank you in advance!

## 4. Decile rank

The Institute for Personality and Ability Testing (IPAT) uses decile scores in some of its norms tables. A *decile* is defined as any one of nine points separating the frequency distribution into ten groups of equal size. Thus the first decile $(D_1)$ equals the tenth percentile, the second decile $(D_2)$ equals the twentieth percentile, and so on. R. B. Cattell modified this meaning of decile to include a band (or range) of 10 percent of the cases, 5 percent on each side of the actual decile point; for example, a decile score of 1 includes values from the fifth to the fifteenth percentile. (Values below $P_5$ are given a decile score of 0; values above $P_{95}$, a score of 10.) IPAT believes that these scores should be used in preference to percentile ranks when the range in raw scores is very small. In order to prevent confusion between decile and decile score, I prefer to use the term *decile ranks* because of their similarity to percentile ranks.

## 5. Normalized standard scores (area transformations)

Normalized standard scores are derived scores that are assigned standard-score-like values but are computed from percentile ranks. With *linear* standard scores, the shape of the distribution of raw scores is reproduced faithfully; if additional baselines were drawn for a frequency polygon, we would find that the values of any of those standard scores would lie in a straight line below the corresponding raw-score values regardless of the shape of the raw score distribution. With *normalized* standard scores, this is true only when the raw-score distribution is normal, as shown in Figure 8.2 of Chart 8.3.

Normalized standard scores have the property of making a distribution a closer approximation of the normal probability distribution. This is accomplished in similar fashion for all normalized standard scores, so we consider the general procedure here rather than treating it separately for each score.

**Area transformations.**   As we can see from the computation procedures in Chart 8.5, these scores are known as *area transformations* because they are based on standard-score values that would correspond to specified cumulative percentages in a normal distribution (and area indicates frequency of cases).

> Saying that 23 percent of the cases lie below a specified score is the same as saying that 23 percent of the area of a graph showing that distribution lies below that same score value. In finding a normalized standard score, we are merely substituting for that score value a standard-score value that would be at a point below which falls 23 percent of the area under the normal probability curve.

**(a) *T*-scaled score.**   In a normal distribution, this has exactly the same properties as the *T*-score (including its mean of 50 and standard deviation of 10). In fact, this score often is called a *T*-score. It has all the advantages and limitations of the normalized standard scores already mentioned. It has the additional limitation of being confused with the *T*-score, which is of practical significance only when the original distribution of raw scores differs appreciably from the normal probability model.

**(b) Stanine score.**   Developed by World War II psychologists for use with the U.S. Air Force, stanine scores were intended to maximize the information

*CHART 8.5*   **How to Compute Normalized Standard Scores**

---

1. Find the percentile rank for each raw score.
2. Use the Conversion Table (pp. 177–182); locate the percentile rank in the extreme right column; then read the corresponding value from the appropriate column to the left.

---

about test performance that could be entered into a single column of an IBM punched card. Obviously a card could hold more one-digit scores than two- or three-digit scores. Whereas other standard scores have indicated specific values, stanines (from **sta**ndard score of **nine** units) were intended to represent bands of values; except for the open-ended extreme stanines of 1 and 9, each stanine was to equal one-half standard deviation in width, and the mean was to be the midpoint of the middle stanine, 5.

Apparently some Air Force psychologists used the stanine as a linear standard score at first, thereby giving it the properties mentioned above; however, others treated it as a normalized standard score, and it is so used today. When distributed normally, stanines have a mean of 5 and a standard deviation of 2; in addition, all stanines except 1 and 9 are exactly one-half standard deviation in width. With distributions that are not normal, these values will be only approximated.

In general, stanines have the advantages and limitations of other coarse-unit scores. It is unlikely that a person's obtained score is many units away from his or her true score, but a test interpreter is perhaps more likely to put undue confidence in the accuracy of the obtained score. For computation, see Chart 8.6.

**Flanagan's Extended Stanine score.**   For use in reporting scores on its *Flanagan Aptitude Classification Tests,* London House splits each stanine value into three units by using plus and minus signs. Stanine 1 is made into three stanine values—1–, 1, and 1+—and every other stanine is treated similarly. In this way, John Flanagan achieves a 27-unit normalized-standard-score scale. This scale has certain obvious advantages over the usual stanine scale, but it is not in general use. The percentile equivalents of these extended stanine values differ slightly for each test in the *FACT* battery; they may be found in the *FACT Examiner's Manual.*

**(c) C-scaled score.**   J. P. Guilford developed a C-scale that provides one additional unit at each end of the stanine scale. The C-scale has eleven units, assigned values of 0 to 10. This scale is used in the norms tables of tests published by the Sheridan Psychological Services. C-scores are computed exactly as stanines are, except for the two extremes. See Chart 8.7. Note that the C-values are identical with stanines except at the two extremes.

**(d) Sten score.**   Similar in rationale to the two preceding scores is the *sten* (a normalized **sta**ndard score with **ten** units). This system provides for five normalized-standard-score units on each side of the mean, each of them one-half standard deviation in width except for the sten values of 1 and 10, which are open-ended. Since this is a normalized standard score, these interval sizes apply exactly only in a normal distribution. This metric is used for norms of some of the tests published by the Institute for Personality and Ability Testing.

*CHART 8.6*    **How to Compute Stanines**

> The purpose is to assign stanines according to the designated percentages; these are the normal-curve percentages that fall into each unit one-half standard deviation in width when we set up stanine 5 to extend from a z-score of −0.25 (one-fourth standard deviation below the mean) to a z-score of +0.25.
>
> The ideal percentage for each stanine is shown on the top line below. The stanines to be assigned are shown in the boldface type. The bottom line shows the ideal cumulative percentages up through each stanine. We can only approximate these figures with real data—especially when either range or number of cases is small.

| Lowest | Next | Next | Next | Middle | Next | Next | Next | Highest |
|---|---|---|---|---|---|---|---|---|
| 4% | 7% | 12% | 17% | 20% | 17% | 12% | 7% | 4% |
| **Stanine 1** | **Stanine 2** | **Stanine 3** | **Stanine 4** | **Stanine 5** | **Stanine 6** | **Stanine 7** | **Stanine 8** | **Stanine 9** |
| 4% | 11% | 23% | 40% | 60% | 77% | 89% | 96% | 100% |

Cumulative Percentages

### Steps in Computing Stanines

1. Draw up a frequency distribution.
2. Find the cumulative frequency up through each score value.
3. Change these cumulative frequencies to percentages by multiplying every $cf$ value by $100/N$.
4. Assign stanine values by approximating the *ideal* cumulative percentages on the bottom line above as closely as possible.
5. Remember: Each person with the same raw score must receive the same stanine score, regardless of how well each value "fits" the ideal percentages.

Stens may be computed in the same way as stanines, except that the values given are as shown in Chart 8.8.

**(e) Deviation IQs (sometimes).**    So far as I know, no intelligence test presently uses the deviation IQ in this normalized-standard-score sense; however, the *Fourth Edition Stanford-Binet* uses the Standard Age Score (Type II B 5 g), which amounts to the same thing.

**Wechsler subtests.**    Something similar to deviation IQs of the sort mentioned in the previous paragraph is already found in the subtests (or scales) of the Wechsler intelligence tests: Each of the separate scales on these tests uses a normalized standard score with a mean of 10 and a standard deviation of 3.

*CHART 8.7*

| Lowest 1% | Next 3% | Next 7% | Next 12% | Next 17% | Middle 20% | Next 17% | Next 12% | Next 7% | Next 3% | Highest 1% |
|---|---|---|---|---|---|---|---|---|---|---|
| C = 0 | C = 1 | C = 2 | C = 3 | C = 4 | C = 5 | C = 6 | C = 7 | C = 8 | C = 9 | C = 10 |
| 1 | 4 | 11 | 23 | 40 | 60 | 77 | 89 | 96 | 99 | 100 |

Cumulative Percentages

However, these scale scores are used mainly in finding totals on which the Wechsler IQs are based, and the subtest scores themselves are seldom interpreted.

**(f) ITED-score.** The *ITED*-score was developed for use with the *Iowa Tests of Educational Development*, but it is now also used with the *American College Testing Program (ACTP)* and some other tests. This score has a mean of 15 and a standard deviation of 5 and is based on a nationally representative sample of tenth- and eleventh-grade students.

**(g) Standard Age Score.** Now used in connection with certain Riverside Press tests (such as the *Fourth Edition Stanford-Binet*), the Standard Age Score has a mean of 100 and a standard deviation of 16. Thus it has the same properties as the 1960 *Stanford-Binet* metric, except that the SAS is a normalized standard score.

**(h) Normal curve equivalent (NCE).** The NCE is a type of score developed by the RMC Research Corporation for use by the United States Office of Education. Its use by educators and psychologists engaged in research pro-

*CHART 8.8*

| Lowest 2% | Next 5% | Next 9% | Next 15% | Low Middle 19% | High Middle 19% | Next 15% | Next 9% | Next 5% | Highest 2% |
|---|---|---|---|---|---|---|---|---|---|
| Sten 1 | Sten 2 | Sten 3 | Sten 4 | Sten 5 | Sten 6 | Sten 7 | Sten 8 | Sten 9 | Sten 10 |
| 2 | 7 | 16 | 31 | 50 | 69 | 84 | 93 | 98 | 100 |

Cumulative Percentages

jects for the USOE is strongly recommended. It is not intended for interpretation of an individual's test results.

The NCE is a normalized standard score with a mean of 50 and a standard deviation of 21.06. NCE values can be found by calibrating the baseline of a normal curve from 1 to 99 in equal units—when 1 and 99 are made the equivalent of percentiles of 1 and 99. Thus, NCE values and percentile ranks are identical at 1, 50, and 99, as shown in Figure 8.4.

## Type II C: Inter-Individual Comparison Considering Range

Only one derived score, the percent placement score, is based on inter-individual comparisons considering the range of raw scores. It is used in rare instances to express scores on classroom tests of achievement, and nowhere else.

The *percent placement* score indicates a person's position on a 101-point scale where the highest score made on a test is set at 100 and the lowest score made is set at 0.

*Formula:*

$$X_{\%pl} = 100 \frac{(X - L)}{(H - L)}$$

where
    $X$ = any specified raw score
    $L$ = lowest raw score made
    $H$ = highest raw score made

*Example*: On a 300-item test, there is a range from 260 to 60; range = 260 − 60 = 200. Barry's raw score was 60; the percent placement score is 0. Harry's raw score was 260; the $X_{\%pl}$ = 100. Carry's raw score was 140; the $X_{\%pl}$ = 40 [i.e., 100(140 − 60)/200 = 40].

## Type II D: Inter-Individual Comparison Considering Status of Those Making Same Score

Type II D scores include age scores and grade-placement scores. These are set up to express test performance in terms of averages of groups that differ in status (either in chronological age or in grade placement). Thus examinees' scores are not a statement of how well they have done when compared with some designated group. Instead, a score tells which group (among several) an examinee is most like in terms of level of performance.

Type II D scores are used most commonly with standardized tests of achievement and intelligence for children of school age. They are not suited for use with informal tests, and no computation guide will be given.

Although Type II D scores seem easy to understand, they have many limitations that are not immediately apparent.

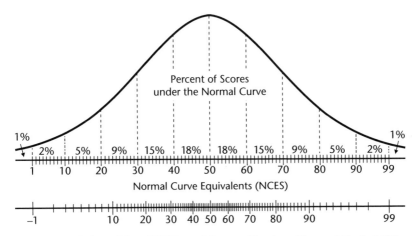

Percent of Scores
under the Normal Curve

**FIGURE 8.4**    **Relationship of NCEs and Percentiles in a Normal Probability Distribution.** (Tallmadge and Wood, *User's Guide, ESEA Title I Evaluation and Reporting System.*) The research worker will prefer to consult the conversion table in Tallmadge and Wood's *User's Guide, ESEA Title I Evaluation and Reporting System* from which Figure 8.4 was obtained.

## 1. Age scores

*Age scores* can be developed for any human characteristic that changes with age; however, they are used most frequently with intelligence and achievement tests for children of school age or below. The most common age score is the *mental age (MA)*, a concept developed by Alfred Binet about 100 years ago for use with the earliest successful intelligence test.

An age score is an expression of an examinee's test performance stated in terms of the developmental level characteristic of the average child of that corresponding chronological age.

> Moya gets an MA of seven years six months (expressed as 7-6) on an intelligence test. This means that Moya's level of performance is equal to the average score made by children with a chronological age of 7-6. Alternatively, although less frequently, an MA may be defined as the average chronological age of individuals making a given raw score. By this definition,Moya's MA of 7-6 would indicate that the average chronological age of children with the same raw score as hers was 7-6.

When used with young children, age scores are reasonably easy to understand. The logic is straightforward and simple. On the other hand, age scores are easily overinterpreted. A five-year-old who obtains an age score of 7 on a test is still only five years of age in most respects. There can be no assumption that all people with the same age score have identical abilities.

Test makers have difficulty in getting good representative samples for age norms because some children are located a grade or two ahead of (or behind) their age peers. These youngsters must be included if the norms are to be meaningful, but they can be difficult to locate, especially when they do not attend the same schools as their age peers.

An age score by itself tells us little about the individual's potentiality, but it may be used in combination with chronological age or other measure to form a quotient score that will do so.

**(a) Mental age.**    Although the MA served Binet's need for a score that could be understood easily, it has been extended beyond reason. As originally conceived, MA units were credited to a child for each task that was passed. The sum of these units yielded an MA; this MA had the property of being equal on the average to chronological age. There are better types of score today.

We must use considerable caution when interpreting MAs. Within the range of about five and fifteen years, MAs may be reasonably meaningful for children of approximately those same chronological ages; however, it is not correct to think of a mentally disabled adult who has, let us say, an MA of 6-0 as being equal to the average child of that age. The adult will have habits and motor skills that differ greatly from those of the typical child, and the child will probably be able to grasp new ideas much more readily than the retarded adult.

One difficulty with the interpretation of MAs is the fact that the standard deviations differ from test to test and even from age to age within the same test. Therefore, there is no way of generalizing age-score values that are any stated distance from the mean; for example, an MA of 13-3 for a child of 12-3 does not indicate the same degree of superiority as does an MA of 6-3 for a child of 5-3.

In recent years, though, the MA has been used by some school systems in connection with the mainstreaming of special education pupils. And special education teachers, by and large, do a superior job of working with their students.

**(b) Educational ages, etc.**    Very similar to the mental age is the educational age. An *educational age (EA)* indicates test performance at a given level, which level is expressed as the age of individuals for whom this is average performance.

> Krista Kitsinis has an EA of 8-6 on a test. In other words, her achievement on this test is equal to the average (mean or median) performance of children in the norm group who were eight years six months of age when tested; or, less frequently, this may mean that the average chronological age of children earning the same score she did is 8-6.

Actually, what we are calling simply *educational age* goes under many different names: *achievement age, reading age,* or (any subject matter) *age.* All the difficulties and limitations mentioned for the MA hold for the EA at least equally as well.

The EA is not in common use today.

## 2. Grade-placement scores

One score that is still commonly used in reporting performance on standardized achievement tests is the *grade-placement* (or *grade-equivalent*) *score*. This is unfortunate! In spite of their intrinsic appeal and apparent logic, these scores are confusing and lend themselves to erroneous interpretations.

The basic rationale for grade-placement scores is similar to that for age scores, for their values are set to equal the average score of school pupils at the corresponding grade placement. They are established by (1) testing youngsters at several grade placements with the same test; (2) finding the average (mean or median) for each grade-placement level; (3) plotting these averages on a graph and connecting these plots with as straight a line as possible; (4) extending (extrapolating) this line at both extremes to account for scores below and above the averages found; (5) reading off the closest grade-equivalent values for each raw-score value; and (6) publishing these equivalents in tabular form.

Grade-placement scores are usually stated in tenths of a school year; for example, 8.2 refers to the second month of grade eight. (This system gives a value of 1.0 to the beginning of the first grade, which presumably should be the true zero point in school grade placement.) A basic assumption seems to be that children learn more or less uniformly throughout the school year, but that they learn nothing during the summer vacation.

Grade-placement scores are intrinsically appealing. It seems reasonable at first glance to think of children who stand high in comparison with others in their school grade as doing the same quality of work as youngsters who are more advanced in school. And in a sense they are. But that does not mean that these children should be promoted immediately to a higher grade. These grade-placement scores are based on the average performance of pupils having that actual placement in school. In obtaining that average, we had some better scores and some poorer scores.

Furthermore, regardless of how high a child's grade-placement score is, the child has been in school for only a given amount of time. And there are probably breadths and depths of understanding and competency that are closely related to one's experiences and to the length of one's exposure to school. A child's higher score is more likely to mean a more complete mastery of (and therefore fewer errors on) material taught at his or her grade. When this fact is considered, we see that the direct meaning of grade-placement scores is more apparent than real.

Standard deviations for different subject matters are bound to differ even when the tests are included in the same standardized achievement test battery and based on the same normative groups. Students are much more like-ly, for example, to have grade-placement scores several grade equivalents higher than their actual grade placement in reading and in English than in arithmetic and in science. The latter subjects depend much more on specific, school-taught skills. The result is that standard deviations are almost certain to be larger for English and reading than for arithmetic and science; similar, although less extreme, differences exist for other subjects.

The test manuals of all major publishers of achievement tests carefully point out these differences in standard deviations. Many test users, though, do not understand the critical importance of these differences in any inter-pretation of scores. Among many other points, these different standard devi-ations reflect the greater possible range in grade-placement scores on some tests of an achievement battery than on others. Grade-placement scores on one test may extend up 4.5 grade equivalents, as compared with only 2.5 grade equivalents for another test in the same coordinated achievement bat-tery.

Grade-placement scores are so confusing that a lower score on one test may indicate relatively higher performance than does a higher score on another test. Because of the difference in size of standard deviations, the fol-lowing might easily happen: a grade-placement score of 8.5 on reading may be equal to a percentile rank of 60, but a grade-placement score of 8.2 on arithmetic fundamentals may be equal to a percentile rank of 98. Especially for higher elementary grades and beyond, grade-placement scores cannot mean-ingfully be compared from test to test, even within the same battery!

Best conclusion: *Use another type of score.*

## TYPE III: INTRA-INDIVIDUAL COMPARISONS

All Type III scores are unique in that they are based on two measurements of the same person; all are found as ratios or fractions.

### Type III A: Ratio IQ (Intelligence Quotient)

Although we have considered the IQ twice before and will return to it once again (under Type IV), this is the original IQ—the one first proposed by Wilhelm Stern and first used by Lewis Terman in 1916. The *ratio-type intelli-gence quotient* is found by the formula $IQ = 100\ MA/CA$, where *MA* is a men-tal age found from an intelligence test, and *CA* is the examinee's chronologi-cal age at the time of testing (with an adjusted *CA* used for older adolescents and adults). It is rarely used today.

The rationale of the ratio-type IQ is widely understood, but its many lim-itations are less well known. The score depends on an assumption of equal-sized mental-age units, and these may not exist. Ratio-type IQs work reasonably well between the ages of about five and fifteen years, but tend to be of questionable value outside those approximate limits. Adult IQs of necessity are based on artificial mental ages (as explained earlier) and "adjusted" chronological ages.

The most telling argument against the ratio IQ, however, is that standard deviations differ from one age level to the next. If standard deviations are permitted to vary (and this cannot be controlled with the ratio IQ), the same IQ indicates different degrees of superiority or inferiority at different ages. The deviation IQ (Type II A or II B) is much better than the ratio IQ.

## Type III B: Intellectual Status Index

This was a sort of IQ substitute with the denominator changed from a child's actual chronological age to the average chronological age of children with the same grade placement in school. It is no longer in use.

## Type III C: Educational Quotients

An *Educational Quotient* is found by dividing an educational age (EA) by chronological age (CA) and multiplying by 100. Just as we may have subject-matter ages of all sorts, so may we have all sorts of subject-matter quotients. EQs have never been very widely used, for grade-placement scores have been preferred.

## Type III D: Accomplishment Quotients

There is almost unanimous agreement that the *Accomplishment* (or *Achievement*) *Quotient* (AQ) is a poor type of score. Not only is it based on two test scores, each with its own errors of measurement, but it also gives illogical results. It compares a pupil's achievement test score with an intelligence test score, and it is presumed to indicate how completely one is working up to capacity.

*Formula:*

$$AQ = 100 \, \frac{EA}{MA}$$

where
$EA$ = educational age, determined by an achievement test
$MA$ = mental age, determined by an intelligence test

The ideal *AQ* is 100, indicating that a pupil is realizing his or her complete potential. How, then, do we explain an *AQ* above 100? Although logically impossible, *AQs* above 100 can occur—suggesting that some pupils are achieving more than they are capable of achieving! A much more reasonable explanation, of course, is that the two scores entering into the *AQ* are fallible measures and that errors of measurement have combined to produce this "impossible" result.

## TYPE IV: ASSORTED ARBITRARY BASES

Although the three main bases for expressing test scores are sufficient to account for most commonly used scores, there are other bases that are unique. We shall mention three very briefly.

### Type IV A: Nonmeaningful Scaled Scores

Several publishers use scaled scores that are nonmeaningful in themselves but that are extremely useful in giving a common basis for equating different forms and/or levels of a test.

We shall consider only one example: the *SCAT*-scale developed by the Educational Testing Service. This is a nonmeaningful scaled score used with ETS's *School and College Abilities Tests* (*SCAT*) and *Sequential Tests of Educational Progress* (*STEP*). ETS deliberately sought a scale that would use numbers that would not be confused with scores from other scales. The scale was constructed so that a scaled score of 300 would equal a percentage-correct score of 60; and a scaled score of 260, a percentage-correct score of 20. These scaled-score values are used as a statistical convenience for the publisher, but percentile bands are used for interpreting results.

### Type IV B: Long-Range Equi-Unit Scales

None of the scores already mentioned has a scale with equal units except within a narrow range or under certain assumptions. For some purposes, it is most desirable to have a single equi-unit scale covering a wide span of ages.

An early attempt at constructing such a scale resulted in the *T*-score mentioned earlier. As originally conceived by W. A. McCall, this scale was to use 50 for the mean of an unselected group of twelve-year-olds. The mean for older groups would be higher, and that for younger groups lower. The standard deviation would be 10 at all age levels.

Another early attempt was made by Heinis, who developed mental growth units that he believed were more nearly uniform in size than mental age units. These, in turn, were made to yield a Personal Constant, which he felt was more consistent than the IQ over a period of years.

One more example of such a scale is the *K*-score scales developed by Gardner. The average score of tenth graders is set at 100, and the unit of measurement is set at one-seventh the standard deviation of fifth graders. The rationale underlying the scale is too technical to go into here, but it has been applied to the *Stanford Achievement Tests* (published by The Psychological

Corporation). The principal advantage of such long-range equi-unit scales is to be found in various research applications. For the most part, they do not lend themselves well to direct interpretation. Their underlying rationale is usually very involved and their development complicated.

### Type IV C: Deviation IQ (Otis-Style)

It is fitting, perhaps, to come to the end of our long succession of scores with another IQ—the fourth one we have mentioned. (Is it any wonder that the IQ seems confusing sometimes?)

The deviation IQ as used on earlier Otis intelligence tests and certain others is basically different from the Type II deviation IQs. In the development of the Otis-style deviation IQ, a norm (or average) is found for each age group. We obtain an examinee's IQ by finding the raw score, subtracting the age norm, and adding 100; the result shows deviations of examinees from their age norms in raw-score units.

*Formula:*

(Otis) $IQ = 100 + (X - \text{age norm})$

where

$X =$ any person's raw score on an Otis intelligence test

age norm = average raw score for those in the norm group whose chronological age is same as the examinee's

This deviation IQ has a mean of 100, but the standard deviation is not controlled as were the standard deviations of the Type II deviation IQs. Because of this, the standard deviations of Otis-style IQs may vary from age to age and make interpretations difficult (or, perhaps, impossible). Note: This score is no longer used. The current Otis-Lennon intelligence tests do *not* use this metric.

## A FINAL WORD

We have considered many types of test score in this chapter. The personnel worker in industry is likely to encounter relatively few of them—probably only Types II A and II B (inter-individual comparisons considering mean and standard deviation, and considering rank within group). The schoolteacher or the guidance worker may very well encounter almost any of them.

Test scores would be much easier to interpret (for all of us, experts and novices alike) if we could only agree upon a single type of score, or even on just a few.

Considering all factors, I should like to see the day when we would use only percentile ranks or percentile bands in test interpretation. This score has limitations, to be sure, as all scores do. But the score has some inherent meaning and is easy for the layperson to grasp. If we had a single type of score, we could direct our attention to educating everyone concerning its meaning and its principal limitation, the difference in distances between various percentile points. We could stress, too, the importance of knowing the composition of the norm group (or groups).

There is little question but that percentile ranks can do everything that the IQ can. Percentile ranks within grade or within age have many advantages over grade-placement and age scores.

We might still have need of special warnings about the use of percentile ranks on very short tests where the difference of a single raw-score value may mean a great difference in percentile rank, but the percentile band, of course, is a protection here. We would still need other kinds of scores for research, because percentile ranks do not lend themselves well to mathematical manipulation; indeed, we cannot even average them.

We must remember that a test score must be understood before it can be interpreted. It would be easier to learn one score thoroughly than to try to learn something about many varieties of score.

Even more significant than any of these considerations is, of course, the quality of the test itself. A good test is one that will do the job we want it to, will do so consistently, and will possess those practical features (such as cost, time required, and the like) that make it usable for our purposes.

# *Test Profiles*

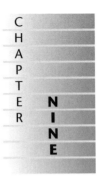

It is not always necessary to draw profiles of test results, but profiles often can help an examinee to better understand the results. Indeed, the profile often seems to be a great boon to the counselor who is interpreting test data to others.

A test profile is a graph that shows the test scores for an individual (or, less often, the average scores of a class or some other group). Years ago, most profiles were drawn locally, usually by a teacher, personnel worker, or clerk. Today almost all profiles are computer-produced, most typically by the test publisher. These profiles usually are accompanied by an interpretation of the results prepared by the professional staff of the test publisher. The test taker who pays attention to those printed interpretations can usually understand the meaning of the results reasonably well on her or his own; however, I recommend that a counselor also discuss the results with the individual.

Figure 9.1 shows a computer-prepared profile for the *Differential Aptitude Tests*. These results are for Pat Paraskevopoulos, who was tested in the spring semester of the eleventh grade. The profile proper shows percentile bands for each of the tests in that battery; these bands are similar to score Type II B 2, and extend one standard error of measurement in each direction from the raw score obtained by the examinee.

# Differential Aptitude Tests FIFTH EDITION

| | | |
|---|---|---|
| SCHOOL: | WATERTOWN H.S. | |
| DISTRICT: | WATERTOWN | |

GRADE:    11
TEST DATE: 04/98
NORMS: GRADE 11  SPRING
LEVEL:   2      FORM:  C      CAREER INTEREST INVENTORY LEVEL:   2

| DIFFERENTIAL APTITUDE TESTS | FEMALE | | NATIONAL PERCENTILE BANDS | MALE |
|---|---|---|---|---|
| | NP | PR-S | 1    5    10    20    30    40    50    60    70    80    90    95    99 | PR-S |
| VERBAL REASONING | 40 | 66-6 | | 64-6 |
| NUMERICAL REASONING | 40 | 75-6 | | 76-6 |
| ABSTRACT REASONING | 40 | 84-7 | | 84-7 |
| PERCEPTUAL SPEED & ACCURACY | 100 | 40-5 | | 58-5 |
| MECHANICAL REASONING | 60 | 89-8 | | 59-5 |
| SPACE RELATIONS | 50 | 83-7 | | 78-7 |
| SPELLING | 40 | 86-7 | | 92-6 |
| LANGUAGE USAGE | 40 | 63-6 | | 75-6 |
| | | | | |
| SCHOLASTIC APTITUDE (VR + HR) | 80 | 72-6 | | 75-6 |

## EDUCATIONAL PLANS

The Scholastic Aptitude score gives you some information about your ability to learn the subjects taught in school. Your score is in the average range. When you took the DAT, you indicated that your future educational plans included attending a college or a university. You should do well.

## UNDERSTANDING YOUR DAT RESULTS

Recently, you took the Differential Aptitude Tests (DAT). This brief description of the scores presented above tells how you did compared with other female students in the same grade from across the country.

You scored in the average range on the Verbal Reasoning and Numerical Reasoning tests. Verbal Reasoning measures your ability to see relationships among words, and Numerical Reasoning measures your ability to perform mathematical reasoning tasks. Both abilities are important to success in school, and your scores show that you are capable of doing well.

Your score on the Mechanical Reasoning test is in the above-average range. People who have this ability can usually figure out how things work and how to fix them.

Your score on the Abstract Reasoning test is in the above-average range. People who have this ability can recognize relationships that do not depend on language or numbers.

Your score on the Space Relations test is in the above-average range. People who have this ability do well when the task involves using patterns to build things.

You scored in the above-average range on the Spelling test. Many courses and careers require good spelling skills.

Your Language Usage score is in the average range. People who do well in this area are usually very good at writing and using correct English. Because many courses and careers require this ability, you may want to improve your ability by taking courses in English grammar or writing.

You scored in the average range on the Perceptual Speed & Accuracy test. This test measures how quickly and correctly you can compare and mark written lists.

It is important to remember the DAT scores give only one indication of your aptitudes at this time. Aptitudes can change as you learn and do more things. Keep this in mind as you think about what courses to take and what plans to make for the future.

Scores based on Normative Data Copyright © 1990 by The Psychological Corp. All rights reserved.

**FIGURE 9.1**

# Career Interest Inventory

INDIVIDUAL REPORT
FOR
PAT PARASKEVEKOPOULOS
GENDER FEMALE

16 YRS 10 MOS

UNDERSTANDING YOUR CAREER INTEREST INVENTORY

Your highest interest is in the Clerical Services area. Most people in this field work in offices, doing things such as preparing and keeping records, operating office machines, and arranging schedules. People who are in this field tend to have aptitudes like yours. Also, some of the subjects you like, such as word processing or typing, bookkeeping, office practices, or business law or management, relate well to this career field. However, many careers in Clerical Services do not require as much schooling as you are planning; but, some careers may require additional schooling or training. Given your interests and aptitudes, this might be a good career field for you to explore.

Your second highest interest is in the area of Management. Workers in this field establish goals, direct operations, and control activities within an organization. They usually work with different types of people, motivating them and directing their activities. Most of the careers in the Management field require either a college education or additional schooling or training beyond high school, which is the amount of education you are planning. Also, people who are in the Management field tend to have aptitudes like yours, and some of the subjects you like relate well to this career field. Given your interests and future plans, this might be a good occupational area for you to begin to explore.

Your third highest interest is in the Mathematics and Science area. Many workers in this field often do research that involves observing things and doing experiments. Most of the careers in the Mathematics and Science area require specialized training or a college education, which is the amount of education you are planning. People who are in the Mathematics and Science field tend to have aptitudes like yours. Also, some of the subjects you like, such as science, mathematics, electronics or electrical trades, and courses in computer technology, relate well to this occupational field. Given your interests, this might be a good career field for you to explore.

When you plan what courses to take or select what careers to explore, you need to consider your abilities, interests, goals, and what you know about yourself. This report might help you. Remember, however, it can only tell you how things look at the present time. Your interests, goals, and educational plans may change.

**INTEREST PROFILE**

| OCCUPATIONAL GROUPS | LOW | MEDIUM | HIGH |
|---|---|---|---|
| Clerical Services | | | |
| Management | | | |
| Math & Science | | | |
| Social Science | | | |
| Agriculture | | | |
| Fine Arts | | | |
| Health Services | | | |
| Benchwork | | | |
| Educational Services | | | |
| Transportation | | | |
| Legal Services | | | |
| Sales | | | |
| Building Trades | | | |
| Customer Services | | | |
| Machine Operation | | | |

| SUBJECT AREAS | DISLIKE | NEUTRAL | LIKE |
|---|---|---|---|
| Bookkeeping/Office Pract. | | | ✓ |
| Business Law or Management | | | ✓ |
| Computer Programming | | | ✓ |
| Creative Writing | | | ✓ |
| English or Foreign Language | | | ✓ |
| Marketing or Sales | | | ✓ |
| Photography | | | ✓ |
| Word Processing or Typing | | | ✓ |
| Cooking or Sewing | | | ✓ |
| Newspaper Writing | | | ✓ |
| Mathematics or Science | | ✓ | |
| Music or Art | | ✓ | |
| Speech or Drama | | ✓ | |
| Automotive Repair | ✓ | | |
| Carpentry or Home Building | ✓ | | |
| Electronics | ✓ | | |
| Farming or Livestock Care | ✓ | | |
| Haircutting or Styling | ✓ | | |
| Health Care | ✓ | | |
| Plumbing or Welding | ✓ | | |

The Occupational Groups represent types of career interests. The Groups are listed in the order of your interests, with the Groups that interest you most at the top of the list. The bars across from each Group tell you whether your degree of interest in the Group was low, medium, or high.

By looking at the ✓ across from the some of the school subjects and/or activities, you can also compare your degree of interest.

PROCESS NO. 12281911-0000-00472-1

**FIGURE 9.2**

Although only same-sex percentile bands are shown graphically, the form lists same-sex and opposite-sex percentile ranks and stanines (national norms). Raw scores are available from the publisher as an option (but are not shown here). Additional valuable information about the meaning of the profile is printed at the bottom of the form. Most counselors still will want to add their own oral interpretations.

Figure 9.2 shows the results of the *Career Interest Inventory* for the same student. Statements at the bottom of both forms remind examinees that they should use *all* available information when making educational and vocational plans.

## GENERAL PROFILES

Once upon a time, it was common practice to list and graph all tests taken by an individual on a single profile form. The careful counselor would note the presence of any different norms groups that were involved. Nevertheless, it was easy to neglect the gross differences among the various norms groups. When the norms groups are not the same, separate profile sheets should be used. (Note again what a difference different norms can make. See page 82.) It is not essential, of course, to show all test results on profiles; but profiles often do make the results easier to visualize.

Even today a general profile form can be useful within a school or other organization in displaying the results of an examinee who has been tested on a variety of tests, when local norms are involved. Note well: Although different tests have been used, *all individuals are being compared with the same group(s).* A form such as Figure 9.3 can be used in such instances. Note the variety of metrics (types of score) that can be used with a form such as this one.

## THE GOOD PROFILE

What is a good profile? The examinee's name, of course, must appear, together with any other identifying information that is appropriate (perhaps date of birth, grade and school, company and department, and so on). The *examiner's* name is very important when an individual test has been given. The date(s) of the testing should be indicated. A note should be attached indicating any deviation from standard testing procedure that may have occurred.

Although not all test authorities would agree, I believe that all raw-score values should be shown, regardless of the metric used in the profile. If scoring and profiling are done locally, the cautious user may want to double-check the scoring.

It is always wise to be a bit compulsive in checking test results. One of my doctoral candidates, as part of her research, had examined several hundred *WAIS-R*

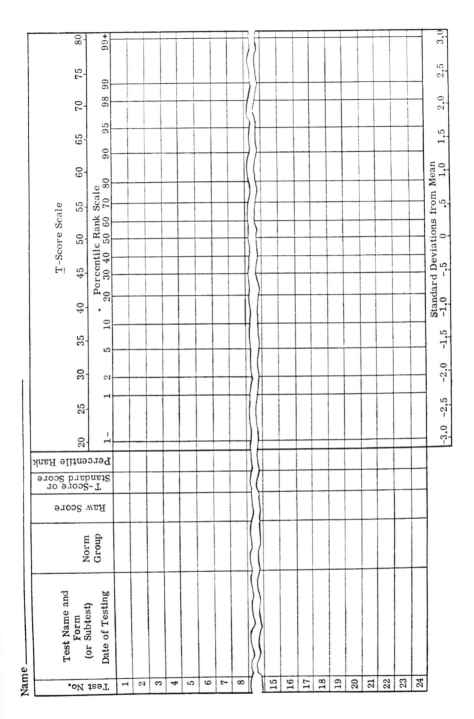

*FIGURE 9.3*

protocols. She decided to check the arithmetic on each form before going further with her study—and found mistakes in arithmetic, usually small, on fully 25 percent of the forms. Do you wonder that I have taught my own graduate students to be compulsive when scoring tests that are to be used in practical settings!

## SIGNIFICANT DIFFERENCES IN PROFILE POINTS

I under... that there is a professional cartographer (mapmaker) who deliberately draws some nonexistent feature—perhaps a tiny village, lake, or stream—on each of his maps in an effort to trap any would-be copier. The place, of course, does not exist after it appears on the map any more than it did before it appeared there. A good map *reflects* features that exist in reality, but it does not create them.

In exactly the same way, we must guard against overemphasizing slight differences that we see in a profile. Remember: The profile only reflects differences in test scores—it never creates them. It never makes them more real than they were before testing. In interpreting test scores from profiles, one must be careful not to overinterpret apparent differences. We need specifically to consider the standard error of measurement. The difference between test scores may not be so great as it looks on a profile. If the norms for two tests are not the same, there is no way to tell whether the scores are truly different. Nor can we tell unless the tests use the same metric. We can't, for example, directly compare an IQ with a percentile rank.

Every test score includes some amount of error. If one were to take a large number of comparable forms of the same test, the scores would vary somewhat from form to form even if the forms were designed to give identical results on the average. As noted in Chapter 6, the standard error of measurement is an estimate of what the standard deviation of a person's scores would be if one were to take these many forms.

When two tests are involved, both scores are subject to measurement error, and we must consider the fact that both tests have standard errors. We can be reasonably certain that a given difference is a true difference (one that is not caused solely by the unreliability of the tests) if bands extending out one standard error of measurement from each obtained score do not overlap. Looking at Figure 9.1, we can see quite easily that Pat did far less well on *Perceptual Speed and Accuracy* than on most of the other tests.

## PROFILE ANALYSIS

Whenever there are several scores reported for an individual (as in a profile), one may be tempted to try a profile analysis—that is, to try to find additional meaning through a study of the relative peaks and dips in the scores. On the *Wechsler Adult Intelligence Scale—Revised*, for example, some clinical psychologists believe that relationships between scores on certain of the eleven sub-tests can be used as a basis for personality diagnosis; however, except when the differences are very large, there is little clear-cut evidence that such diag-noses are meaningful.

Hundreds of studies involving profile analysis of the *Minnesota Multiphasic Personality Inventory II* have been published, and some of them seem very rewarding. Similarly, Harrison Gough proposes interpretations for various combinations of scores on his *California Psychological Inventory*. So, too, does John Holland for his *Self Directed Search*, and, of course, one must recognize the elaborate studies of Cattell and his *16PF* at the Institute for Personality and Ability Testing. Profile analysis, in other words, is commendable and desirable if the data are adequate, but dangerous when attempted by the neophyte.

The meaningfulness of any sort of profile analysis depends in part upon the reliability of the tests that enter into the analysis and the reliability of the differences in score. No difference can have psychological or educational sig-nificance unless the difference is sufficiently large to be considered statistical-ly significant (i.e., probably due to something other than pure chance).

There are many circumstances in which scores may be used jointly to obtain better prediction of criterion values than can be obtained through the use of any one variable by itself; however, this topic (multiple correlation and multiple regression) is beyond the scope of this book.

In summary, don't attempt to perform profile analyses unless you know what you are doing. And show commendable caution when reading the ana-lytical work of others.

# Don't Forget Common Sense

Test results and "common sense" sometimes seem at odds with each other. In such instances, the test results may be wrong—or our common sense may be faulty. Neither is perfect.

All testing programs should be checked at every stage where mistakes can be made. As test users, we should be prepared to check the scores that are put into our hands. If the test results do not seem reasonable, they may be wrong; check them!

> Years ago I was looking over a multiple-score preference inventory taken by a college student as part of a campuswide testing program. I was surprised that this student had no scores above the median. Upon checking, I discovered that one of the scoring clerks had not understood the directions for using the norms table. She had taken raw-score values from the test, entered these in the percentile-ranks column, and read out the corresponding entries in the raw-score column as percentile ranks. Since there had been no systematic checking of results, more than 1,000 test sheets and profiles had to be reexamined!

Even today, with machine and computer scoring the norm and very little hand scoring being done, mistakes still occur. We need to check thoroughly—especially if some results seem suspicious in any way.

Years ago I had several hundred admissions tests scored by a commercial scoring service. Just as a precaution, I personally hand-checked every fiftieth test paper. On more than half of the papers there were small errors. I insisted that the agency rescore all of the tests—even though the agency director assured me that the differences were so small that "they wouldn't make much difference." We did not use that agency after that!

And consider this situation:

A company for which I was a consultant had tested several people for a junior-level management position. Al Athol had been an employee of the company for several years, had a good work history, and was well liked by fellow employees and by management. The other candidates were recent college graduates and new to the firm. Al did as well as the other candidates except on a spatial relations test; on this, he did very poorly. The personnel director decided to select one of the other men because of this one very low score—and it is doubtful whether spatial relations skill was even involved in the management position! This personnel director should have used common sense, for Al was clearly superior to the other men on the various nontest factors that should have been considered.

In this following situation, common sense did prevail:

Cathie Cudder had worked in the divisional offices of Crowder Grocery for nearly ten years. Her job required little typing and no shorthand, but it did keep her in telephone contact with all stores within the division. When the divisional vice president fired his personal secretary, none of the more than eighty other secretaries in the office dared to apply for the vacancy; they were afraid of the "V.P." Ms. Cudder wasn't afraid, but the personnel manager wouldn't recommend her for the position because her secretarial speeds were below those required. Cathie called the vice president directly and requested an interview. Despite her slowness on typing and shorthand tests, she got the position because the vice president noted her strengths: (1) She was not afraid of him; (2) she knew company policy; and (3) she knew every store manager, assistant manager, and head cashier in the division. She could reacquire the secretarial skills. She worked successfully for the vice president until his retirement years later.

When test results and common sense seem to be in conflict, we need to check all possibilities: (1) The tests may be wrong, (2) common sense may be wrong, (3) both may be wrong, or (4) neither may be wrong.

Let us see how common sense can be wrong. Are we sure that our preconceptions are correct? Is this really an able person, or has the person succeeded by saying the right thing at the right time? Is this student really good or merely an "apple polisher"? Are these tests as valid for our purpose as they should be? What makes these test results seem unreasonable?

Sometimes we find that questioning the results will help us to find errors in both our reasoning *and* the results. In such situations, checking really pays off, for it enables us to get a better understanding of the entire situation.

What about those situations, though, where test results seem unreasonable, and yet both our reasoning and the test results seem correct even after checking? In such situations we should probably stop to consider whether there is really a discrepancy between the two. Closer scrutiny may prove that the tests are giving us just a slightly different slant from the one we had been considering. Or perhaps the discrepancy is not so great as we had thought. If these lines of reasoning fail to resolve the discrepancy, we may want to get further information from other tests, interviews, and/or additional sources— provided that the situation is important enough to justify the effort.

## INSTITUTIONAL AND INDIVIDUAL DECISIONS

Tests are often used as tools in reaching decisions. Some decisions are *institutional*; that is, the decisions are made on behalf of an institution (school, college, corporation, etc.), and such decisions are made frequently. Two examples of such institutional decisions are (1) which persons to select and which to reject, and (2) where to place a particular examinee. Tests can be extremely effective in such situations because they help the institution to make a higher percentage of appropriate personnel decisions. And an occasional bad decision is not likely to have any adverse effect on the institution. Tests can be used more effectively to predict the performance of a group than to predict the performance of an individual.

> Let us test a random sample of 1,000 fifth-grade pupils. Let me have the top fifty pupils, and you take the bottom fifty pupils. You may decide what these 100 pupils are to be taught. You may have a team of experts help you teach your pupils; I will teach mine myself. At the end of one semester, we will give both groups the same final examination. Regardless of the subject matter taught, I am sure that my group will score higher *on the average*. Some of your pupils may outscore some of mine, despite that tremendous initial difference in ability. Which of your pupils will show this tremendous response to superior teaching? Which of my pupils will lag far behind the others? We cannot predict accurately which ones these will be; however, we can have considerable confidence in predicting that my *group* will have the higher average achievement.

A second general type of decision is the *individual* decision. Here, people make decisions that will affect themselves, or perhaps a daughter or son. The individual has no backlog of similar decisions and may never have to reach a comparable decision again. The situation is unique insofar as the individual is concerned, and a wrong decision may have a lasting effect. Typical examples of individual decisions include whether to accept a certain job offer, whether to go to college, which college to attend, which curriculum to study, and which course to take. Tests sometimes may help, but they are rarely so helpful as in institutional decisions. Tests are far less accurate in individual situations.

## SOME COMMON MISTAKES

Besides the measurement error inherent in any test, there are many possibilities for mistakes to be made in the administration and scoring of a test and in reporting its results. The test user should make it part of the regular routine to check reported test scores whenever feasible.

Some sort of check should be made at every stage of testing to ensure near-perfect accuracy of conditions for administration, scoring, and recording. Most of the mistakes are relatively simple things: failing to start the stopwatch used in timing, failing to wind the stopwatch, failing to stop at the proper time limit, omitting part of the directions, using the wrong answer sheet, using the wrong scoring key, lining up the scoring key incorrectly, making a mistake in counting, using an incorrect scoring formula, using the wrong norms tables, reading the norms table incorrectly, misreading a handwritten score, making an error in copying, and so on. Over the years I have discovered some classic mistakes. I shall pass a few of them along, partly for comic relief and partly to show that one cannot be too compulsive in checking on tests.

> I shall never forget the chaos created when a package of 500 machine-scoring answer sheets proved to have been printed a little off center—not enough for the eye to discern, but more than enough to throw the scoring machine off. Hand-scoring a sample of answer sheets showed that something was wrong, but it took us several days to discover the cause.
>
> One national testing program once sent me a set of the wrong tests. The tests were not to be opened until the morning of the examination, and when they were—did we have fun!
>
> From a major and reputable test publisher, I once received three successive batches of a standardized test that had been printed just a bit too small; unfortunately, the scoring key was of standard size, and the two did not match.

Errors in the scoring keys of standardized tests are rare today, for they are very carefully checked; however, mistakes have been known to occur even here. There is even the story (true, I think) of several people who managed to steal a preliminary scoring key for an important national examination that they were to take; they were caught and found guilty when they turned in perfect papers—except for the three items that had been incorrectly marked on that preliminary scoring key!

And, of course, I have made a few mistakes myself. It is human to err, we are told. Most mistakes, though, can be prevented.

## OTHER SOURCES, TOO!

Tests are only one source of information. And test scores are only bits of information. In any important decision, we should make full use of *all* the information available to us. As information collectors, tests do have certain advantages—most especially their objectivity. But tests are fallible instruments, and test scores are fallible bits of information.

If tests are to be used, they should contribute something. People managed to exist and to make decisions without the aid of tests for many years, and they can do so today. *If tests provide helpful information, we should use them; if they do not, we should not!* And even when we do use tests, let us not forget to consider all nontest factors as well—they, too, can be important.

The message is even stronger for those using tests in industrial or personnel settings. There must be evidence of the validity of the test (or other procedure) if it is used in selecting or rejecting people for employment or for promotion. The federal government insists on it.

# What Can We Say?

Throughout the book to this point, we have been concerned primarily with the task of helping test users to understand the meaning of test scores. Additional skill is needed when one must interpret the results to others.

School counselors and guidance workers, among others, have the responsibility for communicating test results to other people—especially to school pupils and their parents. Such interpretation is more involved and requires more skill than merely understanding test results oneself.

No amount of reading, of course, is going to make us expert at interpreting test scores. Written admonitions can't substitute for personal experience. Even so, it is possible to learn some general principles and "tricks of the trade." Our primary emphasis in this book is directed at enabling people with limited backgrounds in psychological and educational testing to understand the nature of test scores. No book can substitute for a course in tests and measurements or for courses in counseling and guidance techniques. These and other courses, along with practice and experience, are needed before a person is prepared to get full meaning from test data.

There are two main topics in this chapter: (1) Who is entitled to test information? and (2) What do we say?

# WHO IS ENTITLED TO TEST INFORMATION?

As a starting point, examinees themselves are entitled to receive information about their test results. In educational settings, federal law underscores that right.

## The Examinee

Information given to examinees should be as detailed as is warranted by the test and as the examinees are likely to understand. Specific scores should be given only when examinees are also given a thorough explanation of both what the scores mean and what their limitations are. The legal requirement that schools must make test results available upon request imposes an additional professional responsibility. School personnel must ensure that all results released are accompanied by meaningful interpretations!

Except within the clinical-counseling or court-legal frameworks, examinees should be told the results of the tests in as much detail as they are likely to understand; however, information should not be forced on those who cannot assimilate it. This incident, for example, never should have happened:

> Barbie, a third grader, was skipping down the corridor at school and chanting, 'I'm a genius! I'm a genius!" Barbie did not know what the word meant, but she did know that it must be something good because her parents had been so pleased when ". . . a lady came to our house and gave me a test. And then she said, 'Why, she's a little genius!'"

## Parents of Minors

In the case of minors, parents must also be told the test results if they make such a request—as is provided in the Buckley Amendment (Federal Family Educational Rights and Privacy Act of 1974). Parents, too, should be given reasonably detailed results, but the counselor should use good judgment in deciding how much detail the parent can understand.

## Agency Policy

School and other agencies are likely to have their own policies regarding the interpretation of test results. These policies should be made known to all people within the agency who have access to test scores, including secretaries, file clerks, and receptionists. As a rule, only professional-level workers should interpret scores to examinees, parents, or other laypersons; however, in a well-run agency, there may be provision for routine release of scores to professional people outside the agency under stated conditions. (By *professional* in this chapter, I mean to include teachers, personnel workers, and others whose positions involve working with people; but to exclude general office workers.)

## Schools and Colleges

With schools and colleges, routine test results should be handled in the same way as grades and personnel files. In the event of transfer to another institution or system, these routine test results should be sent along. It is imperative that furnished test information include the date of testing, names of tests (with form, level, and edition), and raw scores; if derived scores are included, the norm groups should be identified.

On the other hand, tests given for counseling purposes (especially at the college level) should not be transferred automatically. This is testing that has been done for the student's personal benefit, and test scores must not be transmitted without the written permission of the student or (if the student is under eighteen) of his or her parents.

## Professional Colleagues

Within any given agency (including a school system), any professional worker who has a need for test data should have access to the scores. If there is reason to believe that the data are being misused, the access should be denied or withdrawn.

> Merry Melody, a music teacher at a college where I once taught, used to come to my counseling office toward the end of each semester and request intelligence test scores for her students. After a semester or two, I found that she had been using these scores as a basis for assigning course grades to her students. I told her that this practice was inadvisable and unethical. When, after two subsequent sessions, she still used the scores in this fashion, I denied her further access to all test data.

When professional workers outside the given agency request test data on a person, the request should be cleared through channels. These channels should include a release (in writing) from the examinee or her or his parents. Scores should not be released to nonprofessionals outside the agency.

## Personnel

Certain differences may be noted in the handling of test data in personnel settings. Although the company or agency may employ the psychologist or the personnel specialist, it seems clear that the applicants or employees may demand to see their own test results. At least in certain types of setting (for example, civil service), examinees must be shown their test papers and a copy of the test.

The American Psychological Association's Society for Industrial and Organizational Psychology recommends that reports to management *not* include specific scores, but only provide an interpretation of the results. The society further recommends that employee files be purged every few years so that obsolete data do not introduce bias into employee matters. Personally, while recognizing the sincerity of their intent, I disagree with this latter point, believing (perhaps naively) that the data can be used as evidence of employee growth. On the other hand, I agree completely with the intent of their recommendation: that obsolete data should not be used to the disadvantage of the employee.

Test data should not be released to anyone outside the company without the written permission of the individual.

### In Conversation

We do not discuss, either publicly or in casual conversation, the test results of any of our examinees. It is permissible, of course, to identify the individual and test scores in a case conference in a school, personnel, or clinical setting. But we cannot ethically continue our discussion of the individual outside the conference room!

## COMMUNICATING THE RESULTS

The two essential steps in test interpretation are (1) understanding the test results and (2) communicating these results orally or in writing (or both) to another appropriate individual. And, in all instances, remember to get the examinee's permission in writing.

### To a Trained Professional Worker

When the other person is trained in testing, the task of communicating results is relatively simple. We may start by giving the test name (including form, level, and edition) and the raw scores. We may include derived scores, if desired, along with the norms group(s) used. If both of us know our tests, there is every reason to believe that the information will be communicated accurately. If the information is communicated orally, we may take a few shortcuts; however, if the report is made in writing, it should be complete. Nowadays photocopiers are so common that the following procedure is a good one to emulate:

> I include a photocopy of test results and a short letter of transmittal pointing out any unusual aspects of the case (either about the person or about the test results); I also note irregularities (if any) in the testing procedures. If the examinee has been in counseling with me, I may include on a separate sheet a brief summary of our contacts to date, together with my observations about probable major problem areas and my expectation of outcome. I address this material to the professional worker personally and mark it "CONFIDENTIAL," both on the report itself and on the envelope. In my own files, I note the referral and the written permission of the examinee.

When there is the slightest doubt about the testing knowledge of the person to whom we send test scores, we should add some further explanation of the tests and the scores. For example:

> The *NEW Test* is a new scholastic aptitude test put out by the PDQ Company. We have been trying it out this year to see how well it compares with the *OLD Test*. The norms groups seem to be reasonably comparable, and we have found that our students tend to do about the same on both tests; however, the *NEW* is a little more highly speeded, and some of our teachers do not like it so well for that reason. You will note, too, that the publisher's national norms are given in stanines. I do not know whether you have been using stanines at your school, so I have included a table that shows approximate percentile values for each one. Please let me know if I can be of further help. . . .

The aim of test interpretation is, after all, to ensure that the other person understands the test results. We do not fulfill that purpose unless we take all reasonable steps to state the results meaningfully.

## To a Professional Person Untrained in Testing

When test data are being given to a professional worker who is relatively untrained in testing, it is advisable to give both a written report and an oral interpretation. Unquestionably some of the best work of this sort is done by school psychologists in their reports to school principals and teachers. By and large, school psychologists do a remarkably good job of working with individual children and of reporting their findings. They seem much more interested in delivering informative and helpful reports than in showing off their erudition through overuse of technical jargon.

Reports to schoolteachers, to members of management, to personnel workers, to academic deans, and to others who typically have limited training in testing should be drawn up very carefully. We cannot assume that they know the difference between percentage-correct scores and percentile ranks; they probably do not. We cannot assume that they know what a standard score is—or an IQ—or an age score. Our reports must be informative. At the same time, we must be careful to avoid the appearance of "talking down" to such people.

> "Betty's PR on the *BAT* was 82" is a statement that will not mean much to a person who does not know that PR means percentile rank, does not know what percentile rank means, and has no idea what the *BAT* might be!

This form would be more helpful:

> "On the *Blank Aptitude Test*, Betty did as well as or better than 82 percent of the recent applicants for data processing positions with our company. We find that about 70 percent of the people with similar scores have obtained at least 'Satisfactory' ratings after six months on the job."

Or perhaps this:

"On the Blank Aptitude Test, Betty did as well as or better than 82 percent of the students entering our college this past September. This score suggests that she should be capable of doing the work required in her program."

## To a Mature Examinee

Trained and experienced counselors will have developed skills and techniques of their own, and new counselors should be developing them through specialized training and in-service supervision. We are concerned here with techniques that can be used effectively and safely by relatively untrained test users.

Individuals who are suspected of severe maladjustment or very limited ability should be referred to specialists wherever possible. Our examinees are presumed to be adolescents or adults who have no disabling problems.

The following list of suggestions is not exhaustive, but I think that most of them would be accepted by nearly all experienced test users:

1. Test interpretation usually is done within some greater purposeful context; examples include counseling, guidance, placement, and selection. There are times, however, when the test interpretation itself is sufficient reason for the interview—especially with high school students.
2. Look over the test results before the interpretation interview. Make sure that you understand them and that you have some idea of what you want to say.
3. Establish rapport (a comfortable working relationship) with the examinee and make certain that you gain her or his interest and attention, but don't spend an unreasonable length of time in doing so. It's been my experience that new counselor-trainees have a tendency to take too much time in establishing rapport. Ordinarily one can establish reasonable rapport with a few words of greeting—and that should rarely take longer than a minute or two.
4. Be careful of your words. Examinees can be depended upon to remember your careless remarks and to misunderstand what they do not want to hear. Your care can keep distortion to a minimum. (Repetition also often helps to keep meanings clear.)
5. Explain something about every test variable you interpret. The examinee may know nothing about the various types of test and probably knows nothing about the *specific* tests taken.
6. Explain the nature of the norms groups being used, especially when they differ for the various tests.
7. Sometimes, especially in a counseling setting, an opening like this is helpful: "How do you think you did? Which tests do you think you did best on?"
8. If you feel comfortable in doing so, show the examinee the profile sheet(s); use this (them) as your basis for interpretation.

9. Do not force the interpretation on the examinee. When you try to interpret test results to a reluctant examinee, you are wasting your time. Point out that you may be available later, but that you feel it is pointless to continue under such circumstances. (I can think of some exceptions, but not many; the point is that, desirable though it might be for the examinee to know the test results, he or she is unlikely to understand them under coercion.)

10. Interpret all of the test variables, not just those on which the examinee has done a good job. The examinee has a right to learn both personal limitations and personal strengths. (Even a well-trained counselor, though, may prefer not to interpret some personality test variables.)

11. It is more difficult to interpret low scores than high ones. Designations of high and low are somewhat arbitrary, but not entirely so. (See the suggestions at the end of this chapter.)

12. Low scores are more easily accepted if they are stated in objective terms, such as: "Of people with scores like yours, only 10 percent have managed to maintain a passing average and to graduate in that curriculum." (See Expectancy Tables, pages 68–70.)

13. Sometimes low scores may be made easier to accept when the nature of the test is *slightly* distorted. I sometimes point out to a student who has done poorly on an intelligence or scholastic aptitude test: "This means that you are very low in book-learning ability when compared with other high school juniors nationally. A few students with scores like yours may succeed in college through very efficient planning and extra-hard studying, but your high school grades suggest that you have not been achieving well in actual class situations, either."

14. At times low scores can be communicated successfully through an analogous statement: "Mr. Dean, director of admission at Ourstate University, is like anyone else. He likes to bet on the winners. He knows that students with better high school grades and higher test scores than yours are more likely to do well in college. Like a gambler, he will sometimes play a long shot and will be delighted when one pays off. But, for the most part, he has to select those people who seem most likely to succeed."

15. *Never* make a direct prediction, such as: "This score means that you will never make it to college," or "This test score proves that you would never succeed on this job," or "With scores like these, you are a cinch to get through college with flying colors." You can be very, very wrong! You are much safer talking in group terms, such as: "Very few students with such scores . . ." or "Most students with scores such as these are able to do well in college if they study reasonably hard."

16. Do not assume that your examinee will remember everything. Try to help the person remember the important elements by summarizing

the results, perhaps saying something like this: "In general, then, you show average or better ability to learn, and you show near-average achievement in most areas. But you seem to be somewhat lower in dealing with abstract or mathematical reasoning."

17. If appropriate, make helpful suggestions: "Our company likes to promote only people who have higher scores on tests of verbal ability. Have you considered going to night school? You could pick up an English course or two that might be helpful—and our company policy is to pay at least part of the expense." Or, perhaps: "Your scores suggest that you may have difficulty in getting into medical school. On the other hand, you do have good grades here in high school, and this is important. You might be wise to select a small liberal arts college where you can hope to get more individual attention and try for high grades in premedical courses. Perhaps you will make it. Just to be on the safe side, though, you may want to consider some possible options if you do not make med school. Sometimes people find it very difficult if they have given no thought to alternative goals and then have to change plans at the last minute." Or, perhaps: "You have scored very high on the various English tests. Have you ever thought of working on the school paper? You might find it very rewarding." Be thoughtful and creative!

18. Do not forget: The examinee decides what will be done. As a test interpreter, you may make suggestions, but not decisions. (As an academic dean, placement director, and the like, you may make institutional decisions, but the examinee still makes the individual decisions.)

19. Test interpretation often provides a good way of opening a discussion of the examinee's problems, plans for the future, and so on. If you are not a trained counselor, decide in advance how far you can go in receiving the examinee's confidences.

20. Don't interpret an examinee's scores solely in writing. Supplementary interpretation, especially through interpretive folders, may be very helpful. Most counselors feel strongly, however, that we should not rely exclusively on written interpretations because they provide no opportunity for counselee feedback and, especially, no chance to observe whether the examinee appears to be understanding the results.

21. Most important of all: Know what you are doing, do what seems natural and effective to you, and try to be genuinely helpful to the examinee.

## To a Child

Some teachers try to explain achievement test results to elementary school children, especially when using the results in deciding to which areas the pupils may need to give special attention. Other than this, little effort is made to interpret tests to children who are below junior high school age.

I think that this reluctance is unfortunate. Children have considerable capacity for understanding, and they have tremendous curiosity. Some people may disagree, but I believe that some basic interpretation can be done effectively with children as young as ten years of age. The teacher may discuss the general nature of the tests with the class as a group. This can be followed up by an individual conference with each pupil, perhaps focusing attention mainly on areas of highest and lowest achievement and a statement about achievement relative to ability (without saying much about the intelligence level itself). Such interpretations need to be handled carefully, but can help youngsters in their search for an understanding of themselves.

Even with children of junior high school age, most test interpretation should be couched in general terms. Children like to see things in clear-cut terms and are likely to oversimplify or overgeneralize. They are not likely to remember the test limitations as well as they remember specific facts that are mentioned casually or incidentally.

Superior students can handle somewhat more detailed interpretations. The interpretation can perhaps be used as an opportunity to emphasize the importance of developing good study habits in preparation for future education. Special care must be used when interpreting results to children of below-average ability in order not to discourage them from trying to do their best. In dealing with this problem, the skilled counselor should be able to help the older child come to an acceptance of his or her limitations and to an appreciation of what he or she can *reasonably* accomplish through sustained effort. There is little kindness in encouraging unrealistic ambitions in the below-average child, but it is cruel to make the child feel worthless and stupid. There is ample evidence that children tend to grow up to our expectations—so it may be advisable to overemphasize the positive.

Encouragement can be especially helpful to the young child. Perhaps a set of low scores can be explained, "You may have to study harder and longer than some boys and girls do to get good grades." There is lots of evidence that young children respond positively to encouragement.

> One of my graduate students recently reported the following incident to me. Her son, Tommy, came home and said that he had gotten an A on a standardized achievement test battery. Tommy's second-grade teacher, it developed, had announced aloud in class letter-grade equivalents (including Fs) for the test performance of every pupil. Such letter grades existed only in the teacher's mind—they do not appear in the manual!

This incident, of course, is an example of bad interpretation. No second grader is likely to learn much from such a procedure, and with few exceptions (such as a scholarship competition), public announcement of test scores is both grossly unethical and sadistic!

I think that it is best to have the parents present when interpreting tests to a student. Sometimes, though, parents are impatient and refuse to allow the counselor or school psychologist enough time for decent interpretation.

## To Parents

Very much the same considerations involved when interpreting test scores to mature examinees are involved when interpreting scores to parents. Parents, though, are more likely to be argumentative and to question the accuracy of the test results. Parents of children with low test scores are likely to be very defensive, and special care must be taken to get the parents to view the results as objectively as possible. They must not be allowed to develop hostility toward the child because "he's so dumb," nor should they be given encouragement that "she's just passing through a phase."

Parents of a child of superior intellect may question why Paul is not doing better work and getting better grades if he is so intelligent. They may also question whether the school is doing its part in challenging the child to do his best work. (Consider carefully whether some such criticism may not be justified. Is the school doing what it can to meet the needs of the superior youngster?)

Parents differ markedly in their ability to understand and accept test results. I have no hesitancy in discussing actual scores (IQs, percentile ranks, or whatever) with some mature parents. Others are defensive from the start, and I shudder at even the thought of giving them any sort of interpretation! Be careful! And try to know beforehand how detailed an interpretation you will give.

Also, remember that the law says that you must make those data available to parents.

## HIGH AND LOW

How high is high? Your answer is probably as good as anyone else's. Except for a few considerations, it is an arbitrary decision.

First, we need to remember that scores are never perfect. Therefore, we should never say that any score is high unless it is at least one or two standard errors of measurement above the mean; otherwise, the above-average score may very well differ from the mean only by chance. The same line of reasoning, of course, operates in calling scores low.

Second, we must remember the way in which scores tend to cluster about the mean in typical distributions of test scores. The distance between successive percentile values is very small near the middle of the distribution. Thus, a given difference in percentile ranks reflects only a slight change in raw scores near the average but a large change in raw scores near the extremes.

Third, we have to remember that scores used in reporting standardized tests are relative rather than absolute. A given raw score may place an examinee high when compared with one group, but low when compared with another group.

Fourth, because of the greater reliability (and relatively smaller standard errors of measurement) of some tests, we may have more confidence in our use of "high" and "low" with those tests than with other, less reliable tests.

Typically I use something like the following descriptive scale:

| Percentile Ranks | Descriptive Terms |
|---|---|
| 95 or above | Very high; superior |
| 85–95 | High; excellent |
| 75–85 | Above average; good |
| 25–75 | About average; satisfactory or fair |
| 15–25 | Below average; fair or slightly weak |
| 5–15 | Low; weak |
| 5 or below | Very low; very weak |

This is not an inflexible standard, but I find it a helpful one. Sometimes we vary these designations, or apply more (or less) rigorous standards.

If a graduate engineer were being compared to company norms for general clerical employees (perhaps the only norms the company has for the test), we might regard a percentile rank of 88 as being only "satisfactory" or "reasonably good."

In the same way, a graduate student who scores near the eightieth percentile on national undergraduate norms is probably only "about average."

## IN SUMMARY

1. The person who interprets test results, however casually, must understand the nature of the tests and of the test scores. If you don't understand them yourself, you can't explain them to others.
2. Examinees and/or their parents are entitled to an interpretation of all tests taken, in as much detail as they are likely to understand.
3. Test interpreters should try to avoid hurting people. Whenever possible, they should aim at giving some sort of *realistic* encouragement to examinees.

# *Closing Remarks*

**C**
**H**
**A**
**P** **T**
**T** **W**
**E** **E**
**R** **L**
**V**
**E**

## THINGS TO KEEP IN MIND

Here are some of the more important principles for the new test user to bear in mind:

### Know the Test

There is no substitute for knowing about the test that is being given. Test titles are not always descriptive of the actual test content; furthermore, many terms can be defined differently by different people. The underlying rationale for a test may be very important to our understanding of it. Our interpretation of test results may differ for power and speeded tests, for individual and group tests, and the like. We should study the manual of any test we plan to interpret. Whenever practicable, the selection of tests to be used should be made by people with sufficient background in measurement to understand the technical data describing the tests.

### Know the Norms

It is especially important that we know what norms are being used. We cannot interpret test scores satisfactorily if we do not understand what group(s)

144

our test scores are being compared with. We may want to use several different norms groups. For example, we may want to compare a high school senior's scores with both high school seniors and college freshmen, or a person's aptitude test results with both applicants and present employees. In some situations, we may want to develop our own local norms.

## Know the Score

It is always good to "know the score" in the colloquial sense of that term; however, here we are being literal. We need to know whether a given number is a standard score (and what kind), a percentile rank, a raw score, or something else. Fantastic misunderstandings can result from confusing the various metrics (for example, confusing percentage correct and percentile ranks).

## Know the Background

Test results do not tell the entire story, and we should not expect them to. We must consider all available information—whether it comes from a test or from some other source (grades, teacher or supervisor evaluation, portfolio contents, etc.).

## Communicate Effectively

In many settings, we have to communicate test results to others. To get the interpretation across to examinees, we must be certain to give them all pertinent information. Examinees may very well resist accepting any interpretation that differs from their own conceptions of themselves. Some techniques that I have found helpful are listed in the previous chapter.

## Use the Test

Not too surprisingly, we can come to a better understanding of what a test is like by using it. As we develop more experience in working with tests, we can attempt some simple studies to see how well a particular test works for our own specific purposes. As we develop competence in such research, we can have increased confidence in our interpretations.

## Use Caution

Test scores reflect ability; they do not determine ability. Test scores may suggest, but they never prove. We are much safer when we make interpretations based on the actual performance of those who have had similar scores (see expectancy tables on pages 68–70) than when we try to tell an examinee, "This score means that you *will* . . ."

## EXPERTS STILL NEEDED

Testing can be very technical, and there are many subtleties that are not even hinted at in this book. There is still need for a testing specialist wherever tests are widely used. This specialist should be freely available to those who would like this assistance.

For example, we have barely mentioned tests of typical performance. When properly used by qualified persons, typical-performance tests may give clues to the personality dynamics of both normal and disturbed people. Interpretation of these tests demands skills and knowledge beyond those covered in this book (although doing a reasonable job of interpreting interest tests and some simple inventory-style personality tests should not be much beyond the competence of most readers).

Projective tests, certainly, should be interpreted only by licensed psychologists or suitably trained psychiatrists. The diversity of projective techniques is great, and some degree of training in each of the specific techniques that are going to be used is needed. Projective techniques are not parlor games or classroom exercises for the personal amusement of the tester.

Even with tests of maximum performance, there are some areas that are best left to the expert. Individual tests of intelligence, for example, require special training of the examiner. The trained examiner should also be the one to report the results of individual intelligence tests, for the report should include much more than a mere test score; if a test score alone had been sufficient, an individual test would not have been required in the first place.

We have said almost nothing about exceptional (now called "challenged") children. Although much that has been said about testing applies equally well to them, there is much that does not. Special skills are demanded when we test these children. It can be helpful to consult with people in special education for assistance.

The child with a severe language handicap cannot be tested fairly on a verbal test. Children who are hard of hearing and those who have visual disabilities are similarly at a disadvantage when taking tests. And children with other disabilities or behavior problems may experience greater difficulty on tests than do "normal" children.

Exceptional children often have been assigned to special schools or to special classes. In such classrooms, they have been taught by teachers with special qualifications (special education teachers, for the most part). Federal legislation, first implemented in 1977, now decrees that such children must be taught in the least restrictive classrooms that are appropriate. This means that efforts will be made to mainstream them in "regular" classrooms.

Thus, regular classroom teachers, counselors, and the like may need to become more involved in the testing of (and test interpretation with) exceptional children. Extra knowledge and special skills are involved. Consult the testing expert whenever possible to see that the children receive fair treatment. School psychlogists and special education personnel are often excellent resources.

Throughout this book, we have considered briefly some implications of testing for guidance and counseling. On the other hand, we have recognized that the most effective use of tests in guidance and counseling situations requires much more knowledge than can be acquired solely from this book. There is a need for professional counselors and guidance workers—people who can extract the fullest meaning from test results and employ this meaning in their interviews.

Experts in tests and measurements are needed also to construct and validate new tests, to conduct research with tests, to advance measurement theory, and so on.

There should be at least one top-flight test specialist within each school system, each college, and each large personnel office. This specialist and his or her staff should have such varied duties as the following:

1. Staying current on theoretical measurement; there is some excellent work being done that has not as yet trickled down to the test user.
2. Maintaining a file of tests, both old and new, that can be consulted by other professional workers; this file should include manuals and catalogs as well as reprints related to some of the tests.
3. Maintaining a library of books and periodical publications on tests and measurements.
4. Directing any major research activities that involve tests.
5. Serving as advisor or consultant to people who want to do their own test-related research.
6. Evaluating new tests for possible use within the organization.
7. Selecting new tests for use within the organization.
8. Preparing local norms for tests.
9. Discussing test-related problems, issues, and questions with interested personnel both within and outside the organization.
10. Conducting in-service training programs for all people in the organization who work with tests.
11. Maintaining contact with governmental agencies concerned with tests and test-related activities.
12. Serving as a liaison with test publishers, informing them of any difficulties with tests, and staying current with their plans.

So many tests are available that experts are needed to evaluate them, and to select those that best meet local needs. There is a need for someone who can serve as a resource person for all those who use tests within an organization.

Because of the ever-increasing governmental interest in responsible test usage, every agency/institution using tests in the hiring and promotion of large numbers of employees must have such an authority available full-time to keep apprised of governmental regulations and changes. Smaller organizations may find it more feasible to retain an industrial or consulting psychologist to perform similar services.

The next few years will see more changes in policies. Some will come as various agencies acquire more experience and expertise. Others will come through court decisions. In my opinion, most governmental workers try to be fair to all concerned: examinees, examiners, and the public; however, agencies still have some personnel who themselves are not knowledgeable about tests.

> An issue of *The Industrial Psychologist* related the story of two (hypothetical, we hope!) companies that used the same test for employment selection. Validity studies at the companies yielded identical validity coefficients between test score and production on the job. But the smaller company was found guilty of discrimination and eventually was forced out of business, while the larger company was found innocent of discriminatory policies. Why? Simply because of the difference in the number of people tested at the two companies! (Larger values of a correlation coefficient are needed for statistical significance when the number of people involved is small.)

## GO AHEAD AND TRY!

I hope that I have been able to communicate to you some of the love and enthusiasm I feel for psychological and educational testing. I find this field of work fascinating. It's dynamic, and it's challenging. It is criticized, and it is challenged. One of my fondest hopes is that some of my readers will "catch" my enthusiasm and decide to specialize in psychometrics.

There are many pitfalls in the use of tests and their proper interpretation. There are all sorts of limitations to tests and to test scores. But tests can be helpful. Do not be overly cautious or you will never get any testing done.

**Go ahead and try!**

# *Appendix*

Glossary of Terms    *150*

Selected Test Publishers    *162*

Bibliography    *164*

Code of Professional Responsibilities in Educational
    Measurement    *167*

Conversion Table    *176*

# Glossary of Terms

This glossary is intended primarily for readers who have had little formal training in testing. I have tried, therefore, to keep all definitions as nontechnical as is feasible. Because most of the terms are discussed elsewhere in the book, I have kept these definitions brief. The designation of various derived scores according to types refers to the classification presented in Chapter 8.

**accordion key:** See *strip key.*

**accountability:** (1) The state or condition of being responsible for those actions and behaviors and performances that are expected of a person because of the office or job held by that person. (2) Being held responsible or liable for performing the duties of one's office or job.

**achievement battery:** A battery of achievement tests. (See *battery.*)

**achievement test:** A test designed to measure the amount of knowledge and/or skill a person has acquired, usually as a result of classroom instruction; may be either informal or standardized.

**adaptive testing:** The act or process of ensuring that the test items that an examinee will be asked to answer are of appropriate difficulty for the examinee. *Syn.:* tailored, individualized, branched, programmed, staged, response contingent, dynamic, selective.

**adjustment inventory:** See *personality test.*

**age equivalent:** The chronological age for which a specified raw score is the average.

**age norms:** Norms that give age equivalents for raw-score values.

**alternate-form reliability:** A method of estimating test reliability by correlating two equivalent (parallel) forms of the test.

**alternative:** One of the choices for a multiple-choice item—either the correct response or a distracter.

150

**anchor:** A test or other variable used to ensure the comparability of two or more forms or editions or levels of a given instrument.

**aptitude:** That combination of characteristics, both native and acquired, that indicates the capacity of a person to develop proficiency in some skill or subject matter after relevant training; usually, but not necessarily, implies intellectual or skill aspects rather than emotional or personality characteristics.

**articulation:** The act or process of developing different editions, forms, and (especially) levels of the same test that will yield results that are comparable.

**assessment:** The act or process of determining the present level (usually of achievement) of a group or individual, typically on the basis of multiple sources of information.

**average:** General term for any central tendency measure; e.g., the mean, median, or mode.


**bar graph:** A type of graph often used for displaying a discrete variable; resembles a histogram used for displaying distributions of a continuous variable.

**Barnum effect:** The act or practice of stating a test interpretation in such general and favorable terms that it is readily accepted as appropriate by almost everyone; named after showman P. T. Barnum, who reputedly said, "There's a sucker born every minute"; sometimes called "Aunt Fanny Effect."

**basal age:** (Especially on older editions of the *Stanford-Binet*) the highest age level at which a given examinee correctly answers all items.

**battery:** (1) A set of tests standardized on the same group, so that the results will be comparable; such a battery is called *integrated*. (2) A set of tests administered at about the same time to an individual or group; e.g., an employment battery or a counseling battery.

**bell-shaped curve:** See *normal distribution (curve)*.

**bias:** Unfairness, real or imagined, in an item or set of test items.

**Buckley Amendment:** A federal law passed in 1974 that decrees (among other provisions) that school records, including test data, must be made available to students and/or parents upon request.

**Buros, Oscar K.:** Late founder and, until 1978, editor of the *Mental Measurements Yearbooks*; MMY is now published by the Buros Institute of Mental Measurements in Lincoln, Nebraska.


**C-score:** A normalized standard score (Type II B 4 c) of eleven units.

**chronological age (CA):** Any person's age; i.e., the length of time the person has lived. The CA is a factor to consider when interpreting certain types of score, especially age scores.

**class interval:** The unit of a frequency distribution, especially when the unit is greater than one; a band of score values assumed to be equal for purposes of computation or graphing.

**coaching:** The act or process of preparing one or more individuals for a test—perhaps even to the extent of teaching the specific content of actual items known to appear on the test.

**coefficient of correlation:** An index number indicating the degree of relationship between two variables; i.e., the tendency for values of one variable to change systematically with changes in values of a second variable; no relationship = 0.00, a perfect relationship = ±1.00. [Although there are different coefficients for various purposes, the basic type is the Pearson product-moment correlation ($r$), which is used when both variables are continuous, distributed symmetrically, etc.]

**cognitive factors:** Those characteristics of the individual that imply intellectual ability, as contrasted with affective or personality characteristics.

**composite score:** A total score consisting of the sum of scores on two or more variables; (less commonly) an average of such scores.

**concurrent validity:** Criterion-related validity when both test scores and criterion values are obtained at about the same time; contrast with *predictive validity.*

**construct validity:** Test validation based on a combination of logical and empirical evidence of the relationship between the test and a related theory; concerned with the psychological meaningfulness of the test; increasingly the term is being used to embrace *all* evidence of a test's validity.

**content-referenced:** (1) Describes a test on which scores are interpreted directly in terms of performance on some achievement continuum (e.g., "can type 55 words per minute"). (2) *Syn.:* criterion-referenced.

**content reliability:** The consistency with which a test measures whatever it measures; may be estimated by a reliability coefficient based on (a) split halves, (b) alternate forms, or (c) internal consistency.

**content validity:** Logical (as opposed to statistical) evidence that the item content of a test is suitable for the purpose for which the test is to be used; concept is used principally with achievement tests.

**continuous variable:** A variable capable, actually or theoretically, of assuming any value, as opposed to a *discrete variable,* which may take only whole-number values; test scores are treated as being continuous, although they are less obviously so than time, distance, weight, etc.

**convergent thinking:** Refers to a test that is scored for the "right" or "best" answer; used in opposition to *divergent thinking.*

**correction-for-guessing formula:** A formula sometimes used in scoring objective tests to make an allowance for items that have been "guessed" correctly; general formula is $X_c = R - (W/A - 1)$, where $X_c$ = corrected score, $R$ = number of items right, $W$ = number of items wrong, and $A$ = number of alternative choices per item. Although the underlying reasoning is dubious, the formula has considerable merit when examinees differ greatly in number of items left unanswered; use of the formula does not change the order of scores when no examinees omit any items.

**correlation:** The tendency for two (or occasionally more) variables to change values concomitantly. Note: Evidence of correlation is *not* evidence of causation. (See *coefficient of correlation.*)

**creativity:** See *divergent thinking.*

**criterion** (plural, **criteria**)**:** A standard against which a test may be validated; e.g., grade-point average is an obvious criterion for a scholastic aptitude test.

**criterion-keying:** The act or process of developing a scoring key empirically by noting differences in answers made by contrasting groups.

**criterion-referenced:** (1) Testing that is not *norms-referenced,* but where test performance is described directly in terms of performance at any given level on the continuum of an external variable. (2) *Syn.*: content-referenced, edumetric.

**criterion-related validity:** Test validity based on a correlation coefficient between test scores and criterion values. *Syn.*: empirical validity.

**cross-cultural test:** A test believed to be suitable for use in different societies because it is relatively free from cultural influences (such as language).

**cross validation:** The act or process of verifying results obtained on one group (or one study) by replication with a different, but similar, group (or study).

**culture biased:** Describes a test on which the items, whether intentionally or not, are easier for one cultural subgroup than for another or others.

**culture fair:** Describes a test that is relatively unbiased; no test can be completely *culture free*. *Ant.*: culture specific.

**curriculum validity:** See *content validity.*

**cutting score:** The minimum passing score, usually determined through research, for some practical situation (e.g., college entrance or job selection). *Syn.*: cutoff score.

**decile:** Any one of nine points that divide a distribution into ten subgroups of equal frequency; e.g., the fifth decile ($D_5$) is the same as $P_{50}$ or the median.

**decile rank:** A derived score (Type II B 5) expressed in terms of the nearest decile.

**derived score:** Any type of score other than a raw score.

**deviation:** The amount by which a score differs from a specified reference point (usually, but not always, the mean or other average).

**deviation IQ:** (1) A standard score (Type II A 5) with a mean fixed statistically at 100 and standard deviation fixed by the test's author; has advantages over the *ratio IQ*, which it is designed to approximate. (2) A *normalized standard score* (Type II B 4 e) designed to resemble a *ratio IQ*, but possessing certain advantages. (3) Rarely, a derived score (Type IV C) in which IQ is equal to 100 plus (or minus) the amount by which an examinee's raw score deviates from the norm for his or her age.

**diagnostic test:** (1) A test (usually of achievement) designed to identify specific educational difficulties. (2) A test given as a part of counseling or psychotherapy as an aid in determining the nature of an individual's mental disorder, maladjustment, etc.

**difficulty value:** A statement of a test item's difficulty, usually expressed as the percentage of individuals in a group who answer the item correctly.

**discrete variable:** A variable obtained through counting rather than measuring; thus, it can take only whole-number values (e.g., number of students in each classroom), unlike *continuous variables*, which can assume any value.

**discrimination value:** Any statistic used to express the extent to which a test item shows a difference between high-ability and low-ability examinees.

**distracter:** Any incorrect alternative in a multiple-choice item.

**distribution:** See *frequency distribution; normal distribution.*

**divergent thinking:** Refers to a test in which novel or creative responses are desired; contrasts with the more common *convergent thinking* tests.

**domain:** See *population.*

**domain-referenced measurement:** See *content-referenced.*

**edumetric:** Measurement of learning outcomes through criterion-referenced measurement. *Ant.*: psychometric.

**EEOC:** Equal Employment Opportunity Commission.

**empirical validity:** See *criterion-related validity.*

**equivalent form:** Any of two or more forms of a test, usually standardized on the same population and published at the same time, that are designed to be similar in item content and difficulty so that scores on the forms will be comparable.

**error:** A generic term for those elements in a test and testing situation that operate to keep a test from being perfectly reliable: (a) *constant errors* have a direct adverse effect on validity, but may not affect reliability (e.g., having arithmetic items on an English test); and (b) *variable* (or *random*) *errors* reduce reliability directly and validity indirectly (e.g., nonstandard conditions of test administration, chance passing or failing of items, ambiguous wording of test items). **Note: Errors are inherent in all measurement, but mistakes are not.**

**evaluation:** A statement of test results that includes a judgmental factor (e.g., "The class is achieving higher than others in the school" or "Maria is doing better in arithmetic than in English").

**expectancy table:** Any table showing class intervals of test scores (or other predictor variable) along one axis and criterion categories (or similar information) along the other axis; entries show number or, more typically, the percentage of individuals within specified score intervals who have achieved at given levels on the criterion variable.

**extrapolation:** The act or process of estimating values beyond those actually obtained; e.g., extreme values for both age- and grade-placement scores have to be established in this manner.


**face validity:** Superficial appearance of validity; i.e., a test *looks* as if it should measure what is intended.

**factor:** (1) Strictly and technically, an element or variable presumed to exist because of its ability to help explain some of the interrelationships noted among a set of tests. (2) Equally properly, the ability or characteristic represented by a factor (definition 1). (3) Loosely, anything partially responsible for a result or outcome (e.g., "Study is an important factor in obtaining good grades").

**factor analysis:** Any of several complex statistical procedures for analyzing the intercorrelations among a set of tests (or other variables) for the purpose of identifying the factors (definitions 1 and 2), preferably few in number, that cause the intercorrelations.

**frequency:** The number of individuals obtaining any specified score or falling in any specified class interval.

**frequency distribution:** Any orderly arrangement of scores, usually from highest to lowest, showing the frequency with which each score (or each class interval) occurs.

**frequency polygon:** A type of graph commonly used to portray a distribution of test scores (or values of some other continuous variable).

**grade norm:** The average test score for pupils with a given grade placement.

**grade-placement score:** A derived score (Type II D 2) expressed as the grade placement of those pupils for whom a given score was average.

**halo effect:** An unwarranted generalization of test interpretation; e.g., inferring that an examinee is highly intelligent because of a high score on one aptitude test, or inferring low ability because of a single observation.

**heterogeneity:** Possessing great variability; thus, in testing, a test with a great variety of content, or a group that varies considerably in the attribute tested. *Adj.*: heterogeneous.

**histogram:** A type of graph often used for displaying distributions of continuous variables such as test scores; resembles a *bar graph* used for displaying discrete data.

**homogeneity:** Having relatively little variability; thus, in testing, a test composed of items that vary little in type, or a group that varies little in the attribute tested. *Adj.*: homogeneous.

**individual test:** A test that usually, if not always, can be administered to only one examinee at a time.

**inferential statistics:** Statistics used to test hypotheses, establish confidence limits, etc. (e.g., *t*, chi square, or analysis of variance).

**informal test:** Any test intended primarily for the use of the test constructor or in a single setting; used in opposition to standardized test.

**intelligence:** An abstraction variously defined by different authorities; in general, the capacity or set of capacities that enables an individual to learn, to cope with the environment, to solve problems, etc.

**intelligence quotient (IQ):** See *deviation IQ; ratio IQ*.

**internal consistency:** Any of several techniques for estimating the content reliability of a test through knowledge of item analysis statistics.

**interpolation:** The act or process of estimating a value that falls between two known or computed values; this practice is often followed in establishing age- and grade-placement scores, so that the norms table will cover all possible ages or grade placements.

**inventory:** (1) Most commonly, a paper-and-pencil test of personality, interest, attitude, or the like. (2) Less commonly, an achievement test designed to "take an inventory" of student or class knowledge or skill on a specific task.

**ipsative:** A type of test or score in which a person's performance on one variable is influenced (usually inversely) by scores on one or more other variables within the same test battery.

**item:** (1) Any individual problem or question on a test. (2) Usually the basic unit to be scored on an objective test.

**item analysis:** The act or process of examining a test item empirically to determine (a) its difficulty value and (b) its discrimination value. Note: Such values will differ somewhat from group to group, from time to time, and according to the particular item statistic used.

**item bank:** A collection of questions available for use on a test; especially, a file of items stored in a computer and available for retrieval.

**job sample test:** A test that involves the operation of equipment that one might find in the actual workplace or, perhaps, a model (or an element) of the equipment.

**key, scoring:** (1) The collection of correct answers (or scored responses) for the items of a test. (2) The device or sheet, containing the scored responses, which is used in scoring the test.

**Kuder-Richardson formula:** Any of several formulas developed by Kuder and Richardson for estimating content reliability through internal-consistency analysis.

**latent trait scaling:** The act or process of developing test items that can be demonstrated to have similar discriminating power when used with groups of widely differing ability. *Syn. or closely related*: item response theory; item response curve theory; Rasch model.

**local norms:** (1) Test norms that are based on people tested locally (e.g., by a school system or industry) in the hope that such norms may give more helpful information than the norms provided by the publisher in the test manual; (2) norms that are developed for use with a locally prepared test.

**machine scoring:** The act or process of scoring a test with the aid of a mechanical or electrical device that counts and may record the scored responses of a test (or subtest); the most common machines involve one or more of these processes: (a) *mark sensing,* (b) *punched hole,* or (c) *electronic scanning.*

**mark sensing:** Descriptive of a system for machine-scoring tests that uses an electrical contact to "sense" responses to be scored.

**mastery testing:** Content-referenced measurement aimed at assessing the degree of accomplishment of a stated skill.

**maximum-performance test:** Any test on which the examinee is directed, at least implicitly, to do the best job he or she can; e.g., intelligence, aptitude, and achievement tests. *Ant.*: typical-performance test.

**mean:** Most widely used measure of central tendency; equals the sum of scores divided by the number of examinees.

**median:** Next to the mean, the most common measure of central tendency; the point on the scale of score values that separates the group into two equal subgroups; the fiftieth percentile ($P_{50}$), the second quartile ($Q_2$), and the fifth decile ($D_5$).

**mental age:** A derived score (Type II D 1 a). Rarely used today.

**modal age:** The chronological age that is most typical of children with a given grade placement in school.

**mode:** A measure of central tendency; that score value which has the greatest frequency; i.e., that score obtained by more examinees than any other.

*N*: Symbol for the number of examinees in any specified group.

**NCE (normal curve equivalent):** A normalized standard score with a mean of 50.00 and a standard deviation of 21.06; intended for research use only.

**norm:** Average, normal, or standard for a group of specified status (e.g., of a given age or grade placement).

**normal distribution (curve):** Useful mathematical model representing the distribution expected when an infinite number of observations (e.g., scores) deviate from the mean only by chance; although a normal distribution can never be attained in reality, many actual distributions do approach this model. The curve drawn to portray the normal distribution is a symmetrical bell-shaped curve whose properties are completely known.

**normalized standard score:** Any of several scores (Type II B) that resemble standard scores (Type II A), but that are computed like percentile ranks.

**norms:** A set of values descriptive of the performance on a test of some specified group; usually shown as a table giving equivalent values of some derived score for each raw score on the test.

**norms-referenced:** Descriptive of an objective test that has been standardized on a group of people, so that the performance of examinees can be described in reference to this comparison (i.e., norm) group; such tests are *psychometric*, as opposed to *edumetric*.

**objective test:** A test for which the scoring procedure is specified completely in advance, thereby permitting complete agreement among different scorers.

**omnibus test:** A test, usually of intelligence, in which items of several different types are used in obtaining a single overall score; usually has one set of directions and one overall time limit.

**optical scanning:** Describes a process of scoring in which the scoring machine "reads" the test paper visually to determine the score.

**paper-and-pencil test:** Any test that requires no materials other than paper, pencil, and test booklet; most group tests are paper-and-pencil tests.

**parameter:** A summary or descriptive value (e.g., mean or standard deviation) for a population or universe; i.e., a parameter is to a population as a statistic is to a sample.

**percentage-correct score:** A derived score (Type I A) expressing the examinee's performance as a percentage of the maximum possible score.

**percentile (*P*):** Any of the 99 points along the scale of score values that divide a distribution into 100 groups of equal frequency; e.g., $P_{73}$ is that point at or below which fall 73 percent of the cases in a distribution.

**percentile rank (PR):** A derived score (Type II B 2) stated in terms of the percentage of examinees in a specified group who fall at or below a given score point. *Syn.*: centile rank.

**performance test:** An ambiguous term used variously to mean (a) a test involving special apparatus, as opposed to a paper-and-pencil test, (b) a test minimizing verbal skills, or (c) a work-sample test.

**personality test:** A typical-performance test, questionnaire, or other device designed to measure some affective characteristic of the individual.

**population:** Any entire group so designated; i.e., the total group that is of interest or concern. *Syn.*: universe.

**portfolio:** An accumulation of the products (papers, tests, notebooks, artworks, etc.) belonging to an individual (here, usually a student), probably to be used in evaluating that individual's achievement.

**power test:** Any maximum-performance test for which speed is not an important determinant of score; thus, a test with a very generous (or no) time limit.

**predictive validity:** Criterion-related validity where criterion values are obtained at a later time than the test scores; contrast with *concurrent validity.*

**probable error (PE):** A measure of variability, rarely used today, found by multiplying 0.6745 by either the standard deviation (to obtain the probable error of a distribution) or the standard error (to obtain the probable error of some statistic).

**profile:** A graphic representation of the performance of an individual (or, less commonly, a group) on a series of tests, especially the tests in an integrated battery.

**prognostic test:** A test used to predict future performance (usually success or failure) in a particular task or course of study.

**projective technique:** Any method of personality measurement or study that makes use of deliberately ambiguous stimuli (e.g., ink blots, incomplete sentences, etc.) into which examinees "project" their personality when responding.

**psychometric:** Psychological (or educational) measurement that is norms-referenced, rather than criterion-referenced. *Ant.*: edumetric.

**punched hole:** Descriptive of a system for machine-scoring tests that utilizes holes punched into cards (e.g., IBM cards).

**quartile:** Any of the three points that divide a frequency distribution into four groups of equal frequency. The first quartile ($Q_1$) equals the twenty-fifth percentile ($P_{25}$); $Q_2 = P_{50}$ or the median; and $Q_3 = P_{75}$.

*r*: symbol for Pearson product-moment correlation coefficient; this is the most common correlation method.

**random error:** See *variable error.*

**random sample:** A sample drawn from a population in such a manner that each member of that population has an equal chance of being selected; samples so drawn are unbiased and should yield statistics representative of the population from which they were drawn.

**range:** The difference between the highest and lowest scores made on a test.

**ratio IQ:** A derived score (Type III A) no longer in common use; the formula is 100 (MA/CA), where MA = mental age determined from a test, and CA = chronological age (adjusted for older adolescents and adults).

**raw score:** The basic score initially obtained from scoring a test according to directions given by the test maker; usually equal to number of correct responses, but may be number of wrong answers or errors, time required for a task, etc.

**reliability:** Reproduceability of a set of scores under differing conditions; i.e., consistency or stability of a measuring instrument; necessary, but not sufficient, for validity. Commonly expressed as a reliability coefficient or a standard error of measurement.

**reliability coefficient:** A coefficient of correlation designed to estimate a test's reliability by correlating (a) scores on equivalent forms, (b) scores on matched halves (corrected for length), or (c) scores on two administrations of the same test.

**reproduceability:** A general descriptive term for all types of reliability.

**sample:** A general term referring to a group, however selected, that is assumed to represent the entire population from which it was drawn.

**scaled score:** (1) Loosely, any derived score. (2) More technically, any of several systems of scores (usually similar to standard scores) used in (a) articulating different forms, editions, and/or levels of a test; or (b) developmental research.

**screening:** (1) The act or process of quickly sorting a group of people into two or more subgroups, usually on the basis of scores on some test or the judgment of some supervisor (e.g., screening students into sections of a course on the basis of perceived ability). (2) A test used in screening.

**selection ratio:** The ratio of the number of persons selected to the number of persons tested; other things being equal, with lower ratios, a higher proportion of those selected are likely to prove successful.

**semi-interquartile range (quartile deviation, Q):** A measure of variability equal to one-half the difference between the third quartile ($P_{75}$) and the first quartile ($P_{25}$); i.e., $Q = (Q_3 - Q_1)/2$.

**sigma:** A Greek letter widely used in statistics. Capital sigma ($\Sigma$) means "to add" or "to find the sum of." Lowercase sigma ($\sigma$) is often used as a symbol for standard deviation, especially of a population; however, $s$, rather than $\sigma$, has been used in this book.

**skewed (distribution):** A noticeably asymmetrical distribution of scores. A distribution with many high scores and very few low scores is said to be "skewed to the left" or "negatively skewed"; a distribution with many low scores and few high scores is said to be positively skewed.

**Spearman-Brown (prophecy) formula:** A formula designed to estimate the reliability that a test will have if its length is changed while other factors remain constant; most commonly used in "correcting" split-half (i.e., "odd-even") reliability coefficients.

**specimen set:** Sample kit of test and test-related material that may be available to potential test users from a test publisher.

**speed test:** (1) A test on which an examinee's speed is an important determinant of his or her score. (2) A test on which the score equals the time taken to complete it.

**split-half reliability coefficient:** An estimate of content reliability based on the correlation between scores on two halves of a test; usually, the odd and even items are scored separately to provide these two half-test length scores. Must not be used with a speed test. See *Spearman-Brown.*

**standard deviation ($s$ or $\sigma$):** A measure of variability preferred over all others because of its mathematical soundness and its general usefulness as a basis for (a) standard scores, (b) standard errors, and (c) various statistical tests of significance.

**standard error:** An estimate of what the standard deviation of a statistic would be if successive values were found for that statistic through repeated testings (usually on different, but similar, samples drawn from the same population).

**standard error of estimate:** A standard deviation based on differences between obtained scores and scores predicted (from knowledge of correlation between a predictor variable and a criterion variable); thus, a measure of a test's validity.

**standard error of measurement:** An estimate of the standard deviation that would be found in the distribution of scores for a specified person if that person were to be tested repeatedly on the same or similar test (assuming no learning); thus, a measure of test reliability.

**standardization:** The act or process of developing a standardized test; many stages are involved in careful standardization, among them tryout of items, item analyses, validation studies, reliability studies, development of norms, and the like.

**standard score:** Any of several derived scores (Type II A) based on the number of standard deviations between a given raw score and the mean of the distribution.

**stanine:** A normalized standard score (Type II B 4 b) of nine units, 1–9; in a normal distribution, stanines have a mean of 5.0 and a standard deviation of 1.96.

**statistic:** A summary or descriptive value (e.g., mean or standard deviation) for a sample (rather than an entire population).

**sten:** A normalized standard score (Type II B 4 d), similar to the more common stanine, but having five units on either side of the mean; the mean sten (in a normal distribution) is 5.5, and the standard deviation is about 2.0.

**stencil key:** A scoring key made for placing over the answer sheet, the examinee's responses being visible either through holes prepared for that purpose or through the transparent material of the key itself.

**strip key:** A scoring key prepared in a column or strip that may be laid alongside a column of answers on the examinee's answer sheet or test paper; when several columns of answers are printed on the same scoring key, it becomes a "fan" or "accordion" key.

**subjective test:** A test on which the personal opinion or impression of the scorer is one determinant of the obtained score; i.e., the scoring key cannot be (or is not) fully prescribed in advance of scoring.

**survey test:** A test designed to measure achievement in one or more specified areas, usually with the intention of assessing group understanding—rather than individual measurement—of the concepts, principles, and facts.

**temporal reliability:** Test stability over a period of time, estimated through a test-retest reliability coefficient.

**test:** An examination; a device or process for examining some characteristic of an individual or group.

**test security:** The act or process of ensuring that only authorized people have access to tests, test supplies, and test results.

**true score:** A theoretical concept never obtainable in practice, an error-free score; usually defined as the average of the scores that would be obtained if a specified examinee were to take the same test an infinite number of times (assuming no learning).

**truncated:** Describes a distribution of scores that is cut off artificially or arbitrarily at some point; e.g., if some examinees receive the maximum possible score, these examinees may not be able to score as high as they could have if the test had a suitable ceiling.

**T-scaled score:** A normalized standard score (Type II B 4 a) with a mean of 50 and a standard deviation of 10.

**T-score:** A standard score (Type II A 2) having a mean of 50 and a standard deviation of 10.

**typical-performance test:** Any test designed to measure what an examinee is "really like," rather than any intellectual or ability characteristic; e.g., tests of personality, attitude, interest, etc. *Ant.:* maximum-performance test.


**usability:** That attribute of a test that is concerned with such practical matters as cost of the test, time to administer and score, etc.


**validity:** The extent to which a test does the job desired of it; the evidence may be either empirical or logical. Unless otherwise noted, criterion-related validity is implied.

**variability:** The amount of scatter or dispersion in a set of scores.

**variable:** (1) Any trait or characteristic that may change with the individual or the observation. (2) More strictly, any representation of such a trait or characteristic that is capable of assuming different values; e.g., test scores.

**variable error:** Any deviation from a true score attributable to one or more nonconstant influences, such as guessing, irregular testing conditions, etc.; always has a direct adverse effect on reliability; by definition, variable errors are uncorrelated with true scores.

**variance:** a statistic, equal to the square of the standard deviation; it is used widely in research.


**work-sample test:** A test on which the examinee's response to a simulated on-the-job problem or situation is evaluated; e.g., a pre-employment typing test.


**z-score:** The basic standard score (Type II A); widely used in test-related research; $z = (X - \bar{X})/s$, where $\bar{X}$ = mean score, and $s$ = standard deviation.

# Selected Test Publishers

The following is only a partial list of the reputable test publishers that readers of this book may find of interest. Consult the latest edition of the *Mental Measurements Yearbook* for a much more complete listing. The author's selection of these publishers is subjective.

American College Testing Program, P.O. Box 168, Iowa City, IA 52240.
American Guidance Service, Publishers' Building, Circle Pines, MN 55014.
Consulting Psychologists Press, Inc., 577 College Avenue, Palo Alto, CA 94306.
CTB/McGraw-Hill, Inc., 2500 Garden Road, Monterey, CA 93940.
Educational and Industrial Testing Service (EdITS), P.O. Box 7234, San Diego, CA 92107.
Educational Testing Service, Princeton, NJ 08541.
General Educational Development Testing Service of the American Council on Education, One Dupont Circle, N.W., Washington, DC 20036.
Institute of Personality and Ability Testing, Inc. (IPAT), P.O. Box 188, Champaign, IL 61820.
Jastak Associates, Inc., 1526 Gilpin Avenue, Wilmington, DE 19806.
London House, 1550 Northwest Highway, Park Ridge, IL 60068.
National Computer Systems (NCS), 5605 Green Circle Drive, Minnetonka, MN 55343.
PRO-ED, 5341 Industrial Oaks Boulevard, Austin, TX 78735.
Psychological Assessment Resources, Inc. (PAR), P.O. Box 98, Odessa, FL 33556.
The Psychological Corporation, 555 Academic Court, San Antonio, TX 78204.
Psychological Test Specialists, Box 9229, Missoula, MT 59807.
Reitan Neuropsychology Labs, 1338 East Edison Street, Tucson, AZ 85719.
Research Psychologists Press, Box 984, 1110 Military Street, Port Huron, MI 48061.

162

Riverside Publishing Co., 8420 Bryn Mawr Avenue, Chicago, IL 60631.
Scholastic Testing Service, Inc., 480 Meyer Road, P.O. Box 1056, Bensenville, IL 60106.
Science Research Associates, Inc., 155 North Wacker Drive, Chicago, IL 60606.
Sheridan Psychological Services, Inc., P.O. Box 6101, Orange, CA 92667.
Slosson Educational Publications, P.O. Box 280, East Aurora, NY 14052.
Stanford University Press, Stanford, CA 94305.
Stoelting Co., 1350 South Kostner Avenue, Chicago, IL 60623.
University of Minnesota Press, 2037 University Avenue S.E., Minneapolis, MN 55414.
Western Psychological Services, 12031 Wilshire Boulevard, Los Angeles, CA 90025.

# Bibliography

The books listed here are a sample of the many excellent references that may prove valuable for those who wish to learn more about testing.

Aiken, Lewis R., Jr. *Psychological Testing and Assessment,* 6th ed. Boston: Allyn & Bacon, 1988.

Anastasi, Anne. *Psychological Testing,* 6th ed. New York: Macmillan, 1988.

Buros, Oscar K., ed. *The Eleventh Mental Measurements Yearbook.* Lincoln, NE: Buros Institute of Mental Measurement, 1991. Best single reference for both critical reviews of tests and bibliographic lists of studies using specific tests. Earlier *MMYs* are also needed, for each one is essentially nonduplicative.

Chun, Ki-Taek, et al. *Measures for Psychological Assessment.* Ann Arbor: University of Michigan, 1975. A guide to 3,000 original sources of sociopsychological tests (many of them not standardized).

Cronbach, Lee J. *Essentials of Psychological Testing,* 4th ed. New York: Harper & Row, 1984.

Cronbach, Lee J. and Goldine Gleser. *Psychological Tests and Personnel Decisions,* 2nd ed. Urbana: University of Illinois Press, 1965.

Dubois, Philip H. *A History of Psychological Testing.* Boston: Allyn & Bacon, 1970.

Ebel, Robert L. *Essentials of Educational Measurement,* 4th ed. Englewood Cliffs, NJ: Prentice-Hall, 1986.

Educational Testing Service. *The ETS Test Collection Catalog.* Princeton, NJ: Oryx Press, 1986–present.

Equal Employment Opportunity Commission. *Job Discrimination? Laws and Rules You Should Know.* Washington, DC: EEOC, 1974.

Equal Employment Opportunity Commission. *The Uniform Guidelines on Employee Selection Procedures.* Washington, DC: EEOC, 1973.

ERIC Clearing House on Assessment. *Test Critiques.* Washington, DC: ERIC, 1984–present.

Fabiano, Emily, and Nancy O'Brien. *Testing Information Sources for Educators*. Washington, DC: ERIC, American Institutes for Research, 1987.

Fischer, Joel, and Kevin Corcoran. *Measures for Clinical Practice: A Sourcebook*, 2nd ed. New York: The Free Press, 1994.

Ghiselli, Edwin E., et al. *Measurement Theory for the Behavioral Sciences*. San Francisco: W. H. Freeman, 1981.

Graham, John R., and Roy S. Lilly. *Psychological Testing*. Englewood Cliffs, NJ: Prentice-Hall, 1984.

Guion, Robert M. *Personnel Testing*. New York: McGraw-Hill, 1965.

Gulliksen, Harold. *Theory of Mental Tests*. Hillsdale, NJ: L. Erlbaum Assoc., 1987 (reprint of 1950 text published by Wiley).

Herrnstein, Richard J., and Charles Murray. *The Bell Curve*. Glencoe, IL: Free Press, 1996.

Hopkins, Kenneth D., and Julian Stanley. *Educational and Psychological Measurement and Evaluation*, 6th ed. Englewood Cliffs, NJ: Prentice-Hall, 1981.

Kaplan, Robert M., and D. P. Saccuzzo. *Psychological Testing: Principles, Applications, and Issues*, 2nd ed. Pacific Grove, CA: Brooks Cole, 1988.

Keyser, Daniel J., and Richard C. Sweetland, eds. *A Comprehensive Reference for Assessment in Psychology, Education, and Business*, 2nd ed. Kansas City, MO: Test Corporation of America, 1986.

Lindeman, Richard H., and Peter F. Merenda. *Educational Measurement*, 2nd ed. Glenview, IL: Scott, Foresman, 1979.

Linn, R. L. *Educational Measurement*, 3rd ed. New York: Macmillan, 1988.

Lord, Frederic M. *Application of Item Response Theory to Practical Testing Problems*. Hillsdale, NJ: L. Erlbaum Assoc., 1980.

Love, Harold D. *Psychological Evaluation of Exceptional Children*. Springfield, IL: C.C. Thomas, 1985.

Lyman, Howard B. *Intelligence, Aptitude, and Achievement Testing*. Guidance Monograph Series III: Testing. Boston: Houghton Mifflin, 1968.

Lyman, Howard B. "Metrics Used in Reporting Test Results," in *New Directions for Testing and Measurement* No. 6, ed. S.T. Mayo. San Francisco: Jossey-Bass, 1980.

McLaughlin, Kenneth F. *Interpretation of Test Results*. Washington, DC: USGPO, 1964.

Mehrens, William A., and Irvin J. Lehmann. *Standardized Tests in Education*, 4th ed. New York: Holt, Rinehart and Winston, 1986.

Noll, Victor, et al. *Introduction to Educational Measurement*, 4th ed. Boston: Houghton Mifflin, 1989.

Nunnally, Jum C. *Psychometric Theory*, 2nd ed. New York: McGraw-Hill, 1978.

Samuda, Ronald J. *Psychological Testing of American Minorities*. New York: Harper & Row, 1975.

Shaycoft, Marion F. *Handbook of Criterion-Referenced Testing: Evaluation, and Use*. New York: Garland STPM Press,1979.

Siegel, Jerome. *Personnel Testing Under EEO* (An AMA Research Study). New York: American Management Association, 1980.

*Standards for Educational and Psychological Tests*. Washington, DC: American Psychological Association, 1974; revised,1985.

Thorndike, Robert L. *Personnel Selection*. New York: John Wiley, 1949. Old, but good.

## ON-LINE INFORMATION RETRIEVAL

Identifying and searching test information can be done quickly and efficiently through an on-line database system managed by Bibliographic Retrieval Services in Lantham, NY.

# Code of Professional Responsibilities in Educational Measurement

## PREAMBLE AND GENERAL RESPONSIBILITIES

As an organization dedicated to the improvement of measurement and evaluation practice in education, the National Council on Measurement in Education (NCME) has adopted this Code to promote professionally responsible practice in educational measurement. Professionally responsible practice is conduct that arises from either the professional standards of the field, general ethical principles, or both.

The purpose of the Code of Professional Responsibilities in Educational Measurement, hereinafter referred to as the Code, is to guide the conduct of NCME members who are involved in any type of assessment activity in education. NCME is also providing this Code as a public service for all individuals who are engaged in educational assessment activities in the hope that these activities will be conducted in a professionally responsible manner. Persons who engage in these activities include local educators such as classroom teachers, principals, and superintendents; professionals such as school psychologists and counselors; state and national technical, legislative, and policy staff in education; staff of research, evaluation, and testing organizations; providers of test preparation services; college and university faculty and administrators; and professionals in business and industry who design and implement educational and training programs.

This Code applies to any type of assessment that occurs as part of the educational process, including formal and informal, traditional and alternative techniques for gathering information used in making educational decisions at all levels. These techniques include, but are not limited to, large-scale assessments at the school, district, state, national, and international levels; standardized tests; observational measures; teacher-conducted assessments; assessment support materials; and other achievement, aptitude, interest, and personality measures used in and for education.

Although NCME is promulgating this Code for its members, it strongly encourages other organizations and individuals who engage in educational assessment activities to endorse and abide by the responsibilities relevant to their professions.

167

Because the Code pertains only to uses of assessment in education, it is recognized that uses of assessments outside of educational contexts such as for employment, certification, or licensure, may involve additional professional responsibilities beyond those detailed in this Code.

The Code is intended to serve an educational function: to inform and remind those involved in educational assessment of their obligations to uphold the integrity of the manner in which assessments are developed, used, evaluated, and marketed. Moreover, it is expected that the Code will stimulate thoughtful discussion of what constitutes professionally responsible assessment practice at all levels in education.

The Code enumerates professional responsibilities in eight major areas of assessment activity. Specifically, the Code presents the professional responsibilities of those who:

1) Develop Assessments
2) Market and Sell Assessments
3) Select Assessments
4) Administer Assessments
5) Score Assessments
6) Interpret, Use, and Communicate Assessment Results
7) Educate About Assessment
8) Evaluate Programs and Conduct Research on Assessments

Although the organization of the Code is based on the differentiation of these activities, they are viewed as highly interrelated, and those who use this Code are urged to consider the Code in its entirety. The index following this Code provides a listing of some of the critical interest topics within educational measurement that focus on one or more of the assessment activities.

## General Responsibilities

The professional responsibilities promulgated in this Code in eight major areas of assessment activity are based on expectations that NCME members involved in educational assessment will:

1) protect the health and safety of all examinees;
2) be knowledgeable about, and behave in compliance with, state and federal laws relevant to the conduct of professional activities;
3) maintain and improve their professional competence in educational assessment;
4) provide assessment services only in areas of their competence and experience, affording full disclosure of their professional qualifications;
5) promote the understanding of sound assessment practices in education;
6) adhere to the highest standards of conduct and promote professionally responsible conduct within educational institutions and agencies that provide educational services; and
7) perform all professional responsibilities with honesty, integrity, due care, and fairness.

Responsible professional practice includes being informed about and acting in accordance with the *Code of Fair Testing Practices in Education* (Joint Committee on

Testing Practices, 1988), the *Standards for Educational and Psychological Testing* (American Educational Research Association, American Psychological Association, NCME, 1985), or subsequent revisions, as well as all applicable state and federal laws that may govern the development, administration, and use of assessments. Both the *Standards for Educational and Psychological Testing* and the *Code of Fair Testing Practices in Education* are intended to establish criteria for judging the technical adequacy of tests and the appropriate uses of tests and test results. The purpose of this Code is to describe the professional responsibilities of those individuals who are engaged in assessment activities. As would be expected, there is a strong relationship between professionally responsible practice and sound educational assessments, and this Code is intended to be consistent with the relevant parts of both of these documents.

It is not the intention of NCME to enforce the professional responsibilities stated in the Code or to investigate allegations of violations to the Code. Since the Code provides a frame of reference for the evaluation of the appropriateness of behavior, NCME recognizes that the Code may be used in legal or other similar proceedings.

### Section 1: Responsibilities of Those Who Develop Assessment Products and Services

Those who develop assessment products and services, such as classroom teachers and other assessment specialists, have a professional responsibility to strive to produce assessments that are of the highest quality. Persons who develop assessments have a professional responsibility to:

1.1 ensure that assessment products and services are developed to meet applicable professional, technical, and legal standards.

1.2 develop assessment products and services that are as free as possible from bias due to characteristics irrelevant to the construct being measured, such as gender, ethnicity, race, socioeconomic status, disability, religion, age, or national origin.

1.3 plan accommodations for groups of test takers with disabilities and other special needs when developing assessments.

1.4 disclose to appropriate parties any actual or potential conflicts of interest that might influence the developers' judgment or performance.

1.5 use copyrighted materials in assessment products and services in accordance with state and federal law.

1.6 make information available to appropriate persons about the steps taken to develop and score the assessment, including up-to-date information used to support the reliability, validity, scoring and reporting processes, and other relevant characteristics of the assessment.

1.7 protect the rights to privacy of those who are assessed as part of the assessment development process.

1.8 caution users, in clear and prominent language, against the most likely misinterpretations and misuses of data that arise out of the assessment development process.

1.9 avoid false or unsubstantiated claims in test preparation and program support materials and services about an assessment or its use and interpretation.

1.10 correct any substantive inaccuracies in assessments or their support materials as soon as feasible.

1.11 develop score reports and support materials that promote the understanding of assessment results.

## Section 2: Responsibilities of Those Who Market and Sell Assessment Products and Services

The marketing of assessment products and services, such as tests and other instruments, scoring services, test preparation services, consulting, and test interpretive services, should be based on information that is accurate, complete, and relevant to those considering their use. Persons who market and sell assessment products and services have a professional responsibility to:

2.1 provide accurate information to potential purchasers about assessment products and services and their recommended uses and limitations.

2.2 not knowingly withhold relevant information about assessment products and services that might affect an appropriate selection decision.

2.3 base all claims about assessment products and services on valid interpretations of publicly available information.

2.4 allow qualified users equal opportunity to purchase assessment products and services.

2.5 establish reasonable fees for assessment products and services.

2.6 communicate to potential users, in advance of any purchase or use, all applicable fees associated with assessment products and services.

2.7 strive to ensure that no individuals are denied access to opportunities because of their inability to pay the fees for assessment products and services.

2.8 establish criteria for the sale of assessment products and services, such as limiting the sale of assessment products and services to those individuals who are qualified for recommended uses and from whom proper uses and interpretations are anticipated.

2.9 inform potential users of known inappropriate uses of assessment products and services and provide recommendations about how to avoid such misuses.

2.10 maintain a current understanding about assessment products and services and their appropriate uses in education.

2.11 release information implying endorsement by users of assessment products and services only with the users' permission.

2.12 avoid making claims that assessment products and services have been endorsed by another organization unless an official endorsement has been obtained.

2.13 avoid marketing test preparation products and services that may cause individuals to receive scores that misrepresent their actual levels of attainment.

## Section 3: Responsibilities of Those Who Select Assessment Products and Services

Those who select assessment products and services for use in educational settings, or help others do so, have important professional responsibilities to make sure that the assessments are appropriate for their intended use. Persons who select assessment products and services have a professional responsibility to:

3.1 conduct a thorough review and evaluation of available assessment strategies and instruments that might be valid for the intended uses.

3.2  recommend and/or select assessments based on publicly available documented evidence of their technical quality and utility rather than on unsubstantiated claims or statements.

3.3  disclose any associations or affiliations that they have with the authors, test publishers, or others involved with the assessments under consideration for purchase and refrain from participation if such associations might affect the objectivity of the selection process.

3.4  inform decision makers and prospective users of the appropriateness of the assessment for the intended uses, likely consequences of use, protection of examinee rights, relative costs, materials and services needed to conduct or use the assessment, and known limitations of the assessment, including potential misuses and misinterpretations of assessment information.

3.5  recommend against the use of any prospective assessment that is likely to be administered, scored, and used in an invalid manner for members of various groups in our society for reasons of race, ethnicity, gender, age, disability, language background, socioeconomic status, religion, or national origin.

3.6  comply with all security precautions that may accompany assessments being reviewed.

3.7  immediately disclose any attempts by others to exert undue influence on the assessment selection process.

3.8  avoid recommending, purchasing, or using test preparation products and services that may cause individuals to receive scores that misrepresent their actual levels of attainment.

### Section 4: Responsibilities of Those Who Administer Assessments

Those who prepare individuals to take assessments and those who are directly or indirectly involved in the administration of assessments as part of the educational process, including teachers, administrators, and assessment personnel, have an important role in making sure that the assessments are administered in a fair and accurate manner. Persons who prepare others for, and those who administer, assessments have a professional responsibility to:

4.1  inform the examinees about the assessment prior to its administration, including its purposes, uses, and consequences; how the assessment information will be judged or scored; how the results will be kept on file; who will have access to the results; how the results will be distributed; and examinees' rights before, during, and after the assessment.

4.2  administer only those assessments for which they are qualified by education, training, licensure, or certification.

4.3  take appropriate security precautions before, during, and after the administration of the assessment.

4.4  understand the procedures needed to administer the assessment prior to administration.

4.5  administer standardized assessments according to prescribed procedures and conditions and notify appropriate persons if any nonstandard or delimiting conditions occur.

4.6  not exclude any eligible student from the assessment.

4.7  avoid any conditions in the conduct of the assessment that might invalidate the results.

4.8    provide for and document all reasonable and allowable accommodations for the administration of the assessment to persons with disabilities or special needs.

4.9    provide reasonable opportunities for individuals to ask questions about the assessment procedures or directions prior to and at prescribed times during the administration of the assessment.

4.10    protect the rights to privacy and due process of those who are assessed.

4.11    avoid actions or conditions that would permit or encourage individuals or groups to receive scores that misrepresent their actual levels of attainment.

### Section 5: Responsibilities of Those Who Score Assessments

The scoring of educational assessments should be conducted properly and efficiently so that the results are reported accurately and in a timely manner. Persons who score and prepare reports of assessments have a professional responsibility to:

5.1    provide complete and accurate information to users about how the assessment is scored, such as the reporting schedule, scoring process to be used, rationale for the scoring approach, technical characteristics, quality control procedures, reporting formats, and the fees, if any, for these services.

5.2    ensure the accuracy of the assessment results by conducting reasonable quality control procedures before, during, and after scoring.

5.3    minimize the effect on scoring of factors irrelevant to the purposes of the assessment.

5.4    inform users promptly of any deviation in the planned scoring and reporting service or schedule and negotiate a solution with users.

5.5    provide corrected score results to the examinee or the client as quickly as practicable should errors be found that may affect the inferences made on the basis of the scores.

5.6    protect the confidentiality of information that identifies individuals as prescribed by state and federal law.

5.7    release summary results of the assessment only to those persons entitled to such information by state or federal law or those who are designated by the party contracting for the scoring services.

5.8    establish, where feasible, a fair and reasonable process for appeal and rescoring the assessment.

### Section 6: Responsibilities of Those Who Interpret, Use, and Communicate Assessment Results

The interpretation, use, and communication of assessment results should promote valid inferences and minimize invalid ones. Persons who interpret, use, and communicate assessment results have a professional responsibility to:

6.1    conduct these activities in an informed, objective, and fair manner within the context of the assessment's limitations and with an understanding of the potential consequences of use.

6.2    provide to those who receive assessment results information about the assessment, its purposes, its limitations, and its uses necessary for the proper interpretation of the results.

6.3    provide to those who receive score reports an understandable written description of all reported scores, including proper interpretations and likely misinterpretations.

6.4 communicate to appropriate audiences the results of the assessment in an understandable and timely manner, including proper interpretations and likely misinterpretations.

6.5 evaluate and communicate the adequacy and appropriateness of any norms or standards used in the interpretation of assessment results.

6.6 inform parties involved in the assessment process how assessment results may affect them.

6.7 use multiple sources and types of relevant information about persons or programs whenever possible in making educational decisions.

6.8 avoid making, and actively discourage others from making, inaccurate reports, unsubstantiated claims, inappropriate interpretations, or otherwise false and misleading statements about assessment results.

6.9 disclose to examinees and others whether and how long the results of the assessment will be kept on file, procedures for appeal and rescoring, rights examinees and others have to the assessment information, and how those rights may be exercised.

6.10 report any apparent misuses of assessment information to those responsible for the assessment process.

6.11 protect the rights to privacy of individuals and institutions involved in the assessment process.

## Section 7: Responsibilities of Those Who Educate Others about Assessment

The process of educating others about educational assessment, whether as part of higher education, professional development, public policy discussions, or job training, should prepare individuals to understand and engage in sound measurement practice and to become discerning users of tests and test results. Persons who educate or inform others about assessment have a professional responsibility to:

7.1 remain competent and current in the areas in which they teach and reflect that in their instruction.

7.2 provide fair and balanced perspectives when teaching about assessment.

7.3 differentiate clearly between expressions of opinion and substantiated knowledge when educating others about any specific assessment method, product, or service.

7.4 disclose any financial interests that might be perceived to influence the evaluation of a particular assessment product or service that is the subject of instruction.

7.5 avoid administering any assessment that is not part of the evaluation of student performance in a course if the administration of that assessment is likely to harm any student.

7.6 avoid using or reporting the results of any assessment that is not part of the evaluation of student performance in a course if the use or reporting of results is likely to harm any student.

7.7 protect all secure assessments and materials used in the instructional process.

7.8 model responsible assessment practice and help those receiving instruction to learn about their professional responsibilities in educational measurement.

7.9    provide fair and balanced perspectives on assessment issues being discussed by policymakers, parents, and other citizens.

**Section 8: Responsibilities of Those Who Evaluate Educational Programs and Conduct Research on Assessments**

Conducting research on or about assessments or educational programs is a key activity in helping to improve the understanding and use of assessments and educational programs. Persons who engage in the evaluation of educational programs or conduct research on assessments have a professional responsibility to:

8.1    conduct evaluation and research activities in an informed, objective, and fair manner.

8.2    disclose any associations that they have with authors, test publishers, or others involved with the assessment and refrain from participation if such associations might affect the objectivity of the research or evaluation.

8.3    preserve the security of all assessments throughout the research process as appropriate.

8.4    take appropriate steps to minimize potential sources of invalidity in the research and disclose known factors that may bias the results of the study.

8.5    present the results of research, both intended and unintended, in a fair, complete, and objective manner.

8.6    attribute completely and appropriately the work and ideas of others.

8.7    qualify the conclusions of the research within the limitations of the study.

8.8    use multiple sources of relevant information in conducting evaluation and research activities whenever possible.

8.9    comply with applicable standards for protecting the rights of participants in an evaluation or research study, including the rights to privacy and informed consent.

## AFTERWORD

As stated at the outset, the purpose of the *Code of Professional Responsibilities in Educational Measurement* is to serve as a guide to the conduct of NCME members who are engaged in any type of assessment activity in education. Given the broad scope of the field of educational assessment as well as the variety of activities in which professionals may engage, it is unlikely that any code will cover the professional responsibilities involved in every situation or activity in which assessment is used in education. Ultimately, it is hoped that this Code will serve as the basis for ongoing discussions about what constitutes professionally responsible practice. Moreover, these discussions will undoubtedly identify areas of practice that need further analysis and clarification in subsequent editions of the Code. To the extent that these discussions occur, the Code will have served its purpose.

To assist in the ongoing refinement of the Code, comments on this document are most welcome. Please send your comments and inquiries to:

Executive Officer
National Council on Measurement in Education
1230 Seventeenth Street, NW
Washington, DC 20036-3078

## SUPPLEMENTARY RESOURCES

The following list of resources is provided for those who want to seek additional information about codes of professional responsibility that have been developed and adopted by organizations having an interest in various aspects of educational assessment.

American Association for Counseling and Development (now American Counseling Association). (1988). *Ethical standards of the American Counseling Association.* Alexandria, VA: Author.

American Association for Counseling and Development (now American Counseling Association) & Association for Measurement and Evaluation in Counseling and Development (now Association for Assessment in Counseling). (1989). *Responsibilities of users of standardized tests: RUST statement revised.* Alexandria, VA: Author.

American Educational Research Association, American Psychological Association, & National Council on Measurement in Education. (1985). *Standards for educational and psychological testing.* Washington, DC: Author.

American Educational Research Association. (1992). Ethical standards of the American Educational Research Association. *Educational Researcher, 21*(7), 23–26.

American Federation of Teachers, National Council on Measurement in Education, & National Education Association. (1990). *Standards for teacher competence in educational assessment of students.* Washington, DC: Author.

American Psychological Association. (1992). *Ethical principles of psychologists and code of conduct.* Washington, DC: Author.

American Psychological Association President's Task Force on Psychology in Education. (in press). *Learner-centered psychological principles: Guidelines for school redesign and reform.* Washington, DC: Author.

Joint Advisory Committee. (1993). *Principles for fair assessment practices for education in Canada.* Edmonton, Alberta: Author.

Joint Committee on Testing Practices. (1988). *Code of fair testing practices in education.* Washington, DC: Author.

Joint Committee on Standards for Educational Evaluation. (1988). *The personnel evaluation standards: How to assess systems for evaluating educators.* Newbury Park, CA: Sage.

Joint Committee on Standards for Educational Evaluation. (1994). *The program evaluation standards: How to assess evaluations of educational programs.* Thousand Oaks, CA: Sage.

National Association of College Admission Counselors. (1988). *Statement of principles of good practice.* Alexandria, VA: Author.

# Conversion Table

DIRECTIONS FOR USING CONVERSION TABLE (pages 177–182)

This table may be used to convert from one derived-score system to another, assuming a normal distribution. Enter the table with the score in which you are interested; all entries on the same line are its normal-curve equivalents. **Care must be taken when using the table to compare results from different tests, for different norms groups are likely to be involved.**
*See* odd-numbered pages of the table for an explanation of symbols.

To use this Conversion Table for types of score *not* shown here, follow these steps:

*For a linear standard score (Type II A):*

1. Find the amount by which an examinee's raw score differs from the mean of the group with which you wish to compare the examinee (either from the manual or from the local testing); i.e., $X - \bar{X}$.
2. Obtain the examinee's z-score by dividing this difference by the standard deviation of the same group; i.e., $(X - \bar{X})/s$.
3. Enter this value of z in the first column; all other entries on the same line are linear standard score equivalents (except for the percentile rank in the final column).

*For a normalized standard score (Type II B 5):*

1. Follow the directions for computing a percentile rank (*see* pages 102–106).
2. Enter this value of percentile rank in the extreme right-hand column of the table. All other entries on the same line of the table are now *normalized* standard-score equivalents.

Customarily, none of these scores (except z) is expressed with a decimal. As a final step, therefore, you will usually round your score to the nearest whole number.

**Do not use this table to find IQ equivalents unless "general population" norms are used.**

# Conversion Table for Derived Scores*

| $z$ $\left(\dfrac{X-\bar{X}}{s}\right)$ [Type II A 1][a] | $T$[b] $(10z+50)$ [Type II A2 or II B 5 a][a] | AGCT $(20z+100)$ [Type II A 3][a] | IQ CEEB $(100z+500)$ [Type II A 4][a] | IQ Wechsler $(15z+100)$ [Type II A 5 a][a] | IQ Stanford-Binet $(16z+100)$ [Type II A 5 b][a] | Stanine[c] [Type II B 5 b][a] | C-Score[c] [Type II B 5 c][a] | Sten[c] [Type II B 5 d][a] | Percentile Rank [Type II B 2][a] |
|---|---|---|---|---|---|---|---|---|---|
| 3.00 | 80 | 160 | 800 | 145 | 148 | | | | 99.9 |
| 2.95 | 79.5 | 159 | 795 | 144 | 147 | | | | 99.8 |
| 2.90 | 79 | 158 | 790 | 144 | 146 | | | | 99.8 |
| 2.85 | 78.5 | 157 | 785 | 143 | 146 | | | | 99.8 |
| 2.80 | 78 | 156 | 780 | 142 | 145 | | | | 99.7 |
| 2.75 | 77.5 | 155 | 775 | 141 | 144 | | | | 99.7 |
| 2.70 | 77 | 154 | 770 | 141 | 143 | | | | 99.6 |
| 2.65 | 76.5 | 153 | 765 | 140 | 142 | | | | 99.6 |
| 2.60 | 76 | 152 | 760 | 139 | 142 | | | | 99.5 |
| 2.55 | 75.5 | 151 | 755 | 138 | 141 | | 10 | | 99.5 |
| 2.50 | 75 | 150 | 750 | 138 | 140 | | | | 99.4 |
| 2.45 | 74.5 | 149 | 745 | 137 | 139 | | | | 99.3 |
| 2.40 | 74 | 148 | 740 | 136 | 138 | 9 | | 10 | 99.2 |
| 2.35 | 73.5 | 147 | 735 | 135 | 138 | | | | 99.1 |
| 2.30 | 73 | 146 | 730 | 135 | 137 | | — | | 98.9 |
| 2.25 | 72.5 | 145 | 725 | 134 | 136 | | | | 98.8 |
| 2.20 | 72 | 144 | 720 | 133 | 135 | | | | 98.6 |
| 2.15 | 71.5 | 143 | 715 | 132 | 134 | | | | 98.4 |

*See directions for use on page 176.

[a]Refers to the classification of scores developed for this book; see Chapter 8.

[b]Since this table assumes a normal distribution, these values of $T$ may be either $T$-scores (Type II A 2) or $T$-scaled scores (Type II B 5 a); if the distribution were not normal, $T$-scaled score entries would differ.

[c]This score takes only a very limited number of different values; therefore, it will have the same value for a range of values on other scores.

# Conversion Table for Derived Scores*

| $\left(\frac{X-\bar{X}}{s}\right)$ z [Type II A 1][a] | $T$[b] (10z + 50) [Type II A 2 or II B 5 a][a] | AGCT (20z + 100) [Type II A 3][a] | CEEB (100z + 500) [Type II A 4][a] | IQ Wechsler (15z + 100) [Type II A 5 a][a] | IQ Stanford-Binet (16z + 100) [Type II A 5 b][a] | Stanine[c] [Type II B 5 b][a] | C-Score[c] [Type II B 5 c][a] | Sten[c] [Type II B 5 d][a] | Percentile Rank [Type II B 2][a] |
|---|---|---|---|---|---|---|---|---|---|
| 2.10 | 71   | 142 | 710 | 132 | 134 |   |   |   | 98.2 |
| 2.05 | 70.5 | 141 | 705 | 131 | 133 |   |   |   | 98.0 |
| 2.00 | 70   | 140 | 700 | 130 | 132 |   | 9 |   | 97.7 |
| 1.95 | 69.5 | 139 | 695 | 129 | 131 |   |   |   | 97.4 |
| 1.90 | 69   | 138 | 690 | 129 | 130 |   |   |   | 97.1 |
| 1.85 | 68.5 | 137 | 685 | 128 | 130 |   |   |   | 96.8 |
| 1.80 | 68   | 136 | 680 | 127 | 129 |   |   |   | 96.4 |
| 1.75 | 67.5 | 135 | 675 | 126 | 128 | — | — |   | 96.0 |
| 1.70 | 67   | 134 | 670 | 126 | 127 |   |   | 9 | 95.5 |
| 1.65 | 66.5 | 133 | 665 | 125 | 126 |   |   |   | 95.0 |
| 1.60 | 66   | 132 | 660 | 124 | 126 |   |   |   | 94.5 |
| 1.55 | 65.5 | 131 | 655 | 123 | 125 |   |   |   | 93.9 |
| 1.50 | 65   | 130 | 650 | 123 | 124 |   |   |   | 93.3 |
| 1.45 | 64.5 | 129 | 645 | 122 | 123 | 8 | 8 |   | 92.6 |
| 1.40 | 64   | 128 | 640 | 121 | 122 |   |   | — | 91.9 |
| 1.35 | 63.5 | 127 | 635 | 120 | 122 |   |   |   | 91.2 |
| 1.30 | 63   | 126 | 630 | 120 | 121 |   |   |   | 90.3 |
| 1.25 | 62.5 | 125 | 625 | 119 | 120 |   |   |   | 89.4 |
| 1.20 | 62   | 124 | 620 | 118 | 119 | — | — |   | 88.5 |
| 1.15 | 61.5 | 123 | 615 | 117 | 118 |   |   | 8 | 87.5 |
| 1.10 | 61   | 122 | 610 | 117 | 118 |   |   |   | 86.4 |
| 1.05 | 60.5 | 121 | 605 | 116 | 117 |   |   |   | 85.3 |

| r* | T[b] | | | | | | | | Percentile |
|---|---|---|---|---|---|---|---|---|---|
| 1.00 | 60 | 120 | 600 | 116 | 115 | | | | 84.1 |
| 0.95 | 59.5 | 119 | 595 | 115 | 114 | | | | 82.9 |
| 0.90 | 59 | 118 | 590 | 114 | 114 | | | | 81.6 |
| 0.85 | 58.5 | 117 | 585 | 114 | 113 | | | 7 | 80.2 |
| 0.80 | 58 | 116 | 580 | 113 | 112 | | 7 | | 78.8 |
| 0.75 | 57.5 | 115 | 575 | 112 | 111 | 7 | | | 77.3 |
| 0.70 | 57 | 114 | 570 | 111 | 111 | — | — | | 75.8 |
| 0.65 | 56.5 | 113 | 565 | 110 | 110 | | | | 74.2 |
| 0.60 | 56 | 112 | 560 | 110 | 109 | | | | 72.6 |
| 0.55 | 55.5 | 111 | 555 | 109 | 108 | | | | 70.9 |
| 0.50 | 55 | 110 | 550 | 108 | 108 | | | 6 | 69.2 |
| 0.45 | 54.5 | 109 | 545 | 107 | 107 | | 6 | | 67.4 |
| 0.40 | 54 | 108 | 540 | 106 | 106 | 6 | | | 65.5 |
| 0.35 | 53.5 | 107 | 535 | 106 | 105 | | | | 63.7 |
| 0.30 | 53 | 106 | 530 | 105 | 104 | | | | 61.8 |
| 0.25 | 52.5 | 105 | 525 | 104 | 104 | — | — | | 59.9 |
| 0.20 | 52 | 104 | 520 | 103 | 103 | | | 6 | 57.9 |
| 0.15 | 51.5 | 103 | 515 | 102 | 102 | | | | 56.0 |
| 0.10 | 51 | 102 | 510 | 102 | 102 | | | | 54.0 |
| 0.05 | 50.5 | 101 | 505 | 101 | 101 | 5 | | | 52.0 |
| 0.00 | 50 | 100 | 500 | 100 | 100 | | 5 | 5 | 50.0 |
| -0.05 | 49.5 | 99 | 495 | 99 | 99 | | | | 48.0 |
| -0.10 | 49 | 98 | 490 | 98 | 98 | | | | 46.0 |
| -0.15 | 48.5 | 97 | 485 | 98 | 98 | | | | 44.0 |
| -0.20 | 48 | 96 | 480 | 97 | 97 | — | | | 42.1 |
| -0.25 | 47.5 | 95 | 475 | 96 | 96 | | — | 5 | 40.1 |

*See directions for use on page 176.

[a]Refers to the classification of scores developed for this book; see Chapter 8.

[b]Since this table assumes a normal distribution, these values of T may be either T-scores (Type II A 2) or T-scaled scores (Type II B 5 a); if the distribution were not normal, T-scaled score entries would differ.

[c]This score takes only a very limited number of different values; therefore, it will have the same value for a range of values on other scores.

Conversion Table for Derived Scores*

| $z$ $\left(\frac{X - \bar{X}}{s}\right)$ [Type II A 1][a] | $T$[b] (10z + 50) [Type II A2 or II B 5 a][a] | AGCT (20z + 100) [Type II A 3][a] | CEEB (100z + 500) [Type II A 4][a] | IQ Wechsler (15z + 100) [Type II A 5 a][a] | IQ Stanford-Binet (16z + 100) [Type II A 5 b][a] | Stanine[c] [Type II B 5 b][a] | C-Score[c] [Type II B 5 c][a] | Sten[c] [Type II B 5 d][a] | Percentile Rank [Type II B 2][a] |
|---|---|---|---|---|---|---|---|---|---|
| -0.30 | 47 | 94 | 470 | 96 | 95 | | | | 38.2 |
| -0.35 | 46.5 | 93 | 465 | 95 | 94 | | | | 36.3 |
| -0.40 | 46 | 92 | 460 | 94 | 94 | | | | 34.5 |
| -0.45 | 45.5 | 91 | 455 | 93 | 93 | | | — | 32.6 |
| -0.50 | 45 | 90 | 450 | 93 | 92 | 4 | 4 | | 30.8 |
| -0.55 | 44.5 | 89 | 445 | 92 | 91 | | | | 29.1 |
| -0.60 | 44 | 88 | 440 | 91 | 90 | | | | 27.4 |
| -0.65 | 43.5 | 87 | 435 | 90 | 90 | | | | 25.8 |
| -0.70 | 43 | 86 | 430 | 90 | 89 | | | | 24.2 |
| -0.75 | 42.5 | 85 | 425 | 89 | 88 | — | | 4 | 22.7 |
| -0.80 | 42 | 84 | 420 | 88 | 87 | | — | | 21.2 |
| -0.85 | 41.5 | 83 | 415 | 87 | 86 | | 3 | | 19.8 |
| -0.90 | 41 | 82 | 410 | 87 | 86 | 3 | | | 18.4 |
| -0.95 | 40.5 | 81 | 405 | 86 | 85 | | | | 17.1 |
| -1.00 | 40 | 80 | 400 | 85 | 84 | | | | 15.9 |
| -1.05 | 39.5 | 79 | 395 | 84 | 83 | | | — | 14.7 |
| -1.10 | 39 | 78 | 390 | 84 | 82 | | | | 13.6 |
| -1.15 | 38.5 | 77 | 385 | 83 | 82 | | | | 12.5 |
| -1.20 | 38 | 76 | 380 | 82 | 81 | | | | 11.5 |
| -1.25 | 37.5 | 75 | 375 | 81 | 80 | | — | | 10.6 |
| -1.30 | 37 | 74 | 370 | 81 | 79 | | | 3 | 9.7 |
| -1.35 | 36.5 | 73 | 365 | 80 | 78 | | | | 8.8 |
| -1.40 | 36 | 72 | 360 | 79 | 78 | | | | 8.1 |

| z* | | | | | | | | | |
|---|---|---|---|---|---|---|---|---|---|
| −1.45 | 35.5 | 71 | 355 | 78 | | | | 77 | 7.4 |
| −1.50 | 35 | 70 | 350 | 78 | 2 | | — | 76 | 6.7 |
| −1.55 | 34.5 | 69 | 345 | 77 | | 2 | | 75 | 6.1 |
| −1.60 | 34 | 68 | 340 | 76 | | | | 74 | 5.5 |
| −1.65 | 33.5 | 67 | 335 | 75 | | | | 74 | 5.0 |
| −1.70 | 33 | 66 | 330 | 75 | | | | 73 | 4.5 |
| −1.75 | 32.5 | 65 | 325 | 74 | 2 | — | — | 72 | 4.0 |
| −1.80 | 32 | 64 | 320 | 73 | | | | 71 | 3.6 |
| −1.85 | 31.5 | 63 | 315 | 72 | | | | 70 | 3.2 |
| −1.90 | 31 | 62 | 310 | 72 | | | | 70 | 2.9 |
| −1.95 | 30.5 | 61 | 305 | 71 | | | — | 69 | 2.6 |
| −2.00 | 30 | 60 | 300 | 70 | 1 | | | 68 | 2.3 |
| −2.05 | 29.5 | 59 | 295 | 69 | | | | 67 | 2.0 |
| −2.10 | 29 | 58 | 290 | 69 | | | | 66 | 1.8 |
| −2.15 | 28.5 | 57 | 285 | 68 | | | | 66 | 1.6 |
| −2.20 | 28 | 56 | 280 | 67 | | | | 65 | 1.4 |
| −2.25 | 27.5 | 55 | 275 | 66 | | — | | 64 | 1.2 |
| −2.30 | 27 | 54 | 270 | 66 | | | | 63 | 1.1 |
| −2.35 | 26.5 | 53 | 265 | 65 | | | | 62 | 0.9 |
| −2.40 | 26 | 52 | 260 | 64 | | | | 62 | 0.8 |
| −2.45 | 25.5 | 51 | 255 | 63 | | | | 61 | 0.7 |
| −2.50 | 25 | 50 | 250 | 63 | 1 | 1 | 1 | 60 | 0.6 |
| −2.55 | 24.5 | 49 | 245 | 62 | | | | 59 | 0.5 |
| −2.60 | 24 | 48 | 240 | 61 | | | | 58 | 0.5 |
| −2.65 | 23.5 | 47 | 235 | 60 | | | | 58 | 0.4 |

*See directions for use on page 176.

aRefers to the classification of scores developed for this book; see Chapter 8.

bSince this table assumes a normal distribution, these values of T may be either T-scores (Type II A 2) or T-scaled scores (Type II B 5 a); if the distribution were not normal, T-scaled score entries would differ.

cThis score takes only a very limited number of different values; therefore, it will have the same value for a range of values on other scores.

Conversion Table for Derived Scores*

| $z$ $\left(\dfrac{X - \bar{X}}{s}\right)$ [Type II A 1][a] | $T$[b] $(10z + 50)$ [Type II A2 or II B 5 a][a] | AGCT $(20z + 100)$ [Type II A 3][a] | CEEB $(100z + 500)$ [Type II A 4][a] | IQ | | Stanine[c] [Type II B 5 b][a] | C-Score[c] [Type II B 5 c][a] | Sten[c] [Type II B 5 d][a] | Percentile Rank [Type II B 2][a] |
|---|---|---|---|---|---|---|---|---|---|
| | | | | Wechsler $(15z + 100)$ [Type II A 5 a][a] | Stanford-Binet $(16z + 100)$ [Type II A 5 b][a] | | | | |
| -2.70 | 23 | 46 | 230 | 60 | 57 | | 0 | | 0.4 |
| -2.75 | 22.5 | 45 | 225 | 59 | 56 | | | | 0.3 |
| -2.80 | 22 | 44 | 220 | 58 | 55 | | | | 0.3 |
| -2.85 | 21.5 | 43 | 215 | 57 | 54 | | | | 0.2 |
| -2.90 | 21 | 42 | 210 | 57 | 54 | | | | 0.2 |
| -2.95 | 20.5 | 41 | 205 | 56 | 53 | | | | 0.2 |
| -3.00 | 20 | 40 | 200 | 55 | 52 | | | | 0.1 |

*See directions for use on page 176.

[a]Refers to the classification of scores developed for this book; see Chapter 8.

[b]Since this table assumes a normal distribution, these values of $T$ may be either $T$-scores (Type II A 2) or $T$-scaled scores (Type II B 5 a); if the distribution were not normal, $T$-scaled score entries would differ.

[c]This score takes only a very limited number of different values; therefore, it will have the same value for a range of values on other scores.

182

# Index

Ability, test scores and, 145
Abscissa, 52, 57
ACCENT (*American Cross Cultural Ethnic Nomenclature Test*), 29
Accomplishment quotients (AQ), 117–118
Accountability, competency and, 35–36
Achievement, intelligence test performance and, 22
Achievement age, 114–115
Achievement quotient, 117–118
Achievement tests
    classifications for, 26–29
    increase in, 40
    use of, 22–23
ACTP (*American College Testing Program*), 111
Adaptive testing, 31, 34–35
Administration of test
    directions on, 75
    mistakes in, 131
Administrators, lack of good judgment by, 1–2
AGCT-score, 99

Agency policy, on test result information, 134
Age scores, 113–114
Ambiguity, of test items, 25–26
*American College Testing Program* (ACTP), 111
*American Cross Cultural Ethnic Nomenclature Test* (ACCENT), 29
American education, deterioration of, 1–2, 36–37
American Personnel and Guidance Association, 29
American Psychological Association, 29, 135
Aptitude, 21
Aptitude tests
    batteries, 40
    use of, 22
AQ (accomplishment quotients), 117–118
Area transformations, 108–109
Arithmetic mean, 55, 64
*Armed Services Vocational Aptitude Battery* (ASVAB), 22
*Army General Classification Test*, 99

Assessment, achievement testing and, 22
Average deviation, 58
Averages. *See also* Norms
  measures of, 55–57
*Ayers Handwriting Scale*, 33

Bibliographic references, in test manual, 87
Bimodal distribution, 56
Branched or adaptive testing, 31, 34–35
Buckley Amendment (Family Educational Rights and Privacy Act of 1974), 35, 134

Canada, educational difficulties in, 38
CBTI (computer-based test interpretation), 32
CEEB-score, 99–100
Centile rank. *See* Percentile rank
Central tendency, measures of, 55–57
Challenged children, 146
Cheating, 17
Children
  exceptional or challenged, 146
  parents of (*See* Parents)
Class intervals, 50, 51
Code of Professional Responsibilities, in educational measurement, 72, 167–174
College Entrance Examination Board tests, 99–100
Colleges, test result information handling, 135
Communication, of test results
  to child examinee, 140–142
  effective, 145
  to mature examinee, 138–140
Comparisons
  content difficulty, 89, 90, 94
  inter-individual (*See* Inter-individual comparisons)
  intra-individual, 89, 90, 94, 116–118
Competency, accountability and, 35–36
Computer
  online services, test information from, 87
  testing and, 31–32
  test-item banks and, 34
Computer-based test interpretation (CBTI), 32
Concurrent validity, 13

Confidence interval, 66
Confidence limits, 66
Construct validity, 13, 77
Content difficulty comparison scores, 80, 89, 94
  letter grades, 96–97
  percentage correct, 95–96
  relationship with other scores, 91
  use of, 92
Content-referenced tests. *See* Criterion-referenced tests
Content validity, 10
Continuous values, 50–51
Conversations, about test result, 136
Conversion table, 176–182
Correlation coefficients
  reliability, 14
  variability, 11
Course validity, 10
Covariability, measures of, 59–63
Creativity, 41
Criterion differences, criterion-related validity and, 11
Criterion keying, 24
Criterion-referenced tests, 22, 40
  acceptance of, 31
  evaluation of, 34
  history of, 33
  individualized instruction and, 33
  philosophy of, 33–34
Criterion-related validity, 11–13
C-scaled score, 109
Cultural homogeneity, 29
Culture-bound tests, 7
Culture fair or free tests, 29
Curricular validity (content validity), 10

DAT (*Differential Aptitude Tests*), 22, 76–77
Decile rank, 107
Decisions, institutional and individual, 130
Derived scores. *See also specific derived scores*
  rationale for using, 88
Descriptive statistics, 53–54
  measures of covariability, 59–63
  measures of position, 54–57
  measures of variability, 57–59
Deviation, average or mean, 58
Deviation IQs, 100–101, 110–111, 119

*Differential Aptitude Tests* (DAT), 22, 76–77
Discrete values, 51
Domain-referenced tests. *See* Criterion-referenced tests
Dynamic or adaptive testing, 34–35

EA (educational age), 114–115
Edition, test, 81
Educational age (EA), 114–115
Educational quotients, 117
Educational Testing Service (ETS), 45, 118
Educational tests, role of, 2
Edumetric tests. *See* Criterion-referenced tests
*Edwards Personal Preference Schedule*, 24
EEOC (Equal Employment Opportunity Commission), 5, 35–36
Electronic scoring, 31–32
Empirical validity, 11–13
Employers, personality test administration, 44
Environmental influences, 40
Equal Employment Opportunity Commission (EEOC), 5, 35–36
Errors
    in scoring keys, 131
    *vs.* mistakes, 67
Error variance, 14
    examinee-incurred, 14
    examiner-scorer influence, 15
    sources, interrelationship of, 17
    test content, 15–16
    time influence, 16
Estimate, standard error of, 67–68
ETS (Educational Testing Service), 45, 118
Evaluation, achievement testing and, 22
Examinee
    child, communicating test results to, 140–142
    indecisiveness of, 25
    mature, communicating test results to, 138–140
    motivational pattern of, 25
    test result information for, 134
    variable errors, 14
Examiner
    name, on test profile, 124
    variable errors, 15
Exceptional children, 146

Expectancy tables/charts, 68–70, 81
Experts, test, 146–148

Face validity, 10
FACT (Flanagan Aptitude Classification Tests), 109
Fairness, test, 45–47
Family Educational Rights and Privacy Act of 1974 (Buckley Amendment), 35, 134
Flanagan Aptitude Classification Tests (FACT), 109
Flanagan's extended stanine score, 109
Forced-choice items, 24–25
Form, test, 81
Frequency, 52
Frequency distribution, 50–51
Frequency polygon, 53

Gender differences, in test scores, 45
Grade-placement scores, 115–116
Grades, letter, 96–97, 106–107
Grading, on curve, 107
Great Britain, educational difficulties in, 38
Group differences, criterion-related validity and, 12
Group tests, 28
Guidance workers, 133

Heterogeneity, reliability and, 18
Histogram, 52–53

Inborn ability, measurement of, 7
Incremental validity, 12–13
Individual decisions, 130
Individualized or adaptive testing, 34–35
Individual tests, 28
Inferential statistics, 64–68
Informal tests, 27
Information
    about tests, 29–30
        publishers and, 72–73
        test catalogs, 71–72
        in test manual (*See* Test manual)
    additional, criterion-related validity and, 12–13
    test result, entitlement to, 134–136
    from tests and other sources, 131–132

Innate ability, measurement of, 7, 40–41
Institute for Personality and Ability Testing (IPAT), 107
Institutional decisions, 130
Instructor's manuals, 34
Integer, 50
Integrated test batteries, 85–86
Intellectual status index, 117
Intelligence
    effective, 41
    levels, labeling, 42–43
Intelligence quotients. See IQs
Intelligence tests
    creativity measurements and, 41
    history of, 85–86
    use of, 21–22
Interest tests, 21
Inter-individual comparisons (type II scores)
    interrelationships, 89
    linear standard scores, 94
    of mean and standard deviation, 90, 94, 97–101, 119
    other scores and, 91
    of range, 90, 94, 112
    of rank, 90, 94, 101–112, 119
    of status of those making same score, 90, 94, 112–116
    use of, 94, 97, 119
Interpretation of test, 3–4
    computer-based, 32
    directions, in test manual, 86
    by experts, 146–148
    in industry, 4
    mistakes in, 2–3
    raw scores in, 5–6
    score selection and, 119–120
Interval, real limits, 50
Intra-individual comparisons (type III score), 89, 90, 94, 116–118
*Iowa Tests of Educational Development*, 111
IPAT (Institute for Personality and Ability Testing), 107
IQs
    changes in, 6
    deviation, 100–101, 110–111, 119
    heredity and, 7
    Otis-style deviation, 119
    ratio-type, 116–117
    Stanford-Binet, 101
    Wechsler, 100–101
ITED-score, 111

Item banks, 34
Item characteristics curve theory, 35
Item response theory, 35
Items, possible, universe of, 51

K-score, 118
Kuder-Richardson formulas, 15

Labeling, 42–43
Lake Wobegon effect, 46–47
Language disabled persons, tests for, 37–38
Latent trait scaling, 35
Length of test, reliability and, 18
Letter grades, 96–97, 106–107
Level, test, 81–82
Linear standard scores (type IIA), 94, 97–101, 108
Local norms, 84–85
Logical validity, 10
Long-range equi-unit scales, 118–119

MA (mental age), 113, 114
Mastery, 33
Maximum-performance tests, 20
    measurements from, 40–41
    score determinants of, 21
    type I scores and, 95
    types of, 21–23
Mean, 55, 64
Mean deviation, 58
Measurement, standard error of, 65–67
Median, 55–56, 57, 64
Mental age (MA), 113, 114
*Mental Measurements Yearbooks*, 30
Midpoint, 50
*Minnesota Multiphasic Personality Inventory*, 24
*Minnesota Multiphasic Personality Inventory II*, 127
Minorities, 7, 45–46
Misinterpretation, 47–48
Mistakes
    in administration/scoring, 131
    in test results, 128–130
    *vs.* errors, 67
Misuse, of test, 42–43, 47–48
Mode, 56, 57, 64
Multi-modal distribution, 56

Multiple-aptitude test batteries, 85–86
Multiple-choice items, 43

NCE (normal curve equivalent), 111–112,
    113
Negative skew, 55, 56
Nonlanguage tests, 28
Nonverbal tests, 28
Normal curve equivalent (NCE),
    111–112, 113
Normal distribution, 89, 92–93
Normalized standard scores, 108
Normal probability curve, 63–64
Norm-referenced tests, 33, 40
Norms, 144–145
    articulation of, 81–82
    definition of, 77–78
    importance of, 6
    local, 84–85
    selection/use of, 84
    unisex or separate, 85
Norms groups, 82–84
Norm tables
    abbreviated, 81
    condensed, 81
    definition of, 78
    multiple-group, 79, 80
    multiple-score, 79, 81
    simple, 78–79

Objective-referenced tests. *See* Criterion-
    referenced tests
Objective test, 26
Odd-even reliability coefficient, 15–16
Oral tests, 27
Ordinate, 52
Otis-Lennon intelligence tests, 119
Otis-style deviation IQ, 119
Outcome-based education, 37

Parents
    communicating test results to, 142
    test result information for, 134
Pearson product-moment correlation
    coefficient (r), 59
PE (probable error), 59
Percentage-correct score, 6, 95–96
Percentage placement score, 112
Percentile, 102, 104
Percentile band, 102, 106

Percentile ranks, 106
    advantages of, 102, 103, 120
    averaging, 102–103
    computation of, 104–105
    definition of, 54
    limitations of, 102, 103, 106
    *vs.* percentage-correct score, 6
Perfect negative correlation, 61
Perfect positive correlation, 60
Performance tests, 27
Personality testing, invasion of privacy
    and, 43–44
Personnel workers, 4, 5, 135–136
Ph.D. degree, 36
Physically disabled persons, tests for, 38
Polygon, frequency, 53
Portfolios, in evaluation, 38
Position, measures of, 54–57
Positively skewed distribution, 93
Positive skew, 55, 56
Power tests, 27–28
Practical factors, criterion-related validity
    and, 12
Predictive validity, 13
*Preliminary Scholastic Aptitude Test* (PSAT),
    45
*Principles for the Validation and Use of
    Personnel Selection*, 29–30
Privacy, invasion of, 43–44
Probability curve, normal, 63–64
Probability statistics, 64–68
Probable error (PE), 59
Professional workers
    colleagues, test result information for,
        135
    definition of, 134
    trained, communicating test results to,
        136–137
    untrained, communicating test results
        to, 137–138
Profiles, test
    analysis of, 126–127
    examples of, 121–124
    general, 124
    good, 124–126
    points, differences in, 126
    in test manual, 86–87
Programmed or adaptive testing, 34–35
Projective tests, 26, 146
Psychological tests, role of, 2
Publishers, test, 72–73
    computer-based test interpretation
        and, 32

Publishers (*Continued*)
  control of interpretation programs and, 32

Quartile deviation, 57–58

Range, 57
  inter-individual comparisons of, 90, 94, 112
  semi-interquartile, 57–58
  validity/reliability and, 7
Rank, 54, 101. *See also specific types of rank*
Rasch model, 35
Ratio IQ, 116–117
Rationale, for test, 74
Raw scores, in test interpretation, 5–6
Reading age, 114–115
References, test manual, 87
Reliability
  data for test, in test manual, 76
  definition of, 14
  dimensions of, 14–17
  importance of, 13
  influencing factors, 17–18
  range in scores and, 7
  temporal, 16
  *vs.* validity, 6–7, 18–19
Reliability coefficients, 14
  differences in, 18
  split-half or odd-even, 15–16
  test-retest, 17
Resources, for information on tests, 29–30
Response-contingent or adaptive testing, 34–35
Results, test
  background information for, 145
  changes in, 45
  checking, 128–130
  common sense and, 128–132
  communicating
    to child, 140–142
    to mature examinee, 138–140
    to parents, 142
    to trained professional worker, 136–137
    to untrained professional worker, 137–138
  conversations on, 136
  expressing, bases for, 89

"high," 142–143
information, entitlement to, 134–136
"low," 142–143
profiles (*See* Profiles, test)
reproducibility of (*See* Reliability)
Rorschach inkblots, 26

Sampling statistics, 64–68
Scaled scores, nonmeaningful, 118
SCAT (*School and College Abilities Tests*), 118
*School and College Abilities Tests* (SCAT), 118
School counselors, 133
Schools, test result information handling, 134–135
Scorer. *See* Examiner
Scores, 2. *See also specific types of scores*
  ability and, 145
  access to, 4
  classification scheme for, 88–95
  determinants, for maximum-performance tests, 21
  interpreters for, 3–4
  interrelationships of, 91–93
  knowledge about, 145
  low, 139
  order of, reliability and, 14
  percentage-correct, 6
  pretest on, 5–8
  range, validity/reliability and, 7
  type I, 89, 90, 94, 95-97
  type II
    A, 94, 97–101
    B, 94, 101–112
    C, 94, 112
    D, 94, 112–116
  type III, 94, 116–118
  type IV, 94
Scoring
  directions for, 75–76
Scoring, mistakes in, 131
Selective or adaptive testing, 34–35
Select-response tests, 26–27
$SE_{meas}$ (standard error of measurement), 65–67
Semi-interquartile range, 57–58
*Sequential Tests of Educational Progress* (STEP), 118
$SE_{yx}$ (standard error of estimate), 67–68
Shotgun approach, 24
Significant difference, 7

Situation-induced error, 16–17
Skew, 55, 56, 57
Spearman-Brown prophecy formula, 16
Speed tests, 27, 28
Split-half reliability coefficient, 15–16
Staged or adaptive testing, 34–35
Standard age score, 111
Standard deviation, 58–59, 64
Standard error of measurement, 17
Standard errors, 65–68
Standardized tests, 2, 27, 43
*Stanford Achievement Tests*, 118–119
Stanford-Binet IQs, 101
*Stanford-Binet* scales, 28, 34, 100
Stanine score, 108–109, 110
Statistics
    definition of, 49
    descriptive (*See* Descriptive statistics)
    frequency distribution, 50–51
    histogram, 52–53
    inferential or probability, 64–68
Sten score, 109–110
STEP (*Sequential Tests of Educational Progress*), 118
Subjective test, 26
Supply-response tests, 26–27

Tailored or adaptive testing, 34–35
Teachers, lack of good judgment by, 1–2
Temporal reliability, 16, 18
Test/tests. *See also specific types of tests*
    assortments/integrated batteries, 85–86
    attributes of (*See* Reliability; Usability; Validity)
    content, error variance, 15–16
    description of, 74
    difficulty of, 7–8
    good, 120
    interpretation (*See* Interpretation of test)
    interpretation of (*See* Interpretation of test)
    knowledge about, 144
    purposes of, 74
    quality of, 3
    results (*See* Results, test)
    scores (*See* Scores)
    scoring mistakes, 131
    use of, 145
Test catalogs, 29, 71–72, 86
Test Corporation of America, 30

Testing
    allegations, 39
    conditions, reliability and, 16–17
Test-item banks, 34
Test items
    ambiguity of, 25–26
    forced-choice, 24–25
Test manual, 73–74
    administration directions in, 75
    development of test in, 74–75
    information about test in, 29–30
    interpretation data in, 86
    norms and norms tables, 77–86
    profiles in, 86–87
    purposes for test in, 74
    rationale for test in, 74
    references, 87
    reliability data in, 76
    scoring directions in, 75–76
    test description in, 74
    validity data in, 76–77
Textbook validity (content validity), 10
*Thematic Apperception Test*, 26
Theory of Multiple Intelligences, 41
Time
    influence, error variance and, 16
    reliability and, 18
Truncated distribution, 55–56, 57
T-scaled score, 108
T-score, 89, 98–99, 118
Typical-performance tests
    ambiguity of items and, 25–26
    criterion keyed, 24
    forced-choice items, 24–25
    use of, 20, 23

Unfairness, test, 45–47
Unisex norms, 85
Usability, 19

Validity
    coefficient, 11
    concurrent, 13
    construct, 13, 77
    content or logical, 10
    criterion-related or empirical, 11–13
    data for test, in test manual, 76–77
    face, 10
    importance of, 9–10
    incremental, 12-13
    outside variables and, 18–19

Validity (*Continued*)
  predictive, 13
  range in scores and, 7
  *vs.* reliability, 6–7, 18–19
Validity coefficients
  additional information and, 12–13
  size of, 19
Variability
  differences, criterion-related validity
    and, 12
  measures of, 57–59
Variable errors, 19

Variables, test, criterion-related validity
    and, 11
Verbal tests, 28

Wechsler intelligence tests, 28, 74,
    110–111, 126–127
Wechsler IQs, 100–101
Written tests, 27

Z-scores, 89, 98